Paul G. Clifford
The China Paradox

Paul G. Clifford

The China Paradox

At the Front Line of Economic Transformation

ISBN 978-1-5015-1574-3
e-ISBN (PDF) 978-1-5015-0727-4
e-ISBN (EPUB) 978-1-5015-0721-2

Library of Congress Cataloging-in-Publication Data
A CIP catalog record for this book has been applied for at the Library of Congress.

Bibliographic information published by the Deutsche Nationalbibliothek
The Deutsche Nationalbibliothek lists this publication in the Deutsche Nationalbibliografie;
detailed bibliographic data are available on the Internet at http://dnb.dnb.de.

© 2017 Paul G. Clifford
Published by Walter de Gruyter Inc., Boston/Berlin
Cover image: Fei Yang/Moment/gettyimages
Printing and binding: CPI book GmbH, Leck
♾ Printed on acid-free paper
Printed in Germany

www.degruyter.com

Advance Praise

An invaluable and unique account of China's pathway to modernity by someone who has engaged profoundly with this process, living for much of the last three decades inside China. . . . A thoughtful, thought provoking, and, above all else, admirably pragmatic, sympathetic but astutely critical work.

—Dr. Kerry Brown,
Professor of Chinese Studies,
King's College, London

Dr. Clifford is a scholar with a deep knowledge of Chinese history and culture, who entered the business world at a time of dramatic change in China's political economy. His rich business experience in China across a range of industrial sectors combined with his deep scholarly understanding make this a uniquely insightful book. The insights are far more original and interesting than those of other studies in this field.

—Dr. Peter Nolan,
Chong Hua Professor in Chinese Development,
University of Cambridge

In this first-hand account based on years of working in China, Paul Clifford takes the reader deep inside the belly of the beast. . . . This well-written and engrossing inside account should be read by all China watchers.

—Dr. David Shambaugh,
Professor at Elliot School of International Affairs,
George Washington University

The China Paradox combines a highly-informed broad-sweep analysis of China, knitting together the economy, politics and history. Engagingly written and drawing on unique personal experience, it provides a penetrating guide to this most important country.

—Jonathan Fenby,
Author and former editor of the South China Morning Post

Paul G. Clifford's *The China Paradox* reflects the insights, sensibilities, and rich experiences of an individual who began living in China as a student in the late Mao period, and then stayed on as a business practitioner and globally-renowned consultant through the four decades of reform that

Acknowledgments

I should like to acknowledge many friends and colleagues who have contributed ideas and provided encouragement as I researched, shaped, and wrote the book.

I owe a special debt of gratitude to David Shambaugh, Peter Nolan, Fraser Howie, Anthony Saich, Kerry Brown, Edward Steinfeld, and Jonathan Fenby who read the manuscript and provided invaluable advice and support.

I am grateful to so many more. Some of those in my extensive network shall remain anonymous, especially those in China. But I shall mention quite a few (in alphabetical order), even at the risk of missing names that should be included.

Peter Batey, Ira Belkin, Flora Botton, Sabina Brady, Peter Brown, Alastair Campbell, Dane Chamorro, Reuben Chaudhury, Karen Christensen, Andrew Collier, Clifford Coonan, Remi Cornubert, David Dollar, Ian Driscoll, Joel Epstein, Stephan Feuchtwang, John Fitzgerald, Larry Franklin, John Frisbie, Michael Forsythe, Helena Fu Orlik, Steve Ganster, Sam Geall, Amy Gendler, Jeanne-Marie Gescher, Rob Gifford, Fernando Gil De Bernabe, John Gittings, Tom Gold, David Goodman, Jimmy Goodrich, Doug Guthrie, Jon Halliday, Isabel Hilton, John Holden, Ellen Hu, Eddie Huang, Charles Hutzler, Kenneth Jarrett, August Joas, Mark Kadar, Robert A. Kapp, Joan Kaufman, Mark Levine, Roberta Lipson, Borje Ljunggren, Davin Mackenzie, Stephen Markscheid, Robert Martin, Paul Mooney, Chris Murck, Drake Pike, Ted Plafker, Robert Poole, Peter Richardson, Daniel Rosen, Andrew Rothman, Bill Russo, Scott Seligman, David Shohan, Joseph Shohan, Stuart Schonberger, Daniel Senger, Adrian Slywotsky, Dave Sovie, Susan Spindler, Anne Stevenson-Yang, Christopher Sykes, Didi Kirsten Tatlow, Michael Taylor, John Tian, Raymond Tsang, Brett Tucker, Georges Vialle, Stanley Wallack, Jonathan Watts, Adam Williams, Kim Woodard, Gabriel Wildau, David Wolf, Elizabeth Wright, Rod Wye, Gary Van Wyk, Michael Yehuda, Myra Yu, and Yu Yi.

My thanks also to my publisher Walter de Gruyter who were quick to sign me up and have fast-tracked the publication. It has been a pleasure working with their highly professional team: VP Americas Paul Manning, editorial director Jeffrey Pepper, copy editors Mary Sudul and Mark Watanabe, production editor Angie MacAllister, editorial assistant Megan Lester, marketing manager Caitlyn Nardozzi as well as Nick Wallwork in

Asia. Also, my thanks to Esther Baldwin for her thoughtful comments on the book.

Of course, I should hasten to add that I alone bear responsibility for the contents of the book. Any errors or omissions should be laid firmly at my door.

Finally, without the patience, encouragement and support of my wife Miriam, I cannot imagine having had the fortitude to pursue my academic and business life, and to complete this book.

Contents

Chapter 1: The Hybrid Model at the Heart of a Vibrant New China —— 1

Chapter 2: Early Attempts at Industrialization: The Empire and the
   Republic —— 9

Chapter 3: The First Decades of the People's Republic: The Soviet Model
   ... and Worse —— 17
  The Fate of China's Capitalists: From Ally to Enemy —— 18
  The Dysfunctional Soviet Model Is Embraced —— 20
  And Worse ... Beyond the Soviet Model —— 26
  The Brutal Assault on Intellectuals and Science —— 30
  The Dead End of the Mao Years —— 35

Chapter 4: Wrongs Are Righted, the Reforms Take Shape —— 39
  Setting the Boundaries of Change —— 46
  The Initial Reforms—Limited and Tentative —— 47
  The Reforms Go into a High Gear —— 51
  The Reforms Lose Steam (2002 Onward) —— 52
  China's Economic Planning Today —— 53

Chapter 5: What to Do with the State-Owned Enterprises? —— 57
  Weaning the SOEs Off the State (1978–93) —— 57
  Central Planning Fades Away —— 60
  Addressing Ownership and Governance (1993–2003) —— 62
  Selling off the "Dogs" —— 62
  Transforming the Large SOEs —— 64
  Can SOE Culture Be Changed? —— 72
  SOE Reform Falters (2003 Onward) —— 74
  A New Type of SOE Shows the Way Forward —— 78

Chapter 6: The Private Economy Emerges Unannounced —— 83
  TVEs—Engine for Growth as the Reforms Took Shape —— 84
  POEs Flourish, Especially If Far from the Capital —— 87
  Wanxiang—A Pioneering Private Company Forges Its Own
    Path —— 88
  Huawei—A Private Firm as "National Champion" —— 91
  Private Firms Sustain the Economy —— 93

Chapter 7: Magnet for Foreign Investment —— 95
    Why Did China Welcome FDI? —— 96
    Why Has China Been so Attractive to Foreign Investors? —— 97
    China Has Its Cake and Gets to Eat It, Too —— 99
    Win-Win in the Auto Industry —— 100
    Why Did China Neglect Logistics and Resist Its "Opening Up" to
             FDI? —— 107
    The Motorola Breakthrough —— 111
    Why FDI Will Stick with China —— 115

Chapter 8: Business Models at the Heart of China's Emergence —— 119
    Model 1. Learn and Catch Up —— 119
        Disappointment in Auto and Semiconductor —— 121
        The Model Works Well—In Consumer Products, High-Speed Rail,
             and Nuclear Power —— 124
    Model 2. Picking off Underperforming Overseas Assets —— 129
        Obstacles to China ODI —— 130
    Model 3. "China, Inc." in Emerging Markets —— 135
        The Government/CCP —— 136
        Financial Institutions —— 137
        Chinese Firms —— 140
        A Little-Known Firm from Anhui Grows in Africa —— 141
        Transportation, Mines, and Downstream Industry —— 146
        How to Assess the China, Inc. Business Model in Emerging
             Markets —— 148
    Model 4. Novel Product or Technology Breakthrough —— 149
        Implications for the Emergence of Chinese Firms on the Global
             Stage? —— 153

Chapter 9: What Could Disrupt or Sustain the China Paradox? —— 155
    Peace, Stability and the CCP —— 155
        The CCP Has Survived and Adapted —— 156
        How Well Is the CCP Functioning Today? —— 157
        The CCP Is Embedded in Businesses —— 159
        China's Fault Lines and Tensions —— 161
        The CCP and China's Future —— 161
    The Rule of Law —— 166
    Culture, Education, and Civil Society —— 168
        A Cocktail of Confucianism and Leninism —— 169

Anything Goes, as the Market Latches onto Newfound
Freedoms —— **170**
Corruption, Moral Turpitude, and Social Alienation —— **171**
Education Falls Short —— **173**
Business Education Flourishes —— **175**
Economic and Financial Stability —— **175**
Confronting the Environmental Crisis —— **179**
The Mega Domestic Market —— **181**
Gleaming New Ground Transportation Infrastructure —— **181**
Government-Sponsored Research and Development —— **182**
The Mobile Handset Example —— **186**
China's R&D Results Are Patchy —— **188**
Connecting with the Consumer —— **190**
Prospects of Deepening Economic Reform? —— **192**

Chapter 10: Conclusion —— **197**

Endnotes —— **207**

Index —— **219**

Preface

It may be useful to say a few words about who I am and what makes me tick. I have been connected to China since 1966—originally as a modern China historian, then retooled into business roles in banking, strategy consulting, and high tech. Although the bulk of my life has been devoted to China, I have also worked in Africa, Latin America, and other parts of Asia, the US and Europe; a fact that helps me avoid the pitfall of overstating China's uniqueness.

I have an emotional and professional commitment to helping China succeed. I first lived in China in 1973–74 as a student and saw close-up the dismal impact of the Cultural Revolution, as well of as the dysfunctional Soviet-style planning. I returned to live and work in China over several decades, had my children educated there, put up with the choking smog, and had my heart broken by the Tiananmen Square Massacre of 1989. I have invested my time, energy, passion, and patience in helping old Chinese state-owned firms transform themselves, in guiding emerging private Chinese firms, as well as in advising foreign firms that have invested billions of dollars in China.

This work is motivated by a deep-seated desire for China's progress to be balanced and sustainable, permitting the nation to play a constructive role in the world commensurate with its economic scale and muscle. There are obviously contradictory elements in my embrace of China, as my friends and family hasten to point out. On the one hand, I remain closely engaged with China on the business side, while on the other hand I am repulsed by the one-party state, the absence of a true rule of law, and the top-to-bottom corruption that distorts economic activity and pollutes society figuratively and in reality. But I am willing to live with this contradiction. Influencing China's economic progress is superior to watching and just hoping it does not lead to a failed state. If that were to happen to China, it would make all other failed states look like non-events and would have profound global implications.

As I engage with China, I find myself sitting in what is sometimes an uncomfortable middle ground, with my head exposed above the parapet, neither a "panda-hugger" (uncritical friend of China), nor somebody who expects or let alone hopes for China's collapse. My deep wish is that my nuanced position is recognized as both constructive and principled.

Having participated so intimately in China's recent development, I have chosen to tell the story of *The China Paradox* through my own eyes, through the projects I worked on across China and in so many diverse sectors, since this content is vivid, concrete, and hopefully fresh to the reader. While I eschew an ultra-academic approach, I have made sure that the narrative is founded on a rigorous historical framework and is not simply another exercise of show-and-tell.

My goal is to share with the reader the high drama, the twists and turns of China's extraordinary path of reform and transformation over the last four decades; but mindful that readers—in business, students, and others engaging with China, or simply those tracking China's rise—are hungry for guidance on what the future may hold. As you will see, I have also assembled compelling evidence that can shed light on what will determine China's trajectory.

Chapter 1
The Hybrid Model at the Heart of a Vibrant New China

How can we explain China's extraordinary and unanticipated emergence over the past four decades? Why did the ruling Chinese Communist Party (CCP) shed old dogmas and boldly lead the reforms that have permitted China's economic takeoff? How was China, against all the odds, able to throw off the heavy burden of historical legacies, both ancient and modern, and achieve progress that has stunned the world? How has China moved from "perpetual poverty"[1] to a situation where its companies can compete in global markets?

The answers lie in understanding what we term *the China paradox*, an unlikely balancing act or equilibrium between forces, motivations, and interests that under other circumstances would have been deeply inimical.

This unexpected and beneficial alignment of the stars that has underpinned China's hybrid developmental model is still young, having seen the light of day only after Mao Zedong died in 1976 and Deng Xiaoping took over the reins of power in 1978. This balance has been, and remains, an extremely fragile construct, vulnerable to disruption and derailment. Most troubling, based on current trends, the CCP today looks less and less like the CCP under Deng Xiaoping. There is certainly no guarantee that *the China paradox* will stand the test of time and that the China "miracle" can be sustained.

At the core of *the China paradox* has been the role of the CCP. This is not to undervalue the role the Chinese people themselves have played in China's rise. But the centrality of the CCP in creating this balancing act is undeniable. Post-Mao, the CCP was severely chastened and forced to acknowledge the dead end in which China found itself. Also, as part of that rare alignment of the stars, Deng Xiaoping showed remarkable courage in breaking free of old dogmas and allowing the bold experiment to unfold. The CCP displayed a profound pragmatism, unlike the hubris it exhibited under Mao or what we see today. We shall see how the CCP's pragmatic actions unleashed reforms permitting foreign ideas, technology, and skills to be effectively grafted onto China, allowing oxygen to flow to China's economy and society.

This is not to suggest for one moment that the CCP was somehow converted to liberal democracy. It remains unyielding in its absolute rule of

DOI 10.1515/9781501507212-001

China and will not permit any challenge to its power. Superficially, that fact seems to be inconsistent with the changes it has led. Indeed, on occasions during the reform process, its repressive autocratic nature has come close to disrupting the fragile balance of forces and halting the process. But the CCP's willingness to experiment, adapt, and innovate flows directly from its quest for survival. Whatever supports its goal of holding onto power will be considered; whatever undermines that goal will not be countenanced. But at the same time the CCP has proven to be deeply committed to wealth creation, improved health services, and, more recently, to environmental sustainability, which help maintain its popular mandate and its hold on power. There is a strong logic to all this. It explains why *the China paradox*, which to the casual observer seems riddled with contradictory elements, has in fact helped China to hold things together in this transitional period and to achieve extraordinary economic results. While it remains true that if the CCP must choose between its goal of survival on the one hand and the goal of economic development on the other, the former trumps the latter. In recent decades those two goals have proven to be compatible most of the time.

The Chinese developmental model of recent decades is a striking piece of social innovation. Historically, the forces of conservatism had drowned out voices and movements that called for reform. But after Mao Zedong's death and the reforms launched by Deng Xiaoping, China finally turned its aspirations into reality through evolving this hybrid social order. Even though the tensions, compromises, and adaptations that have permitted this model to function have resulted in China actually being an underachiever in some respects, we should not let that detract from its achievements.

Since *the China paradox* is new and fragile, what guarantees are there that it can continue indefinitely? Although commentators, both in China and abroad, hold widely divergent views on China's prospects, it is fair to say that the turn of events in China in recent years has overall increased the pessimism over the future. Some see China continuing to plow forward or at least muddle through, while others prophesy the collapse of China or of the CCP. Based on the evidence we assemble on how *the China paradox* emerged and operates, how confident are we that this model can be sustained and for how long? Will the increasingly assertive role of the CCP in society, and in the economy, disrupt the model that has delivered so much progress?

You may ask why it is so important to understand the China paradox. Although China certainly has its own complexity and distinctive features, we should avoid the mistake of overemphasizing its uniqueness. All societies are a blend of the fresh, new elements and the conservative incrustation of past centuries, creating not only disruptive social fissures but at times also supplying the social cement that smooths the way forward.

Given China's global significance, it is vital that we make the effort to understand what is shaping its emergence and will determine its future. China has entered uncharted waters. Its sheer size—both its geography and its population—and the pace of its emergence put it in a league of its own and make predictions difficult. Although step-by-step experimentation and pragmatism have permitted China to move forward through its reforms without foundering so far, there rightly is a deep anxiety over what it would mean for China *and* the world if things in China became seriously unstuck. If we layer in China's history of volatility, rebellion, and even national fragmentation, then that anxiety is further heightened.

The Chinese themselves wrestle with the conundrum of how to free up creativity while keeping a lid on the volatility. A common expression in China is, "as soon as you relax things, there is chaos, but when you control things, they die." (yifang jiuluan, yiguan jiusi). Though more often than not this is used to justify more control not less, it nonetheless addresses a dark reality in China. Observers often speculate as to why the Chinese people tolerate such an oppressive regime. Well, as Chinese will tell you, their deepest anxiety is that an ungovernable nation would see a return to chaos. They argue that, as it stands, only the CCP can keep the lid on things. They are prepared to set aside the CCP's earlier track record of destruction and failure.

The vibrant economy and society that have emerged inspire admiration and respect. The Chinese people have with energy, confidence, and optimism broken free from the old order with unanticipated speed and scale. This massive burst of pent-up energy has helped raise hundreds of millions out of poverty. What the Chinese (the Chinese people themselves and not just their rulers) have achieved, dwarfs other economic "miracles," including postwar West Germany and South Korea.

China's vibrant side goes far beyond its throbbing new businesses and factories. There was the bright-eyed young professional I met who has adopted the name Ansel out of appreciation of the great American photographer Ansel Adams. Consider China's gleaming new transportation infrastructure, with its network of high-speed rail, new airports, and superhighways. There is the flourishing restaurant scene in which imaginative chefs create fresh twists to China's regional cuisines. We can see and feel a refreshing openness to change, the hunger for new ideas. We should celebrate China's "national revival" (zhenxing) and the achievement of its longstanding goal of "wealth and strength" (fuqiang).

Nor should we underestimate the power of historical legacies from traditional China and from Mao Zedong, which on a psychological level generate a chilly, stifling atmosphere that is the very enemy of vibrancy, antithetical to innovation and boldness. This "stifling" still permeates Chinese society, its traditions and culture, its institutions and organization.

The stifling atmosphere manifests itself in many ways, through reinforcing authority and breeding passivity rather than a questioning attitude. It rewards consensus over boldness, small steps over risk-taking. Social control is all pervasive, finding its way into every nook and cranny of society, so that just the hint of state violence is sufficient to ensure that citizens respond with self-discipline and self-censorship.

Seeing Chinese so happily enjoying the fruits of economic success, it is sometimes easy to forget the quiet Faustian pact they are forced to make with their rulers. Over the past four decades of the China paradox, the energy generated by society, the introduction of foreign technology and business processes, all under the aegis of the reform-minded CCP, has proven a strong antidote to that dark side of China's historical legacy.

But the current leadership of the CCP appears oblivious to just how fragile the balance underlying the China paradox is and seems bent on reverting to a harder, more brutal version of one-party rule—not a return to era of Mao, but certainly not the kind of governance Deng ushered in. The breath of fresh air that the reforms brought may not be that long-lived.

In my analysis of the China paradox and its implications for China's future, I shall focus primarily on China's economic transformation—its industry, commerce, and technology. This large arena provides a vivid illustration of how the vibrant creative forces interact with the choking aspects of traditional and more recent communist society.

I shall also layer in political, social, educational, and cultural factors that are inextricably linked to China's developmental model. It is impossible to make sense of China's economic transformation without a full understanding of the role of the CCP, which has been the chief architect of the reforms while at the same time unswervingly maintaining its grip on its paramount imperative of staying in power. To what degree are the autonomous and newly assertive economic forces outpacing the CCP's ingenuity and its ability to manipulate outcomes and to stay in control? Is China's current increasingly restrictive political governance looking out-of-step with the economic system it should be enabling rather than dominating?

A central and recurring theme in modern China, to this day, has been the effort to import and absorb foreign ideas, technology, and skills that can help transform the economy. I delve briefly into early failed efforts to use foreign ideas to reshape industry and commerce, first during Imperial China (before 1911) and then during the Republic (1911–1949). The traditional aspects of Chinese society vastly outweighed those shallow efforts at change which came to naught.

During Mao's rule (1949–1976) in the first decades of the People's Republic of China (PRC), the pendulum swung the other way, away from traditional values and traditions. The wholesale adoption of the massively flawed Soviet economic and political system, then followed by still more missteps even further to the Left, led the nation down the path to what China's reformers were to characterize as a system that made a virtue of "eternal poverty."

The depth and totality of these failures stand in stark contrast to recent achievements, permitting us to appreciate the boldness with which Deng and the CCP addressed the reforms.

Since the reforms began in 1978, a key component of China's newfound vibrancy and vigor has been an effective introduction of foreign knowledge and skills. Modern business concepts and processes have reshaped state-owned industry. Foreign investment has been absorbed, transforming whole sectors and the workforce. Chinese private firms have been permitted to flourish (within certain bounds), driving productivity and the creation of wealth and jobs. The government has funded Chinese research and development (R&D). Chinese universities now turn out countless MBA graduates, while students returning from overseas bring new attitudes, values, knowledge, and skills.

This wholesale import of foreign knowledge is both broad-based and deep-rooted. Even allowing for the pervasiveness of Chinese authoritarian legacies, this absorption of new ideas provides modest optimism that the clock cannot be turned back and that the gains of the last four decades will not be erased.

Of course, China's adoption of foreign ideas and institutions can serve different objectives, in many cases contributing to positive, irreversible change, but sometimes being hijacked for other goals. A recurring theme of China over the past century and to this day has been the use of foreign ideas and mechanisms to prop up the status quo or, more narrowly, its rulers.

In the process of absorption, ideas may be changed to fit local conditions or distorted to defend the existing order. For instance, China's adoption of the "rule of law" is a thin veneer that is easily trumped by the police state. China's "corporate governance movement," which led to Chinese stock market-listed firms having "independent directors," ended up as a hollow charade designed to win the confidence of the market. China blows hot and cold on foreign direct investment, loosening up the regulations in some respects while continuing to erect new barriers. How can this behavior be explained? Could it be that, once having attracted, absorbed, or stolen vital foreign technology, China is perfectly happy to slam the door shut again to protect its "national champions"? Is that narrowly nationalist approach compatible with China competing in the fast-moving global knowledge economy?

The volume and weight of imported foreign ideas and their positive impact may drown out the goals of those who seek to use them as window dressing for a revamped autocratic CCP-dominated order. On the back of this economic breakout, Chinese firms are developing new business models, finding ways to innovate, organize, and compete.

Some firms, as we shall see, are based on a straightforward but effective "catch up" model; for instance, in railways and nuclear power. Some proved to have mastered the art of acquiring and turning around poorly performing global firms. Yet others, by operating under government patronage, can gain access to minerals, to sell power plants, and to develop consumer markets in emerging countries in Africa and Latin America. Although innovation in terms of truly novel products or technologies remains elusive in China, many Chinese firms exhibit innovation in reshaping business models and tweaking existing technologies.

China is fully entitled to shape its own future. It has its own specific conditions, history, and aspirations. It is not for us to seek to dictate what developmental path it should pursue. China's history will continue to be made by the Chinese people themselves in their own way and at their own pace.

Still, China's huge significance today, its interdependence with the global economy, makes it unavoidable that the world not just observes China's progress, but also offers suggestions and shares concerns. Some views are outright hostile, borne out of resentment at China's new-found power. Others are based on legitimate concerns over China's strident nationalism and growing military assertiveness in Asia.

Other concerns have more to do with China's domestic developmental trajectory. Is the current path sustainable in the long term? What adjustments and choices should China make to avoid a social explosion, the ripples of which would undermine world stability? If further, deeper reform is vitally needed, what barriers stand in the way of such change?

Chapter 2
Early Attempts at Industrialization:
The Empire and the Republic

[Zhang Zhidong] had erected a gigantic cotton-mill at Wuchang with thirty-five thousand spindles, covering six acres and lit with the electric light.... He erected a magnificent iron-works and blast furnaces which cover many acres.... He has iron and coal mines, with a railway seventeen miles long from the mines to the river...."[1]

—Written in 1894 by G.E. Morrison,
an Australian adventurer who travelled up the
Yangtze to Wuhan, where he observed this industrial
complex established by the Qing dynasty
official Zhang Zhidong.

During most of its imperial history China performed well in the steady state of a sophisticated agricultural society but at the cost of leaving industry and commerce undervalued and stunted.

Beginning in the Southern Song dynasty during the 12th and 13th centuries, an autonomous merchant class emerged[2] and in the subsequent Ming and Qing dynasties began to engage in industrial activities—porcelain, cotton, silk—that were distinguished from handicraft production by the scale of their operations, by free wage labor and investment by entrepreneurs, and supported by the existence of a national currency and early forms of banking.

However, these "shoots of capitalism," as Chinese historians describe them, failed to flourish due to a range of factors. Max Weber[3] draws attention to a cultural or religious aspect—the absence in China of the "protestant ethic," which drove early European industrializers to remake the world in a new image, while adhering to frugality and ensuring strong capital accumulation. Others point to the massive power of the autocratic imperial China state, which could strangle or co-opt emerging businesses before they became large enough to challenge the status quo. At the same time, the merchant class lacked a strong identity and was more willing to haggle and make concessions to the scholar-officials than to seek independence. Bribery defined the relationship between the officials and merchants, serving as a way for merchants to obtain immunity from dispossession of a franchise, a pattern that persists to this day. Those in the nascent middle class lacked a "fighting spirit,"[4] and their ambition was limited to achieving social mobility in terms of an official position, if only a lowly one,

DOI 10.1515/9781501507212-002

through investing their commercial profits in land, the traditional measure of wealth and status.

During the 18th century in Yangzhou, the government farmed out its salt production monopoly to merchants who received the exclusive rights to process, distribute, and sell salt in that part of China. Despite its scale and high level of profitability, the Yangzhou salt industry failed to develop since it was seriously undercapitalized due in part to official exactions, coupled with the division of wealth due to the family system. But another key factor in this was the diversion of capital to nonproductive uses, to conspicuous consumption and lavish cultural activities, and, of course, to education, which was the route to becoming a government official.[5]

The arrival of the military and mercantile might of the *great powers* at the gate of China during the late 18th century onward shook China's imperial system to the core and ultimately opened the path to revolution and economic modernization. The Opium Wars forced China to give foreign traders access to the China market under conditions that favored the foreigners and put local Chinese firms at a disadvantage.

China's economic modernization was also held back by the traditional close connections between officials and merchants, a symbiotic relationship that during the mid-19th century became known as "official supervision and merchant operation" (guandu shangban). These enterprises, run by merchants but owned and controlled by officials, failed to achieve long-term success.

The high point of this business model was during China's Self-Strengthening Movement in the last half of the 19th century. The Qing Dynasty externally faced the might of the great powers and internally faced rebellion. To shore up its shaky rule, it imported military technology, adopted half-hearted constitutionalism and introduced some modern education and science. The key slogan was "Chinese learning as the core (Chinese: ti), Western learning for practical applications (Chinese: yong)." That ti-yong concept continues to pervade the thinking of today's Chinese leaders, who, while enthusiastic about foreign science and technology, stand steadfastly against broader Western liberal values that could undermine the political order.

A good example of "official supervision, merchant management" was the establishment in 1872 by Qing minister Li Hongzhang of China Merchants Steam Navigation Company, China's first indigenous modern shipping company. He contracted the operations of the company out to merchants, and by 1887 the firm had about 30 vessels plying the Yangtze River, the China coast, and as far away as Singapore, Manila, and Japan. How-ever, its largest shareholders "mined" the company's income for their own personal enrichment rather than reinvesting the funds to expand the fleet.

In Wuhan, Viceroy of Hunan and Hubei Provinces, Zhang Zhidong built an industrial complex with a steel plant, an iron ore mine, and an ar-senal that produced artillery of German design. He established textile mills, introduced technical education, and helped build a modern army. But after China was soundly defeated in the Sino-Japanese War (1894–95), the Self-Strengthening Movement, which had focused on making weapons and ships for China's defense, was utterly discredited. In fact, the steel in-itially made by Zhang Zhidong's steel plant was of low quality and not suit-able for military applications.

The joint official-merchant approach as exemplified by Li Hongzhang and Zhang Zhidong was "too shallow a font of inspiration"[6] to produce modern enterprises. As the historian McAleavy puts it:

> "The characteristic of this type of industry was that its management was in official hands throughout, or in other words that Li [Hongzhang] or whoever was the founder ran it according to his views through men of his own selection. The public at the most were permitted to buy shares, but had no real say in how the business was carried on. Thus, the modernization movement on the whole had only a minor effect on the development of native capitalism."[7]

Feuerwerker, in his classic work on what he calls China's "retarded indus-trialization" in the late-Qing Dynasty, highlights the absence in China of government subsidies in terms of financing and infrastructure that laid the foundation for industrial development and that had helped the transporta-tion industry flourish in Meiji Japan during the same period. In China, there were only "isolated cases rather than an epidemic of industrialization," fo-cused on arsenals and railroads and, later, telegraph lines. Although the Qing government drew up a Company Law and Bankruptcy Law in 1903 and regulations to protect inventions, it was technically bankrupt and un-able to make needed investments. The official-merchant joint enterprises were over-dependent on capital from Chinese businessmen in the treaty ports or from rural gentry living off land rent. Official appointees to man-agement were unqualified to run a business. "Personal ties such as kinship and one's village were as important as competence and experience." There was a "vulnerability to official exactions," a "proclivity to graft or squeeze," and "a willful absence of initiative."[8]

Later efforts did move Zhang Zhidong's industrial center more in the di-rection of a functional corporate structure. In 1908, a senior official, Sheng

Xuanhuai, merged the steel works and the iron ore and coal mines into the Hanyeping Company, which he ran as his personal business until 1916. The steel works were upgraded using Japanese bank loans and were able to supply steel rails for China's rapidly growing rail network. Today tourists can visit Zhang's former factory complex, described as "at that time the largest integrated steel production base in the Far East and the cradle of modern China's industry." As an illustration of China's recent surge into the modern world, there is nearby a new state-of-the-art steel works that produces special steels for aerospace engines, bearings, and machine tools.

The efforts of those late-Qing dynasty modernizing government officials were too little too late. Independent entrepreneurs were weak and without a voice. But warning bells were ringing. While social Darwinism had initially served to provide justification for 19th century imperialism; for the Chinese, as the victims, the theory of survival-of-the-fittest was transformed into a call to action as China faced being carved up by the great powers, along the lines of what happened in Africa. Soon the Qing reformers were outflanked by Chinese revolutionaries whose priority was to overthrow the dynasty as the first step in national survival. In 1911, the Qing's own modern army seized power and the Republic of China was established.

The industrial efforts of the Self-Strengthening Movement failed not only to achieve the task of propping up the decaying Qing dynasty, but were also shallow in that they tried to graft Western technology onto a Confucian society. Chinese revolutionaries in the early 20th century recognized this failing and called for radical cultural change, including the adoption of Western science and education. Chen Duxiu and other leaders of the New Culture Movement, which began around 1915, called for "Mr. Science" and "Mr. Democracy" to replace "Mr. Confucius." But even before the 1911 Revolution, many Chinese intellectuals began promoting radical views on the merits of industrial society.

In 1907, a group of Chinese anti-Qing revolutionaries established the New Century (Xinshiji) Magazine in Paris. Though imbued with the utopian anarchism of Kropotkin, they pragmatically aligned themselves with the nationalism of Sun Yat-sen, who went on to establish the Republic. An essential part of the New Century's platform was a fervent "industrialism," which was derived from their exposure to Western society and which looked forward to an age of machines. It bore no relation to traditional Chinese utopian thinking, which looked back to an idyll of agricultural self-sufficiency.

Wu Zhihui,[9] one of the leaders of this group, foresaw a world in which electric trains and airships would facilitate worldwide contact between experts who would design a new urban environment, while for short-distance travel, moving pavements, operating day and night, would make cars and trains obsolete. In science, emphasis would be placed on hygiene and medicine to lengthen life. Simplified Chinese characters would be adopted to improve access to knowledge, so that "ten-year-old children could already have the knowledge of present-day scientists."[10]

In 1916, Wu confronted China's traditional separation of intellectual activity from manual work, doubting whether China's youth had ever seen a power lathe. He called on young people to forgo eating out or going to the theatre and instead build workshops in their homes where they could develop machines. He did not suggest total reliance on foreign products, but rather advocated the purchase of single foreign machines for the purpose of copying them.[11] We can see striking echoes of this in China's current "catch up" business model.

In 1924, writing in the Science Weekly, Wu called on friends and compatriots to "take off their long gowns" and "put on the blue cloth of the workers and peasants" so as to achieve a bold industrial transformation. The world he espoused, which sounds a lot like China's pulsating economy today, was:

> "Iron pillars will be cast like ten thousand tree-trunks, concrete will pour out in vast quantities, and experimental equipment will fill factory workshops. Chairs of shiny iron and oiled wood will fill the storehouses."[12]

These radical views on industrialization received pushback from some Chinese conservative intellectuals, who rejected the "material civilization of the Westerners," complaining that many Chinese were dazzled by the West and calling for the defense of what they called "the national quintessence."

Following the establishment of the Republic, the new government in 1912 sent telegrams to each province stating that "industry is the lifeblood for the survival of the Republic."[13] Minister of Industry, Liu Kuiyi, who had studied in Japan in 1903, stated: "We should follow the guidance of scholars and link science to industry as the path to creating a strong nation."[14] He set up universities and high schools devoted to agriculture, industry, and commerce and specialized institutions for shipbuilding, medicine, and pharmaceuticals. He issued laws to protect inventions.[15] Though many of these efforts foundered in the instability of the early Republic, they demonstrate the commitment to science and industry.

During the Republic, just as during the late Qing dynasty, Chinese studying overseas had a strong impact on social change in China. Leaders of the Paris group of revolutionaries mentioned above were instrumental in establishing the Work-Study Movement, which brought hundreds of Chinese students to France, among them the young Deng Xiaoping, the future architect of the post-Mao reforms, who worked at a Renault factory in Paris.

During the Republican period, many Chinese students returned from abroad with scientific knowledge. Hou Debang, having studied at MIT and Columbia in the US, returned to contribute to China's nascent chemical industry. Geologist Li Siguang, who had studied in Japan and then Birmingham in the UK, returned to China in 1920 and played a key role in China's oil and gas discoveries. This theme of returned students has remained ever-present to this day.

The early years of the Republic of China (1911–1949) were blighted by warlordism and national disunity. It was only in the late-1920s that some semblance of central control was established across the whole nation. Between 1928, when warlordism was defeated (or at least contained) and the nation largely united, and 1937, when Japan launched its full attack on China, the Republic had almost ten years of breathing space to begin building a modern state. While politically the regime borrowed heavily from European fascism and traditional Confucianism, in society at-large, enlightened reformers strove to modernize science, education, and healthcare.

Unfortunately, the government was able to focus effectively only on the cities and surrounding areas. Much of China, especially in the interior, was poorly controlled by the central government.[16] The modern economy in terms of industry and transportation accounted for only 5% to 7% of the total economy.[17] Demand for manufactured products was weak. There was a dearth of competent management—only 500 of 4,000 spinning mills in 1931 had managers who had received formal training. Foremen in Chinese factories had "long gown attitudes"* and looked down on manual labor. Senior management resembled that of the late-Qing enterprises. Even within the cities, modernization was shallow. The Republic worked hard at building a modern finance system with a central bank, and it understood foreign trade and commerce. But when it came to industry there was no breakthrough. Progress was narrow in range and skin-deep in technology. Compared to foreign entrants to China, the growth of these businesses in centers such as Shanghai

---

* This is a reference to Chinese intellectuals and officials who typically wore long gowns which precluded participation in manual work.

and Wuhan was "slow and precarious,"[18] hampered by traditional official power and the privileges accorded to foreigners.

Industry was concentrated in the so-called treaty ports controlled by foreign governments, and the enterprises were often run by foreign interests. Many of the businesses owned by emerging Chinese capitalists remained under the thumb of the government bureaucrats. The focus was on services and consumer products: textiles, cigarettes, carbonated drinks, electric power generation, water supply, coal gas production, and ship repair.

Nonetheless, there is evidence of technological and industrial progress during the Republic. The indigenous cotton textile industry, through new machinery and stronger management, managed to double its efficiency in terms of output per employee,[19] becoming one of the largest in the world. Pre-1949 industry provided the later PRC with valuable skilled workers and technicians who were able to work alongside Soviet advisors. Furthermore, small pre-1949 machine building firms in Shanghai helped the PRC sustain itself after the departure of the Soviet advisors.[20]

Although Feuerwerker describes China's economy from 1912 to 1949 as "telling a story in minor key" without any takeoff, he is also careful to stress that while the industry inherited by the PRC from the Republican period was relatively small, during 1953–1957 more than two-thirds of the increase in industrial production was to come from the "expanded output of existing factories."[21] Without the industrial base inherited from the Republic, "China's industrial development in the 1950s and 1960s would have been significantly slower and would have had to rely more heavily on foreign technology ... or both." [22]

The modern chemical industry, which was entirely new to China, began during the Republic. In 1918, having earlier set up a refined salt factory in Tianjin, entrepreneur Fan Xudong established a plant to produce soda ash (sodium carbonate, used with silica—sand—in glass production) using the Belgian Solvay Process with salt as its main feedstock. Even though he imported engineering drawings and key items of equipment from the US, he was unable to make the plant work. He hired Hou Debang, who had studied chemistry in the US, as his chief engineer. The problem had to do with the drying vessel being corroded by the soda. Hou, using what is today known as "Hou's Process," revised the last steps of the process, making it more efficient and also producing ammonium chloride, a fertilizer, as a by-product. His book on his improvement of the Solvay Process was published in the US. The high-quality soda ash made in the plant was exported to Japan and Southeast Asia.[23]

Japan's role in China's early industrialization was also important. Having defeated Russia in the war of 1905 and colonized Korea in 1910, Japan had a free reign in China's north east (Manchuria), which it occupied in 1931, followed by most of the rest of China after 1938 until 1945. Even before that, Japan was tapping into natural resources in the north east and, alongside that, established the process industry. In 1918, the Japanese opened an iron mine in Anshan and, after its full takeover of the north east, created a steel plant as well as a coal mine (in Fushun) to supply it. After the Soviets liberated China's north east from the Japanese in 1945, they dismantled the steel plant and shipped it to the Soviet Union. Ironically, after the PRC was established, the Soviets returned to assist China in building a new steel plant in Anshan.

Taking advantage of locally available raw materials—limestone and coal—the Japanese also created significant cement-making capacity in the north east. Dalian Cement Works, for example, was founded in 1907. When the CCP took power in 1949, that plant, with a capacity of 400,000 tpy (tons per year), accounted for 60% of China's national cement production capacity. When I visited the plant in 1986, its two original Japanese-made rotary kilns were still turning. Understandably, the Japanese role in China's early industrialization is not celebrated. But it certainly left its mark.

Although during the Republican period China may have been a chronic underachiever in industrialization and, more broadly, in social development, there was nonetheless much that the subsequent PRC could have built on. But the CCP chose not to do so, cutting a deep trench between the PRC and earlier China. This was not just about the winning and consolidation of power. The CCP and the many Chinese who brought it to power saw the old society as dark and inhibiting, with few redeeming features. They wanted a clean break.

The establishment of the PRC offered the promise of a parting of the clouds, an injection of vibrancy and hope into the nation that had been called the "sick man of Asia." The CCP promised enlightened rule and a revival of private industry and commerce, only to quickly renege on what it had offered. The Communist Party's rule brought a new layer of Stalinist social control, which neatly dovetailed with China's traditional autocratic legacy.

Chapter 3
The First Decades of the People's Republic:
The Soviet Model ... and Worse

Lacking both vitality and incentive.

> —Gao Shangquan, a senior Chinese government
> official commenting, shortly after the reforms
> began, on the impact of Soviet-style planning on
> Chinese enterprises.

Chaos under heaven is a good thing.

> —A slogan plastered on the wall of a
> Chinese factory visited by the author in
> 1974 during the
> Cultural Revolution.

The period 1949–1978, from the CCP's takeover to the beginning of the reforms following Mao's death, was marked by wave upon wave of revolutionary change that left China's economy severely damaged. Through understanding the depths of the social and economic dysfunction and the institutional cruelty meted out to intellectuals, educators, and scientists, we can appreciate just how remarkable was the subsequent success of the CCP under Deng in unleashing radical change and permitting the emergence of what we term *the China paradox*.

As we examine how China embraced the Soviet-style economic model in the 1950s and then sought to drive China farther along the "socialist" road, we shall find that this massive adventure was neither theoretically sound nor effective in practice. It led to disaster and untold human suffering. This is not to deride the legitimate efforts of citizens and officials as they rebuilt China. Nor is the goal to prescribe what kind of economic order China should adopt. Indeed, after taking power, the CCP had few options open to it, other than relying on the Soviets. But we shall demonstrate that the perverse and dysfunctional system that China adopted was not remotely "scientific," and that it left economic activity in chains, systematically stifling innovation and creativity.

When the CCP triumphantly took power in 1949, it was on the back of the Chinese people's broad-based rejection of Chiang Kai-shek's Republic of China, which had become discredited and despised. To further consolidate its power, the CCP then systematically set about creating a clean break with the past and negating the legitimacy and track record of the previous

DOI 10.1515/9781501507212-003

regime, much as newly established Chinese dynasties had traditionally re-written history to justify their own rebellion. That break with the previous regime is delineated by terms such a "New China" and "After Liberation." Generations of Chinese have been brought up on the slogan "I recall the bitterness of the past and think about the sweetness of today." The CCP's contribution is celebrated by the words "if there had been no CCP, then there would have been no New China."

The Fate of China's Capitalists: From Ally to Enemy

The CCP came to power with a broad popular mandate for change, based on its platform called New Democracy, but quickly abandoned the promises it had made and accelerated the pace of social revolution.

In 1940, in a well-written essay entitled "On New Democracy," Mao Zedong defined the New Democratic Revolution as a stage that would lead to socialism, but "at a later date." New Democracy, the first step, "will need quite a long time and cannot be accomplished overnight. We are not utopians ...," he stressed.[1] While he said that the state would own the large banks and large industrial enterprises, he also stressed that the government would neither "confiscate private property" nor "forbid the development of such capitalist production."[2]

The essay, widely reprinted as a pamphlet and distributed across China including in the areas still controlled by the Nationalist government, proved to be highly effective in creating a broad multiclass alliance, albeit under CCP leadership. It is easy to see how Chinese businessmen were lured into imagining that they had a role to play in the new order.

Foreigners were also impressed by the program. In 1945, Gunther Stein, a German journalist, visited the communists in their remote base and interviewed Mao Zedong who stated,

> "We are firmly convinced that private capital, Chinese as well as foreign, must be given liberal opportunities for broad development in postwar China: for China needs industrial growth."[3]

Stein completely bought Mao's deceitful charm offensive and became a conduit for communicating to the world the myth that Mao was some kind of liberal reformer.

By 1947, with total control of China in his sights, Mao was ready to abandon New Democracy in favor of a more radical and accelerated approach to the revolution. Ironically, it was Stalin who leaned on Mao and got him to continue with the original, more inclusive, transitional policy.[4]

So, as the CCP came to power, New Democracy remained the party's platform. In May 1949, five months before the establishment of the PRC, Liu Shaoqi, number two in the CCP hierarchy, made a speech[5,6] to a forum of Chinese businessmen in Tianjin that set out a program for a mixed economy within which private industry and commerce would be retained and protected. Tianjin, located on the North China coast, close to Beijing, was a modern, westernized city second only to Shanghai. It had a strong industrial base in textiles and chemicals, was a major port and trading center, and, like Shanghai, had a race course! Support from Tianjin's industrialists was critical to getting the economy back on its feet. Liu set out the key task of "reviving and developing production," and stated that "probably the private sector will surpass the state-owned sector, but the government does not fear that."[7]

Seeking to allay the anxieties of his audience, he emphasized that socialism was "several decades" away and added, "You have the right to hire and fire workers." For private businessmen, exhausted from years of war and moved by the patriotic drive to "Revive China," the CCP's platform was compelling and eminently reasonable.

But by 1952–1953 the political mood had changed dramatically. Mao Zedong made it clear that the transition to socialism was to begin *during* the New Democratic period. The collectivization of farmland and the nationalization of industry and commerce were to begin immediately. The Korean War and the encirclement of China by the Western powers likely influenced this. Moreover, the goals of the united front with other classes had been achieved. First, the main enemy (the Nationalist Party) had been isolated and driven off the Mainland. Second, the rehabilitation of the economy had gone much faster than expected. The tactic of a multiclass alliance was cynically discarded and the CCP proceeded to turn up the heat of class warfare. It began its assault on its erstwhile class ally, China's business class.

In the cities, the "Five Antis" campaign was launched against the business class, directed at the "five poisons"—bribery, tax evasion, the theft of state property, theft of state secrets, and cheating on government contracts. Capitalists were urged to "confess all their crimes." and suffered "a routine of denunciation, study, confession, and final deposition."[8]

By 1956, the nationalization of industry was complete. Having brutally coerced factory owners to give up their property, the CCP smartly kept many of them on to run the enterprises.[9]

Nationalization was extended from industry to commerce: trading companies, retail stores, restaurants all came under government ownership. This also meant the end of much of China's traditional, bustling, vibrant street life. Food stalls, cobblers, tinkers, scribes, palm readers, and the like simply melted away. The dreariness and drabness that shocked visitors to China at that time reflected not only the nation's real poverty but also constraints imposed by the CCP which cherished control, uniformity, and blind obedience while punishing diversity and creativity.

Since the economic reforms that began in 1978, the old pattern of life has re-established itself with passion. Back are the sellers of Sichuan snacks, the street dancing, fortune tellers, knife sharpeners, plus of course the new arrivals, those selling DVDs, mobile phone covers, and apartments. Once again you can hear the cry of the scrap metal collector as he passes through the Hutongs (alleyways) in a donkey-drawn cart. Color has returned to the formerly pallid cheeks of city life.

The Dysfunctional Soviet Model Is Embraced

From 1952 onward, having rehabilitated the war-ravaged economy through a process greatly helped by the goodwill of China's private business class, the CCP abandoned the notion of a mixed-economy (state and private) and adopted the Soviet economic model pretty well lock, stock, and barrel.

In 1929, Soviet Russia adopted a "hyper-industrialization" economic strategy, giving priority to heavy industry—metallurgy, machinery and related industry—but only after a protracted debate in which another faction had called for the use of market mechanisms and the development of agriculture, light industry (consumer products), and commerce as a way to create a market that would support industrialization.[10]

In China, there was no such debate. With the Korean War and the encirclement of "Red China" by Western powers as the Cold War intensified, the CCP "leant to one side,"—that is, to the Soviet Union and its heavy industrial model. China may have had no alternative. But it was nonetheless a fateful choice.

The Soviet model was a poor choice, given China's economic backwardness. In 1949, China's gross output of industry and agriculture (a reasonable proxy for GDP) was only RMB* 47 BN (about US$ 10 BN) with per capita output at RMB 66. Agriculture accounted for 70% of output and 80% to 90% of the population consisted of farmers, many living in poverty. Heavy industry was less than 8%.

A heavy industry strategy "conflicted with China's economic reality"[11] since it is extremely capital-intensive, and China's capital was scarce and its economic surplus small. It required the import of equipment, but China had virtually no foreign exchange.

Since China could not rely on the transfer of the economic surplus through fiscal revenues from the backward rural economy, industry had to achieve its own accumulation of revenue to fuel its growth. To this end, macroeconomic policy was "to completely suppress the functions of market mechanisms and to distort artificially the relative prices of factors and products."[12] Input costs were rigged to favor heavy industry whether in terms of access to low-interest loans, low wage rates, cheap raw materials, or energy. Prices for agricultural products and food were kept artificially low to help the urban residents who worked in heavy industry.

The emphasis on heavy industry created a variety of economic distortions. Though economic growth did occur, it was at the expense of construction, transportation, and commerce, all of which stagnated.

Within heavy industry, performance measures stressed simple volume or weight, creating an emphasis on basic materials rather than higher added-value processed or refined materials. Thus, China's steel industry produced sufficient raw steel but had to import rolled steel. That imbalance continued to plague China after the reforms, as it ramped up its auto industry, a big consumer of steel sheet.

---

* The PRC's currency, the Renminbi (RMB) Yuan or People's Currency.

Chinese view of Mao and Stalin in Moscow, 1949. Mao spent two months there negotiating economic and financial support

The Soviet-style economic strategy was enshrined in China's First Five Year Plan (1953–1957), during which heavy industry accounted for 85% of industrial investment. Having systematically driven Western engineers, businessmen, and educators out of China, the Chinese government replaced them with a host of Soviet and Eastern Bloc experts. Soviet loans and aid supported 156 key industrial projects—steel, cement, pharmaceuticals, machine tools, railway locomotives, trucks, and so on.

The sheer scale and speed of the adoption was remarkable. Soviet style organizational structures, official posts, and job titles were faithfully translated from Russian, becoming all-pervasive from the central organs of power down to the remotest rural village, even to this day.

The First Five Year Plan did produce significant achievements whether in creating a comprehensive industrial base or in establishing a new infrastructure in science, education, and health. But the organizational principles of the Centrally Planned Economy, which permitted this initial rapid industrial transformation, in the longer run hampered China's development over the 30 years that it was in operation. Its legacy still creates barriers to progress.

The very principles of central planning lay at the heart of its failure. As the Chinese economic reformer, Professor Wu Jinglian, puts it, state-owned enterprises (SOEs) were:

> "Appendages of high-level executive administrative organs: people, finance, materials, supplies, production, selling all were decided by the State Plan, and [the SOEs] lost their vitality and vigor. At the same time, the quality of service from industry and commerce was creating consumer frustration."[13]

It compartmentalized economic activity into vertical administrative silos or stove pipes. Liu Guoguang, a Chinese economist who should know about Soviet planning since he received a doctorate in 1955 from a Soviet economics institute, in 1984 explained that,

> "The emphasis on vertical leadership created heavy barriers among different departments, trades and areas hampering the development of proper economic connections"[14]

Within the silos, factories that manufactured goods had no control over their destiny. Their governance was entirely in the hands of officials in a central ministry (or its local bureau) to which it reported. The factory was not constituted as a corporation. It had a Chief Accountant but there was no treasury function, and it was not responsible for its own profit and loss. The government injected working capital for salaries and materials, and provided long-term investment funds while it took out surplus cash as it was generated or replaced it if the factory was loss-making. China's SOEs were devoid of any real decision-making power.[15]

In the modern economy, business achieves efficiency and responsiveness to market needs through an integrated supply chain within which information flows freely. In stark contrast, under central planning, factories were not permitted to have direct contact with their suppliers or customers.

Take, for example, a factory producing bicycles. To obtain raw materials, such as steel, it would first have to send the order up through the bureaucratic layers of the silo to its ministry, the First Ministry of Light Industry. The order was then agreed upon at one of the biannual "product ordering meetings" with the Ministry of Metallurgical Industry (which controlled the steel mills) and the Ministry of Materials (which handled all in-bound logistics) after which the decision was communicated down through those other silos so that the steel was delivered to the factory. This ponderous and slow process made it difficult for the factory to respond to changes in consumer demand. It encouraged the factory to err on the side of safety and to over-order and carry excessive inventory.

When it came to selling the finished product, there was a similar process. Information on the bicycles produced was communicated up through the layers to the ministry, which then agreed upon a sale with the Ministry of Commerce, which in turn handled the entire distribution of products through its exclusive control over outbound logistics, wholesalers, and retail stores. Likewise, with export products, there was no direct contact with customers. The factory's ministry worked with a specialist state Foreign Trade Corporation, which had exclusive export/import rights in its sector and met the foreign traders at the biannual Guangzhou (Canton) Trade Fair or at the dreary "Negotiations Building," in northwest Beijing. Cross-border freight forwarding was handled exclusively by a separate state corporation.

As Professor Wu puts it:

> "There was a lack of direct relationships and feedback between producers and consumers and between producers and producers."[16]

A deep irony of the planned economy was that it was very poorly planned. It could be argued that the Chinese economy functioned *despite*, not because of, the planned economy. The bureaucratic process entailed the State Planning Commission drafting the Five Year Plan, including detailed production targets, which were then approved by the State Council and passed to the State Economic Commission for execution. In fact, China often failed to finalize the Five Year Plan in time for the first year of the plan. Essentially, China worked to the rhythm of a series of rolling one-year plans.

The planning cycle was often disrupted by political campaigns and upheavals that punctuated the Chinese political scene. The gathering of statistics to support the decision-making under the plan were (and still are) severely compromised by local authorities cooking the books by reporting either what they thought the "Center" wanted to hear or what best served their local interests.

Short of dismantling the whole system, one route open was the decentralization of economic power, something that occurred periodically but with little success:

> "Each of the multiple attempts at decentralization during the period 1958–76 created chaos and subsequent recentralization. According to the principle of "as soon as you relax things, there is chaos, as soon as you control things, it dies," so we created the vicious circle of relax-chaos-take back to the center-death."[17]

Ponderous and inflexible, the strictures of central planning predictably led to informal "back door" local arrangements, and with them, a culture of deception and corruption. At the local level in such a vast country, life simply went on despite central planning. Informal, direct relationships with other economic silos at the local level were forged, bypassing the centralized flows of the command economy.

Another side effect, in response to the dysfunction of this form of "planning," was the creation of a series of largely self-sufficient economic areas, or autarky, based on major cities. Each area sought to mitigate the inefficiency of the central planning cycle, to assure supply, and to avoid being held hostage by out-of-province agencies and the railway bureaucracy as Chinese economist Xue Muqiao explained:

> "Many of our enterprises, large and small, tend to be all-inclusive because the present system of management compels them to rely on no-one but themselves."[18]

Thus, redundant and subscale industrial capacity was created. Each locality created a comprehensive range of plants, whether iron or steel or motor vehicles, plus all their materials or components suppliers. Autarky led to "duplicate investment and products." In 1978, 80% of China's engineering factories produced their own iron castings. Since it was too risky to outsource, plants aimed for maximum self-sufficiency.[19] The legacy of this today is an economic landscape where regional hubs dominate their own neighborhoods and obstruct firms from other parts of China, a phenomenon termed by the Chinese as "local protectionism" (difang baohu zhuyi). This hampers the development of an integrated national economy in which industry can achieve efficiency and economies of scale.

The Soviet model adopted by China was intrinsically flawed since it replaced lively, rational, and constructive contacts between customers and suppliers with a system of administrative processes that disrupted normal commerce and concentrated power in the hands of bureaucrats. On top of this, the use of government groups, rather than the productive entities, to control the information flow was increasingly ill-fitted to the modern economy, where information on consumer needs, products, technology, competition, talent—everything—needs to be communicated quickly and efficiently.

And Worse ... Beyond the Soviet Model

What could be worse than that dysfunctional Soviet-style economic model? The Chinese found out painfully during the Great Leap Forward (1958–1961) and the Cultural Revolution (1966–1976). Mao led China's society through waves of chaos and campaigns designed to force-march the economy to what was perceived to be a more advanced stage of socialism. During the disastrous Great Leap, China lurched to the left, discarding any semblance of economic reality and embarking on a voluntarist, almost religious, search for economic liftoff. It was hoped that any practical constraints, whether technical, human, or financial, would be compensated for by a mystical belief in the power of the people led by Mao's philosophy, "the spiritual atom bomb." In industry, steel was produced in a myriad of backyard furnaces but it turned out to be unusable. Agricultural collectives were merged into the People's Communes where farmers were forced to destroy their home-cooking vessels and eat in communal kitchens. Bogus science was used to justify unsustainable crop-growing techniques. Economic targets were constantly raised and statistics falsified to fit. What followed was the Great Chinese Famine (1958–1961) during which as many as 45 million Chinese died of "unnatural" causes. State grain stores were left untouched while farmers ate tree bark, died an agonizing death from edema or swelling resulting from starvation, or survived through widespread cannibalism.[20]

Though, on the surface, Mao successfully pushed back within the CCP leadership against the bitter criticism of his Great Leap; this left fissures that would precipitate the Cultural Revolution (1966–1976). Mao may have won the battle but not the war. He was relegated to the role of "philosopher king" and for a time was excluded from the day-to-day affairs of state. He plotted his return to power through the Cultural Revolution when he launched the Red Guards in order to attack and demolish the government and the CCP infrastructure, essentially conducting a coup d'état against his own party.

Mao's actions were driven by two interrelated factors, his opposition to the post-Great Leap measures (backsliding as he saw it) that, for instance, had reinstated workers' incentives; and his desire to win back control of the CCP and to exact revenge on those who had opposed him.

In 1973, I went to study in China as a member of the first batch of British students after the UK normalized relations with China. As we walked down the steps from the plane in Beijing on a chilly October evening and were greeted by officials holding out a long cotton-padded coat for each of us, we entered a world of strict frugality and incessant propaganda, where the day began at 6 a.m. with loudspeakers blaring out the first bars of "The East Is Red," a paean to Mao, China's Red Sun and "savior." We were given the standard student issue of bed quilt, towel, enamel washing bowl and padlock for our room. When summer came around, we were also issued a mosquito net.

By then, the violence of the Red Guards had subsided, though political tensions and "red terror" (people were arrested, sent to prison camps, executed, or otherwise "disappeared") by the Left continued. On the surface, the political scene was going through a period of relative calm. There were signs of a return to a more rational approach to development, in particular the rehabilitation of senior officials who had been exiled from the capital.

On Mao's instructions, Deng Xiaoping, the future architect of China's economic reforms, was brought back from exile in Jiangxi Province to Beijing early in 1973 and rehabilitated in the leadership.[21] During the 1974 January 1st New Year celebrations, we were taken to Beijing's largest gymnasium to see a table tennis tournament. In the VIP row, just across from us, was the unmistakable Deng Xiaoping and, next to him, also diminutive but with a more angular face, Chen Yun, Deng's close mentor on economic matters who had also been brought back from banishment. As my fellow Chinese students and our teachers realized what we were witnessing, there was excited murmuring and finger pointing. The reemergence of Deng was a pivotal moment in modern Chinese history.

But within a few months of my arrival in Beijing, a renewed bout of factional fighting within the CCP broke out, manifesting itself in a new "mass movement" of criticism and denunciation. The Left faction in the CCP felt undermined by more moderate educational and economic policies, not to mention the restoration of officials such as Deng. Moreover, Mao's health was fading and he at times was clearly gaga. So, in early 1974, Mao's wife and others on the Left launched the campaign to "Criticize Lin Biao and Confucius."[22] Lin Biao had been Mao's chosen successor but had died in a plane crash in 1971, allegedly fleeing from a failed attempt at a coup d'état. The denunciation of Confucius was a thinly veiled attack on Premier Zhou Enlai whose efforts to revive the economy were anathema to the Left.

Peking University students return from studying with the People Liberation Army, during the campaign to criticize Lin Biao and Confucius, spring 1974[23]

I had the dubious privilege of visiting a number of Chinese institutions that were celebrated as "models" during the Cultural Revolution. One was The Xinhua Printing Works in Taipingzhuang, Beijing, then on the outskirts of the city, among the fields. It had been selected by Mao as a model for the "cleansing of class ranks," a brutal struggle waged against officials and managers deemed to be "class enemies." A classic SOE, set up in 1949, it was responsible for printing 1.8 million copies annually of the Red Flag, the theoretical journal of the CCP. As part of the political campaign, long essays written by its workers on foreign policy were posted on the walls. Hand-painted slogans were draped across all the walls: "Chaos under heaven is a good thing," "Carry the Criticism of Lin Biao and Confucius through to the End." I visited other factories, the Beijing Jeep Factory (see photo below), for instance, which likewise was festooned with slogans and "big character posters" handwritten by the workers.

Beijing Jeep Factory, 1973.[24]

During the period 1969–1973 (after the initial period of Red Guards chaos) the economy had shown some recovery. In 1974, economic output stagnated due to the political campaigns. On the consumer side, there were shortages of food, cotton, even matches. During the first five months of 1974, at the height of the campaign, there were sharp declines in the production of coal, steel, chemical fertilizer production, as well as a decline in goods shipped by rail.[25]

Some places suffered more severe disruption than others. For the Lunar New Year break in February 1974, we were flown down to the Zhejiang provincial seat of Hangzhou. Our cadre minders had a full program of activities, but we clamored for some time to ourselves ("free activities"). Despite calls for us to "respect the collective" (that is, "Do what you are told!"), we simply said goodbye and headed off on public transportation to explore things.

Downtown Hangzhou was covered in handwritten "big character posters" attacking the city government, calling on the citizens to "Fight People's War," which in China is code for civil war. When we got back to Beijing, the national press had headlines praising the "excellent situation in Hangzhou." This was a good lesson on how to interpret China's Party-controlled press. We knew from close up that things in Hangzhou were on the edge of outright rebellion. The historical record shows that it took over two years for the faction entrenched in Hangzhou to be rooted out. Meanwhile, industrial production in Hangzhou's factories was regularly halted by fighting and strikes. The combined output of Hangzhou's Iron and Steel Works during the three years 1974–1976 was lower than that recorded in the single year of 1973.[26] A senior Zhejiang official has stated in his memoirs that due to disruption caused by the Criticism of Lin Biao and Confucius, grain had to be shipped into that province from North China to avoid famine.[27]

Campaign to Criticize Lin Biao and Confucius. Big character poster in Beijing, 1974, addressed to Dear Chairman Mao and asking for injustices to be righted.[28]

The Brutal Assault on Intellectuals and Science

In 1949, Hu Feng, a well-known writer and literary critic, wrote his poem *Song of Joy* to celebrate the CCP's coming to power:

> "Motherland,
> My motherland
> Today
> At this sacred hour of your new birth
> The entire world salutes you
> The entire universe congratulates you."[29]

But soon his joy turned to disillusionment, and he expressed concern at the political controls placed on writers. He was subjected to violent attacks in the press, made a series of abject self-criticisms, and in 1955 was imprisoned as a counterrevolutionary and head of a "secret anti-party clique," emerging from prison only in 1979, physically and mentally damaged.

The CCP insisted on starting with a clean slate. It fueled its rise to power through fomenting national outrage against all aspects of Western influence, including Christians, who had established many of China's top hospitals and universities. During this cleanout of society, valuable social infrastructure was obliterated, foreigners were deported or fled, while the Chinese who had worked with them were treated as suspect for the rest of their lives.

During the Republican period, the Harvard-trained Minister of Health implemented a program aimed at establishing nationwide healthcare coverage at the county level, with an emphasis on preventive medicine. But on taking power, the CCP swept this system away and started afresh with help from Soviet advisors.

Centers of medical excellence, such as West China Union Hospital in Chengdu and Peking Union Medical College in Beijing, which were founded and flourished during the Republican period, were taken over by the new government and the foreign staff expelled from the country. The same happened with foreign-run universities. Any Chinese with connections to the West became the CCP's punching bag over decades of political campaigns.

As the CCP took power, there was a flight of talent that included many industrialists from Shanghai and Tianjin who ended up in Taiwan, the US, and Hong Kong. The move of Shanghai textile mill owners and their wealth to Hong Kong was largely responsible for fueling the British colony's post-World War II takeoff. During the 1950s, 100,000 refugees a month fled from Mainland China into Hong Kong, some by surviving the short but hazardous swim.

This exodus was counterbalanced by returnees from abroad, who were motivated by patriotism, by the opportunity to help "revive China" after a century of decline. But many became victims of political campaigns.

China opened the door to ethnic overseas Chinese fleeing the violence unleashed against them first in Malaya, then Indonesia and Vietnam. About 210,000 refugees settled in 84 "Overseas-Chinese State Farms" dotted across South China, bringing with them skills in tropical crops, such as rubber and coffee. One refugee from Malaya told a reporter,

> "The seeds brought back by Huaqiao [overseas Chinese] were of superior quality, and together with their technical know-how, the first generation was able to plant high-grade rubber trees and harvest top-quality latex."[30]

But during the Cultural Revolution, ethnic Chinese refugees again became victims of violence, this time in China, accused of being spies and even "foreign devils."[31] For example, in one overseas-Chinese state farm in

Guangxi, hundreds of farmers (including returned refugees) were brutalized until they became disabled or died.[32]

Leading scientists were among the many who returned to help build the "New China." Many fell afoul of the CCP at some stage in their careers. The mathematician Qian Weichang was labeled a "rightist" in 1957 and for the next 26 years, until the verdict was reversed, he repeatedly "received all kinds of humiliation and suffering."[33] During the Cultural Revolution, he was sent to work at the Capital Iron and Steel Works in Beijing.

With regard to the role played by returnees from the West, it is instructive to look at how, in 1965, China made a stunning breakthrough in biochemistry, beating teams in the US and Europe in the race to be the first to achieve the artificial synthesis of crystalline bovine insulin.

In 1938, Wang Yinglai left China for Britain to study biochemistry at the University of Cambridge, gaining a Ph.D. in 1941. He returned to China and after the CCP took power became head of the Institute of Biochemistry of the Chinese Academy of Sciences (CAS). In 1958, collaborating with other returned students, such as Zou Chenglu (Ph.D. from the University of Cambridge), as well as with locally trained scientists, he led the effort that on September 17, 1965, resulted in that extraordinary scientific achievement with insulin. In Spring 1966, Wang, Zou, and another colleague presented their findings to a conference in Warsaw. As Zou put it, "Little did we know that we were to face the 'Cultural Revolution' only two months after we returned home."[34]

During the decade of the Cultural Revolution, Wang and his colleagues were largely cut off from the international scientific community, missed out on being nominated for the Nobel Prize in Chemistry for their breakthrough, and were unable to continue their research. This is one of many examples of how knowledge and ability were squandered and wasted, to the detriment of China's progress.

Through the 1950s China absorbed Soviet science and technology in a variety of ways: through the import of complete plants, Soviet blueprints, Soviet advisors in China, and the training of Chinese in the Soviet Union.[35] This highly integrated approach permitted the speedy assimilation of the technology and a rapid impact on China's industrial infrastructure.

In this period, China sent 38,000 people to the Soviet Union for training, of which 28,000 were technicians. The Soviet Union sent 11,000 scientific and technical personnel to China. China established its Chinese Academy of Sciences modeled exactly on the Soviet Academy of Sciences, whose director, Sergei Vavilov, served as consultant to the Chinese. From

1954 to 1963, China and the Soviet Union met annually regarding more than 100 scientific projects, including those in nuclear science.

Soviet science and technology faced political constraints under Stalin, for instance, when biological research was stymied by Lysenko's pseudo-scientific theories on genetics. But it is generally accepted that in the fields of theoretical chemistry, materials science, mathematics, and physics (including nuclear) the Soviet Union did make significant advances.

China itself went through bouts of pseudoscience. In 1960, at the peak of the Great Famine, CAS was instructed to develop food substitutes and came up with a number of pseudofoods, including acorn flour, powdered roots of corn and wheat, leaf protein, man-made meat essence (from enzymes), dried algae, and insects.[36]

Michael Kochko, the Soviet chemist and academician who spent several years as an advisor in China, criticizes the way China assimilated science and technology in the 1950s, arguing that it "blindly" and "slavishly" followed the Soviet system, focusing on specialized institutes and not on universities. There were not enough trained scientists and China would have been better off teaching new scientists instead. "Better [use] one to train 10. But instead they set up many research institutes, equipped them, but could not staff them." "Instead of a good university in each province … they have set up in each province 'branches' of the China Academy of Sciences, which consist entirely of bureaucrats."[37]

He also faulted the Chinese leaders for their negative attitude to basic research:

> "[They] do not see that basic, pure research is the cornerstone of all applied science. Instead projects of pure science are mercilessly tossed out by the bureaucrats. This dooms Chinese applied science from the start and forces it to imitate foreign prototypes and borrow alien ideas."[38]

Most damning was his view that "the party and government consider all scientists, especially those of the older generation, as 'class enemies' who cannot be trusted."

China also set up a broad range of Soviet-style design institutes that housed China's engineering capabilities. But their high degree of specialization, whereby they operated in one of the ministry-led silos, obstructed rational horizontal expertise and collaboration.

Just as factories were kept separate from R&D, China's universities also were not permitted to conduct research and had to focus on teaching. Research was conducted in separate research institutes. The solid-state physicist Huang Kun returned from the UK to China in 1951 and was "allocated" to the physics department at Peking University where he taught but was prevented from engaging in his own research. It was only in 1977 that Huang Kun could get back to his research, which was to have an important impact on China's semiconductor industry.

Although the Soviet assistance was a poor fit with China's stage of development, presenting challenges in absorbing skills and technology, it did deliver results in kick-starting the construction of a broad industrial base. But in 1960, with the Sino-Soviet Rift, Khrushchev abruptly withdrew some 1,400 Soviet technicians and experts from China.[39] The Chinese, making virtue out of necessity, turned to the concept of "self-reliance."

By the early 1970s, China was repairing relations with the Western powers and Japan (in part to counter the threat from the Soviet Union), bringing opportunities to acquire foreign technology. But this in turn fell foul of China's Left, which deemed such imports to be contrary to the principle of "self-reliance."

This is illustrated by how the issue of chemical fertilizers became a political football. In the 1960s, China made its own significant advances in producing ammonia for fertilizer in small plants using not just coke, but also lignite and coal dust. In the period 1964–1973, production of nitrogenous fertilizers grew almost threefold. Most of this growth came from small plants.[40]

But when compared to Japan, China's wheat and rice yields were low, the ratio (China/Japan) being 100:219 and 100:181, respectively.[41] This was due to the intensive application of chemical fertilizers in Japan (in kilograms of plant nutrients per hectare of crop area: China 60, *Japan 425*). A nationwide survey in China showed that 80% to 96% of land was deficient in hydrogen, compared to 40% to 55% being deficient in phosphorus, and 15% to 24% in potash.[42]

In 1973, Premier Zhou Enlai started the import of complete industrial plants. High priority was given to nitrogenous fertilizer and in 1972, China contracted to import 19 dual ammonia and urea plants. Chinese were sent abroad for training, while staff from the suppliers helped with the construction in China.

China wanted to reduce its dependence on imports of both fertilizers and hydrocarbons and make them in China. Due to the oil crisis in 1973, the world market price of urea (high-analysis nitrogenous fertilizer) rose in 1974 from US\$ 46/ton to US\$ 250–280.[43]

The Left started its attacks. In 1976, after he was purged for a second time, Deng Xiaoping was accused of attempting to "negate the Cultural Revolution" and to "strangle" small fertilizer factories. The same year, the policy of exporting oil to pay for the import of large fertilizer plants was heavily criticized. Jiang Qing (the wife of Mao) is said to have "decried" an imported ammonia plant as "comprador slavishness" and "national betrayal" and "even wanted the Taching [Daqing, a major oil field] to dismantle the plant, which was nearing completion."[44] In October 1976, Jiang Qing and the rest of the "Gang of Four"[†] were arrested. The Daqing urea plant was completed and came on stream.

There were other incidents of this kind. One of the most bizarre cases was that of a second-hand 10,000-ton passenger/cargo vessel bought as scrap on the world market, repaired, refitted, and made ready for service. But the Left is alleged to have said, "The ideology of worshiping foreign things is now spreading everywhere unchecked." The vessel was forced to be left moored in Shanghai, and it was not until six months later, after the "Gang of Four" was arrested, that it could finally set out to sea again.[45]

Farcical though that incident may appear (and putting aside the propaganda rhetoric, which sought to nail the "Gang of Four"), it was a manifestation of a serious pattern of factional political infighting that hampered the absorption of technology and undermined economic development.

The Dead End of the Mao Years

China's economic planners, armed with the towering confidence derived from "scientific Marxism," coupled with massive Soviet support for a time, sincerely believed that they could somehow sidestep basic economic principles.

There were indeed some laudable results. Except for the period of the Great Famine, China was largely able to feed its huge population. From 1952 to 1978 (the first year of the post-Mao economic reforms) China's GDP and output of industry and commerce grew at average annual rates of 8.2% and 6%, respectively. Moreover, this was accompanied by major progress

---

[†] The "Gang of Four" was the label the CCP put on the political faction. Led by Mao's wife Jiang Qing, it also included Zhang Chunqiao, Yao Wenyuan, and Wang Hongwen. They were arrested on October 6, 1976, for helping to pave the way for the economic reforms. Wang Hongwen was said to be behind the 1974 crisis in Hangzhou, mentioned above.

in areas such as women's rights, education and literacy, healthcare coverage, and disease control.

But growth was uneven and certainly not a straight line. After 9% GDP growth during the period 1952–1957, it declined by 2.2% in 1958–1962 due to the Great Leap Forward and the famine it precipitated. In 1963–1965, GDP growth surged back to 14.9%, only to fall back to 6.2% during the Cultural Revolution.[46]

But the growth did not translate into wealth creation. China's *per capita* GNP, starting from a pitifully low base of US$ 52 in 1952, reached only US$ 210 in 1978, 25 years later. How was it that the economic development did not lead to a major improvement in China's living standards or, put another way, "Why did China fail to achieve economic modernization?"[47]

Part of the answer lies in serious structural imbalances. Industry grew annually at an average rate of 11%, while agriculture and commerce grew at only 3% and 4%, respectively. Heavy industry grew 15%, at the expense of light industry. During the First Five Year Plan, investment in heavy industry was nearly 6 times that of investment in light industry and that rose more than 8 times by 1976–1978. China's economy was also highly inefficient. Energy consumption was much higher than that of other developing economies, let alone the developed ones, while the working capital of Chinese enterprises accounted for as much as 26% of total assets due to excessive inventories of raw materials and finished goods.

As a prominent Chinese economist puts it:

> "Because of the bias in the distribution of national income, personal income and people's living standards were persistently suppressed at a low level.... Living standards improved little over more than 20 years. Maximum resources were allocated ... to the production of capital products while the production of consumer products was severely restricted.... In urban areas, people faced the policy of low wages and wage freeze.... In rural areas, because of the urban and rural segregation, people suffered from insufficient employment and lacked incentive for agricultural production."[48]

Some observers still argue that the problem with the Soviet economic model was its faulty execution in China rather than its intrinsic weaknesses.[49] But there is abundant evidence that the Soviet system was not only a poor fit with China's low-level of development, but was also per se an irrational construct that hampered human economic activity.

For many sympathetic observers outside China, China had represented the hope that "socialism" could transcend the defects witnessed in the Soviet Union. The book "The Chinese Road to Socialism" (1971),[50] applauded the Maoist model, taking at face value what the authors were told or shown, while ignoring its fundamental faults. For some, it came as a surprise and a disappointment that China eagerly seized the chance, post-Mao, to ditch both the Soviet economic model and Mao's own variant of it.

So the root of the problem lay in the wholesale and unquestioning import of the intrinsically flawed Soviet economic model, compounded by the Maoist variant, which made a virtue out of poverty. In 1974, the loudspeakers I heard blaring out over the campus in Beijing urged citizens to "pass a frugal New Year" and to avoid "eating or drinking a lot." There was a deep bleakness about that vision of society. Even after several decades of peace and modest economic growth, citizens still had to present ration coupons alongside money, as they purchased rice, cooking oil, wheat flour, and cotton-cloth.

In 1976, shortly before Mao's death, the Chinese government published the eye-catching pamphlet entitled "Why China Has No Inflation."[51] Of course, the answer to this question was blowing in the wind. China's economy had been run into the ground and was largely excluded from the global trade (in part through no fault if its own). The result was no path to wealth creation, but instead bleakness and poverty. As Deng observed later, China's development had been set back several decades.

So the early decades of the PRC, far from ushering in a new dawn, saw China sail to economic ruin. As an ode to Mao Zedong from the Cultural Revolution puts it, "sailing the seas depends on the helmsman." The irony of that revolutionary anthem is now painfully apparent.

The year 1976 was pivotal for China. After Premier Zhou Enlai died, the Left was able once again to remove Deng Xiaoping. But its days were numbered. After Mao died later in the year, the Left found itself isolated and within a month, the "Gang of Four" (as the remaining leaders of the Left became known)[52] had been arrested and, following a show trial, were sent to prison. After a two-year transition, by 1978, Deng Xiaoping had full control of the CCP. He embarked on earthshaking reform of the economy and presided over a rebirth of the Chinese entrepreneurial spirit.

Chapter 4
Wrongs Are Righted, the Reforms Take Shape

To free China from poverty and backwardness, we have for 30 years encouraged people to work hard and lead a simple life.... But hard work and a simple life are meant to achieve speedy progress in production and create the material conditions for a rich and happy life. Perpetual poverty is not what we stand for.[1]

—Xue Muqiao, an architect of China's post-Mao economic reforms, writing in 1981. He had been imprisoned during the Cultural Revolution for calling for modifications to the planned economy.

This is where in our narrative *The China paradox* takes the stage. During the last four decades of reforms, what might on the surface appear to be the incompatible interests of business and a ruling communist party have against all the odds proven to be highly symbiotic, feeding off of and reinforcing their respective strengths and goals.

Somehow, the stars were aligned, permitting the formation of a productive, if precarious, equilibrium between a modern economy and wealth creation, on the one hand, and the CCP-led political system on the other. China's entrepreneurial spirit, which had been suppressed but not extinguished during three decades of Maoism, came pulsing back. Key to the emergence of *the China paradox* was the radically new state of mind in the CCP, which provided the conditions for the economic forces to be liberated. Without the CCP shift toward a strident pragmatism that permitted a wide variety of economic experimentation, China's rise would not have occurred. While the CCP politically never wavered from its absolute autocratic power, it abandoned its economic dogmas in favor of Deng Xiaoping's principle that "to get rich is glorious," thus unleashing the Chinese people's pent-up energy.

After the failures of the Maoist period, the CCP was chastened and humbled by the tough verdict of history. It became highly receptive to new ways to transform China as the only practical route to maintaining its grip on power. Though it has remained true to its Stalinist roots in lashing out at those who might threaten their rule, its overall demeanor showed that it was ready to learn and adapt.

In 1978, Deng Xiaoping launched China on a radical new course called "reform and opening up"[2] (gaige kaifang). Since the Chinese people were exhausted by years of violent political campaigns and economic policies

DOI 10.1515/9781501507212-004

that led to mass starvation, the post-Mao leadership had a very strong mandate to steer China in a fundamentally new economic direction. But the leaders were prudent about controlling the pace and depth of change; nor was there a master blueprint. The approach was extremely gradual and cautious, summed up by Deng's principle of "crossing the river by feeling the stones." It took a great deal of experimentation, trial and error, and social upheaval to arrive at today's economic model, which delivers a GDP of more than US$ 10 trillion, second only to that of the US, and a stunning 50 times China's GDP in 1978, when the reforms began.

Deng made it abundantly clear that the reforms did not extend to the CCP's relinquishing any of its political power. The CCP remains to this day acutely mindful of how the Soviet Union collapsed. It embraces much of what during the Russian reforms was called *perestroika* (economic restructuring) but utterly rejects *glasnost* (political opening up). For the CCP, the economic reforms and the wealth creation they have unleashed are central to its ongoing relevance and to shoring up its hold on power. This is a key aspect of *the China paradox*. Is China pursuing capitalism or autocracy? How can they coexist? In fact, the Chinese model embraces both, though the capitalism is shorn of any liberal democracy and is dominated by state enterprises. For China's rulers, there is no contradiction between the two, as long as the capitalistic tools and levers serve the goal of staying in power. But the model is also sustained by the autocratic side being kept in check, by power being wielded with a relatively light hand. If, as appears to be happening, the political aspect of the equation hardens, then what has been part of a beneficial inter-relationship may well morph into a fatal flaw.

To guide the reader, Table 4.1 shows the broad phases of China's economic reforms, the top leaders who presided over the process, and the country's key milestones.

During the initial years of the reforms (1978–1993), the preoccupation was with liberating China from Maoist dogma, getting the economy back on its feet, and modifying the Centrally Planned Economy so that it could function better. However, once the realization struck home that the Soviet-style economy could not be repaired, the CCP, post-1993, sped up the reforms and moved China further toward a more market-oriented economy.

Table 4.1: China's Post-Mao Economic Reforms

		1976–1978	1978–1993	1993–2002	2002–2012	2012–
Phases of the Economic Reform		Post-Mao transition	**Phase 1** Incremental reform. Trying to make the old system work.	**Phase 2** Speeding up of reform. Focus on hybrid "socialist market economy."	**Phase 3** "Lost ten years." Cronyism. "Vested interests" dominate.	**Phase 4** Despite pledges on reform, little is achieved. Political tightening.
CCP Head		Hua Guofeng 1976–81	Hu Yaobang 1981–87 Zhao Ziyang 1987–89	Jiang Zemin 1989–2002	Hu Jintao 2002–12	Xi Jinping 2012–
Gov. Head (Premier)		Hua Guofeng 1976–80	Zhao Ziyang 1980–87	Li Peng 1987–98 Zhu Rongji 1998–2003	Wen Jiabao 2003–13	Li Keqiang 2013–

Table 4.2: Milestones in China's Reforms

	1976	1977	1978	1988
Milestones of the reforms	February Deng removed for second time. September Mao dies. October "Gang of Four" arrested.	July Deng re-instated.	Deng gains full power, reform agenda set.	Private firms become legal.

	1989	1992	2001	2013
	Tiananmen Square Massacre.	Spring. Deng's Southern Tour revives reforms. Planned economy to be abolished. Deeper SOE reform.	China accedes to World Trade Organization.	CCP sets 60 point agenda for "deepening" reform. But since then main focus on economic rebalancing and anti-corruption. CCP tightens grip. Personality cult around Xi Jinping.

The year 1978 was a truly extraordinary year in China's history. Two years after Mao died and the "Gang of Four" was arrested, Deng Xiaoping[3] was finally able to address a wide range of issues, setting forth his bold reform agenda in a series of impassioned speeches across China. He impatiently and courageously lambasted Mao's policies, issue by issue.

Issue: Maoist dogmatism. The year before, in 1977, Deng had begun the task of overturning decades of dogmatism, criticizing those who insisted on slavishly upholding "whatever" policy or instruction Mao had issued. He called for a verdict on Mao whereby 70% of his contribution was positive and 30% consisted of "mistakes."[4] Though this was a massive break with the past, Deng was extremely careful not to undermine the entire historical legitimacy of Mao and the CCP and deemed Mao's faults to be mistakes (not crimes), which "brought the nation many misfortunes," adding the faint praise that "without him the Chinese people would, at the very least, have spent more time groping in the dark."

He now called for the "emancipation of the mind," smartly adopting for himself what was said to be Mao's original slogan, "Seek truth from facts," as the mantra of his pragmatism and the linchpin for his attack on Mao's policies.[5]

Deng was a passionate pragmatist ("I don't care if it's a white cat or a black cat. It's a good cat as long as it catches mice."[6]), but with the powerful caveat, *only* as long as the actions were aligned with the preservation of CCP power. By 1979, Deng was already articulating the concept of "socialism with Chinese characteristics"[7] that went on to become China's guiding definition of the new economic system, placing the country at the "primary stage of socialism" and in so doing created a pragmatic umbrella under which a mixed economy (private business complementing a dominant state sector) was permitted to flourish. Thus, it could be claimed that China had not abandoned socialism for capitalism. This definition is not just an artifice to justify market reforms since it also reflects the new hybrid order with the dominance of state enterprises and the unyielding political power of the party.

Issue: Status of intellectuals. In a long speech attended by 6,000 scientists, Deng denounced the "wanton sabotage" of science and technology and the persecution of intellectuals by the "Gang of Four." He derided the view that "the more knowledge you have the more reactionary you are" and "we would rather be a laboring class without culture." He stated firmly that in socialist society, "intellectuals are part of the working class."[8]

Even though we may take Deng's intervention at face value (there was a pressing need to bring intellectuals back into the mainstream of society), how do we square it with other actions by Deng? Back in 1957, Deng had enthusiastically implemented the brutal Anti-Rightist Campaign, with more than half-a-million people labeled as anti-CCP, hundreds of thousands sent to the Chinese Gulag, and thousands executed. Then, in 1989, it was Deng who ordered the army to fire on students during the Tiananmen Square Massacre. The key to understanding Deng's motivation is recognizing that his overarching goal was the preservation of CCP rule. What supports this goal is embraced; what threatens this goal is rejected. So, in 1957 and 1989, the CCP felt itself beleaguered and under threat, and it acted against the intellectuals.

But as the reforms took shape, Deng needed the skills of businessmen who, during the Mao-years, had been systematically stripped of their property, livelihoods, and professions. He said "we should allow former capitalist industrialists and businessmen to play a role."[9] A few were rehabilitated, but it had to be left to a new breed of entrepreneurs to revive or reconstitute that former capitalist class, which had been so systematically driven out of existence.

Issue: The restoration of educational standards. Deng showed strong resolve to raise educational standards by bringing back the University Entrance Examinations (gaokao), which had been abolished during the Cultural Revolution.[10] Today, there is enormous competition to get into a Chinese university. The traditional culture, which places huge value on education and learning, has returned. Farmers and taxi drivers all set their target on getting their child through the gaokao and into higher education.

Issue: Combating excessive egalitarianism, restoring incentives in industry. Deng took aim at a key policy of the Cultural Revolution, the rejection of "material incentives" in industry. He stressed the importance of paying people based on the work they do and not their political attitude. "The bonus system should ... be reinstated."[11] Then in September 1978 in a speech in Anshan, Liaoning, the location of China's then-largest steel plant, he pointed out that the plant had 23,000 administrative staff while a comparable plant in Japan had only 600. He called for a system of evaluations for both managers and workers, with larger bonuses for those with the higher ranking. Basic factory practice, we may think, but this was radical in China at that time.

Issue: Empowering factories. Deng took on the issue that Chinese factories had become lifeless extensions of the bureaucracy and argued that they should have "the right to make their own decisions and act independently."[12] This set the stage for the retreat from the planned economy.

Issue: Foreign technology and investment. Deng mocked the "Gang of Four's" view that importing technology was "worshiping foreign things," and stated:

> "... we should be good at studying, and on a large scale take on the help that is available internationally. We should import international advanced technology, advanced equipment, and make it the starting point of our development."

We can detect Deng's impatience as he bemoaned the fact that past mistakes had left China technologically 20 to 30 years behind the developed nations. "We have wasted a lot of time; we now have to develop rapidly. But how can we do this without repeating the mistakes of 1958 [i.e., Mao's Great Leap Forward]?" He called for the "utilization of foreign funds" and invited foreign direct investment (FDI) into China. The Chinese door was being opened to foreigners, but the approach turned out to be highly selective and calibrated to avoid putting Chinese firms at too great a disadvantage.

In the arguments Deng put up to justify the importation of foreign technology, there are echoes of the late-Qing modernizers who imported foreign technology to prop up the collapsing dynasty. So far, Deng and his successors have done a masterful job of sustaining their "dynasty," but the theme of economic progress without political reform, which is reminiscent of the Qing, may yet come to haunt the current rulers in Beijing.

Issue: Setting the boundaries of economic reform. Deng drew a line in the sand, making it clear that he was not retreating from socialism:

> "Effective things that have worked in the past we must keep, especially the basic system, the socialist system, the socialist system of ownership; on that there can be no wavering. We cannot permit the rise of a new capitalist class. We import advanced technology so that we can develop the productive forces, raise the living standards of the people. This is beneficial to the socialist state and the socialist system."[13]

This statement may have been to placate diehard conservatives or Deng may have genuinely believed this. In any case, Deng later came to moderate this stance on capitalists in light of the unexpected emergence of the vibrant private sector that sustained the economy while the CCP sorted out the mess left by the planned economy. But Chinese leaders have not backed down on the primacy of the state sector.

Following Mao's death and the arrest of the "Gang of Four," there also began a process of righting past political wrongs. This was important to the CCP not so much in terms of what we might think of as fairness, but more as a pragmatic way to isolate any residual Maoist elements and forge national unity around the economic reform program. Many Chinese had a deep-seated anxiety that the clock might be turned back and were hesitant to embrace the new mood. Deng's decisive moves served to allay those anxieties. While today the social order remains autocratic, the limits for the tolerance of dissent are clearly set and acts of repression are less arbitrary than before. While this may not be much of a consolation to those who run afoul of the CCP, it does permit citizens to get on with their life peacefully, assuming they don't want to overtly challenge the political order.

In the last years of the Cultural Revolution, some victims of political persecution—officials, scientists, teachers, etc.—were given back their freedom and permitted to return to the cities, and many were reinstated in their jobs. With the death of Mao and the arrest of the "Gang of Four" in 1976, this process was accelerated as political offenders had their "crimes" annulled and were released from prisons, labor camps, or exile in the countryside. I personally met one of these victims.

Interview with a "counterrevolutionary element"

In 1979, I visited Xinhua People's Commune, a rice-growing agricultural unit some 60 km from Guangzhou in south China. The authorities granted me what turned out to be a spine-chilling and disturbing interview.

During my interview of Xu Jiwu, he was closely watched by an official who took copious notes. Smoking heavily and his hands quivering, Xu told me his story, which he had no doubt repeated in front of crowds gathered at countless "struggle" sessions over the years.

The son of a rural landlord, he had, in 1949 at the age of 22, been recruited by an "American espionage organization" at a university in Guangzhou. But it was not until 1951 that his "crimes" came to light. He was forced to write a detailed description of his life, and he confessed and was sentenced to five years in a prison camp for being a "counterrevolutionary element," by Chinese standards a relatively light sentence. His wife also received five years.

In 1957, he was released and returned to his home village, where he was to live for more than 20 years but strictly under supervision or "controlled" conditions. He was permitted to work in the fields but deprived of all political rights. He told me that since 1957, he and his wife had been regularly subjected to bitter criticism and denunciation, especially during the Cultural Revolution. But since the removal, early in 1979, of his "class enemy" status, he had been appointed as a teacher at one of the commune's primary schools, where he was teaching English for a salary of RMB 30, barely equal to the lowest income of local farmers.

Xu rarely looked me in the eye and spoke in a low voice. When I asked what friends he had, he explained that he had no close ones from the "progressive classes." Mr. Xu was a broken and shattered man. For him, the changes had come too late. His life had been blighted by the violence of the revolution. I left the scene feeling somehow tainted as a voyeur of the violence that he had been subjected to.[14]

Setting the Boundaries of Change

When the photo of Deng Xiaoping famously donning a cowboy hat at a rodeo in Texas in 1979 was featured through the 1980s in Time magazine articles with headlines such as "Banishing Mao's Ghost" and "Moving Away from Marx," there was a strong but naive hope in the West that China, in abandoning the planned economy, would somehow at the same time embrace political reform and a truly free market economy so that over time it would increasingly look like us.

But while the government "reversed the verdicts" on victims of political oppression, thus building broad-based support for the reforms, it was in no mood to abandon its monopoly on political power. Those who seized on the loosening up to question the political order were quickly dealt with. Early in the reform process, Wei Jingsheng, a human rights activist, paid a heavy price for testing the limits imposed on public dissent, spending 18 years altogether in jail. Periodically, the CCP tightened the screws on dissent, whether it was the campaign against "spiritual pollution" [i.e., Western ideas] in 1983 or the more recent imprisonment and death of Nobel Peace Prize winner Liu Xiaobo. In June of 1989, the CCP ordered the army to turn its guns on unarmed students who had dared to challenge its authority. All this underscores the fundamental point that, from the CCP's own perverse logic, holding onto power is the overriding priority, even at the expense of citizens' lives or of economic development.

Since the reforms began in 1978, the CCP has played down communist ideology and theory, while clinging to Leninist principles of one-party rule.

The resulting ideological vacuum has undermined the CCP's historical legitimacy and put enormous pressure on it to justify its existence by addressing the nationalist agenda of "revive China" (<u>zhenhua</u>) and to do so by sustaining China's economic growth and rising prosperity.

The Initial Reforms—Limited and Tentative

In the first stage of the reforms (1978–1993), China was still seeking to make the old system work, rectifying the problems associated with the planned economy rather than dismantling it and patching up the state-owned economy.

There was no overt agenda to permit the private sector to compete freely. The full acceptance of a mixed economy ("socialist market economy") only came in the 1990s. Still, while the government was focusing on breathing life back into the SOEs, there was the largely spontaneous flourishing of collective firms sponsored by local government and then ultimately of private enterprises. As one sociologist puts it,

> "The rise of private enterprise and capitalism in China was neither envisioned nor anticipated by its political elite."[15]

The explosion of private or quasi-private economic activity came from below and was not engineered as a central part of the reforms. Having become a fact and helping to prop up the economy while the SOEs were reshaped, the private sector was incorporated into the scheme of things. It came about *despite* the government (which initially put up obstacles) rather than the other way around.

The views of the Chinese economist Xue Muqiao in 1981 illustrate just how limited the reforms were in the initial stage. He certainly did draw a clear line under the Maoist model of development, stating that "perpetual poverty is not what we stand for," echoing Deng, who stated that "poverty is not socialism, to get rich is glorious." But although Xue laid bare the dysfunctional aspects of central planning in China, he also stressed that the reason for changing "this irrational system of economic management" was to "develop the superiority of the socialist system."[16] At that time he saw no apparent alternative to some form of state ownership. Only later on did he come to accept the private, nonstate component of the economy that emerged as if by accident.

So for some time, the centrally planned system continued to set detailed targets and quotas. The sixth Five Year Plan (1981–1985) contained specific production targets for washing machines, watches, TV sets, cigarettes, detergents. Without mention of projected market demand five year out, it stated with supreme bureaucratic confidence:

> "Manufacturing ceramic bathroom fixtures. China will produce 4.5 million pieces of these fixtures in 1985, an increase of 54 percent over 1980."[17]

During this initial period, reforms focused on increasing the autonomy of SOEs and reducing centrally mandated production quotas, price setting, control over foreign trade, and the state-allocation of jobs to graduates.

When in 1978 Deng called for more power to be given to SOEs, he sent a clear signal that central planning was not sacrosanct and that it was fine to experiment at the local level in ways that would ultimately lead to its demise. This is consistent with his style of avoiding issues of reform head on, but instead permitting local variation that, once proven effective, became the new norm.

> "We should increase local power.... Enterprises should have the right to make their own decisions and act independently. For instance, if they should increase the staff a little, if they need to reduce the staff, then they should have the power to handle that. Enterprises should have a little foreign exchange, so that they can order goods themselves and have technology exchange with other countries. There are some things which have to be done in convoluted ways, have to go up through the provincial government, the ministries and the State Planning Commission, which is all too slow. Today there are some comrades who ... will not do anything until they hear the higher authorities say something and they themselves don't dare use their brains."[18]

This sent the message to local factories and government. The cat was out of the bag. In this process, conflict inevitably arose between the central government and the localities. At that time, I witnessed, close-up, one such battle in China's flat glass* industry.

---

* Flat glass is for architectural purposes, for windows and the cladding of high-rise buildings.

A Brave Factory Outguns the Central Government

In flat-glass production, China needed to advance from the vertically drawn process, learned from the Soviets, and adopt the float-glass process, whereby molten glass is floated over a bath of liquid tin to produce a very high quality product suitable for the cladding of modern high-rise buildings. The float process had been invented in the UK and then adopted by US, Belgian, and Japanese firms. China was attempting to develop its own float-glass capability in Luoyang, but this was beset with technical issues and the optimal path forward was to acquire the technology through forming joint ventures (JVs) with foreign firms.

The two protagonists in the state sector were the central ministry responsible for the building materials industry (glass, cement, etc.) and one of the glass works that it nominally controlled, located in Dalian, a major port city in northeast China.

A couple of foreign-invested float-glass plants were already under construction, but were locally sponsored. The ministry wanted to claw back central control and in 1985 had issued a directive mandating that glass technology be first imported by the central government and then licensed out to various Sino-foreign JVs with glass exports paying for the investment. This directive has the ethos and tone of the old centrally planned economy written all over it.

The other protagonist, the glass works, had a long history. Established in 1921 by the Japanese, it became a SOE in 1950. Although it used the relatively backward vertically drawn glass production technology, it nevertheless had a strong reputation in China due to its rigorous quality control and excellent sales, service, and delivery.

The conflict arose because the ministry insisted that one of these new export-oriented glass projects be located in Dalian and had already earmarked a Japanese partner. It was said that China's top leaders had signed off on this program. But my client, a US producer of float glass, had already signed a letter of intent for a new JV plant with the Dalian factory, which refused to work with the Japanese partner foisted on them by the ministry. This attitude at the Dalian level was in part fueled by genuine anti-Japanese sentiment. But beyond that, Dalian wanted the new plant to serve the domestic market, where it correctly projected the emergence of massive unmet demand for float glass as the construction boom began.

Meanwhile, the ministry stuck to its idea of exporting the output.

We could not totally disregard the ministry since we needed its official approval for the project, which had a total investment of US$ 100 MM, way beyond the US$ 30 MM investment approval limit given to the Dalian authorities.

There had already been bad blood between the ministry and the Dalian government over who had the final say in a cement plant project, and now Dalian was seeking to shut the ministry out of the negotiations for the glass project.

Communications between the two sides had broken down, with Dalian essentially turning a deaf ear to Beijing. I shuttled between Beijing and Dalian, becoming a communications channel between these two levels of Chinese government. Both sides fully supported my role. Mainly, it was the ministry that wanted me to convey messages to Dalian. Dalian also used me to leak to my client details of agreements reached by the ministry with the Japanese on their role in the Dalian project, but prudently instructed me to wait until I was outside the PRC before transmitting the information, by telex (yes, it was pre-internet) or by phone.

For the ministry, the game was almost up. As the head of the Dalian factory gleefully commented to me, "There is power at the local level as well as at the central level!" A rising star in the glass industry, she proceeded to work on many fronts. She pledged to conduct "ideological work" on the ministry to get them to cease interference. She met with the dynamic Dalian Mayor Wei Fuhai and won his support.

It turned out to be a case of "follow the money." Dalian's ability to fund the deal independently of the central government made it impossible for the ministry to claw back control. As a result of ongoing economic reforms, the Dalian factory was now permitted to retain a proportion of the foreign exchange it earned from glass exports. Based on this, Dalian International Trust and Investment Corporation agreed to provide debt financing to the Dalian partner to the JV secured by a lien on the assets of its existing factory.

The "center's" position had already been undermined by the calls from China's leaders for increased enterprise autonomy. But it still took strong and charismatic leadership at the enterprise level, coupled with a bold local government, to win the day.

As the government loosened its grip on price controls, distribution, and logistics and foreign trade, centrifugal forces drove SOEs to assert their autonomy and permitted managers and market forces, not faceless bureaucrats, to drive business decisions.

True market prices were established for most goods, an essential step in creating an accurate picture of economic activity, where inputs and output reflected real costs. This permitted industry to measure its actual productivity and competitiveness. But to avoid too much disruption to the economy, this was again a story of gradual reforms starting to unwind the old system. There emerged a two-track system for products, those "within the plan" (jinei) and those "outside the plan" (jiwai). If you had an urgent need and lacked confidence in the ability of the state to deliver the materials on time, then you went "outside the plan" and paid a premium.

As an indication of just how slow the reform process was, in 1985, seven years into the reforms, 98% of steel products were still mandated to be sold to the state and then distributed and sold at the fixed national state price by the State Bureau of Materials. The remaining 2% of steel production, which was surplus to the quotas set by the state, were left to the factories to be sold in the free market, but at a higher price than "within the plan."

The Reforms Go into a High Gear

While 1978 was the momentous year in which Deng launched the reforms, 1992 was the year in which he breathed new life into the process, which was facing serious opposition from conservatives.

Conservatives in the CCP leadership blamed the student movement and political crisis in 1989 on overly hasty and ill-considered reforms, and proceeded to roll back the relaxation in the economy and strengthen central controls. Students I met in Beijing during the protests in 1989 stressed that a key subtext to "democracy and freedom" was a demand for the transparency and accountability needed to counter the corruption that had become all-pervasive since the reforms.

While the conservatives wanted to slow down or even kill off the reforms, in order to curb the emerging "frontier capitalism" mentality that affronted their Maoist principles, Deng took a defiantly different view, adamantly stating that "development is the absolute principle." He argued that deeper economic reform and wealth creation were essential to sustaining the CCP's relevance. In response to the roadblocks to reform and his marginalization in the leadership, he came out fighting and turned things around quite dramatically. During the Lunar New Year festival, and without informing his fellow leaders, Deng made an extensive visit of South China, holding talks and making speeches at every point. He stressed:

> "If we don't have the pioneering spirit, if we are afraid to take risks, if we have no energy and drive, we cannot break a new path, or accomplish anything new.... Try bold experiments and blaze new trails."[19]

This was a barnstorming exercise not unlike his dramatic intervention across China in 1978 to kick off the reforms. It did the trick. Urgency and passion returned to the reform process, and a much deeper transformation of the economy began.

During his "Southern Tour," Deng called for risk-taking and experimentation, confronting the Chinese people's aversion to risk-taking or stepping out boldly, a cultural trait with Confucian origins but massively reinforced by 30 years of the communist straitjacket.

While Deng also made it clear that they should be "vigilant" about going too far to the right (to capitalism), he stressed that the main danger to the reforms was the "Left," that is to say, his conservative opponents who remained defenders of the planned economy.

Deng's view had matured a great deal since 1978, when he had called just for the improvement of central planning. In 1992, he was ready to abandon the last vestiges of the traditional planned economy in favor of what came to be known as the "socialist market economy":

> "The proportion of planning to market forces is not the essential difference between socialism and capitalism. A planned economy is not equivalent to socialism, because there is planning under capitalism, too; a market economy is not capitalism, because there are markets under socialism, too."[20]

Between 1978 and 1992, China's GDP grew only modestly from RMB 0.4 trillion to 3 trillion. The 1992–1993 period, after Deng's Southern Tour, was the critical watershed when China's GDP growth reached its inflection point, soared, and has not looked back, reaching RMB 68 trillion (over US$ 10 trillion) in 2015.

Guided by Deng—the main architect of the changes, who remained in the background but was still hands-on—CCP head, Jiang Zemin, and Premier Zhu Rongji led this impressive second phase of economic reforms (1993–2002). The Centrally Planned Economy was finally dismantled, SOEs got to list their stocks in Hong Kong, and the rights of private enterprises were enshrined for the first time in the PRC Constitution. China opened its door more widely to foreign investment and Zhu Rongji, despite tough resistance from sections of the leadership, pushed through China's accession to the World Trade Organization (WTO).

Jiang also brought some reform to the CCP itself by allowing private entrepreneurs to join the CCP. He even created some lightweight theoretical basis to support this move—pointing out that many such businessmen had originally been workers and that the CCP had to represent the whole nation. But this was not out of generosity to the emerging new capitalist class. As he explained in 2000, this was part of his plan to strengthen the links of the party into the newly emerged private enterprises, 80% of which he said had no party members whatsoever.[21]

The Reforms Lose Steam (2002 Onward)

Under the stewardship of party leader Hu Jintao, China saw little progress on further deepening the reform. Standing still on the reform agenda, in effect, permitted backsliding and heightened cronyism in the state sector. It is true that China had to deal with the Wenchuan earthquake (2008) and also hosted a trouble-free (though fun-less) Summer Olympics in the same year. Since the era of Hu ended in 2013, many Chinese have vented their anger at what they see as "ten lost years" during which the reforms stalled while corruption and vested interests flourished. Of course, earlier they had mainly remained silent.

Much hope was pinned on the current CCP leader, Xi Jinping, who in contrast to Hu, exhibits a bold confidence and some human touch. But, although he began his rule with a broad agenda for further reforms, he has focused more on corruption and factionalism and has been distracted by unrest in Xinjiang and escalating tensions with neighbors in Asia.

Xi has concentrated power in his own hands. While he so far has not sought to set himself up in the imperial style adopted by Mao at his peak, he has abandoned the more highly collective leadership style which had prevailed since the reforms began. Xi chairs two new committees within the CCP (separate from the government), one on security and one on the economy. He has sidelined Premier Li Keqiang who by convention should handle economic matters.

We have seen a slowing of GDP growth, partly because of global market factors and partly because China, after its catch-up growth spurt, is now seeking to rebalance the economy. The goal is to move up the economic ladder and achieve a GDP that has quality, efficiency, and innovation, not just growth at any cost. Xi promised deepening reform, calling for market forces to drive capital allocation, for further freeing up of SOEs, and for enhanced consumer spending as an alternative to infrastructure investment. The CCP set out a plan for "330 reform measures." Xi stated with some honesty that, after more than 30 years, China's reforms had "entered a deep-water zone." "The easy part has been done.... What is left are tough bones that are hard to chew. This requires us to act boldly and progress steadily."[22] But progress on these issues has been slow and certainly not bold, overshadowed by anticorruption and the ever-tightening autocracy. Many in China and abroad have become deeply skeptical about Xi's reformist intent.

China's Economic Planning Today

China's centrally planned system was formally abolished only in 1993. Although there is still a National Development Plan, which sets economic growth targets, these are aspirational since the government no longer can enforce a target simply by direct administrative action. The government still allocates investment for the infrastructure and for science and technology. But mostly it uses indirect levers such as taxation, interest rates, and regional incentives to steer the economy in the desired direction.

In contrast to the old Soviet-style command economy, China's five-year plans today embody the new principle of "macroeconomic guidance" and are littered with terms such as "foster," "promote," "support."[23]

Predictably in some of the less developed parts of China in the interior, the planning authorities may interpret "guidance" rather like an interfering parent telling a grown child "I am just helping." But in regions such as Guangdong and Zhejiang, where private enterprises predominate, local government sounds much as government does in Europe or the US. Take the then Vice Governor of Zhejiang, Wang Zhong, who told me that his provincial government's role was strictly confined to creating the supportive environment and infrastructure in which business can flourish.

Still, the impact of the residual state planning functions coordinated today by the National Development and Reform Commission (NDRC) is felt in a number of ways.

Within the framework of the Five Year Plans, projects are developed and state funds channeled into R&D for semiconductor, mobile handsets, high-speed rail, nuclear power, civil aviation, biotechnology, etc. Priority has been given to nurturing large SOEs to become national champions capable of competing on the world stage.

The NDRC, after consultation with other government departments, still exercises control over prices for basic utilities (electricity, gas, and phone), gasoline, transportation, and, with caps, certain meat or grain prices to combat inflation. While overall the NDRC's power and reach has been waning, its role has been somewhat reinforced by its responsibility for enforcing the recent antimonopoly law.

Over the years, the old Soviet-style manufacturing ministries have gradually been shrunk and consolidated so that today a superministry, the Ministry of Industry and Information Technology (MIIT), provides "guidance" to the manufacturing industry. Working with the State-owned Assets Supervision and Administration Commission (SASAC), which acts as the representative of the state as owner of shares in SOEs, it is sometimes able to force mergers between SOEs and, where overcapacity exists, attempts to bring about consolidation and capacity reductions. But pressures from the central government are often thwarted by fleet-footed SOE management in cahoots with local government, whose top priority is preserving jobs and thus social stability, rather than adjusting capacity to market demand or improving environmental protection.

Enterprises can flex their muscles against government pressure, but we should not underestimate the residual impact of central planning, its institutions, processes, and, above all, its frame of mind. It helps to explain how, despite using capitalist methods, China's SOE-dominated economy remains far from a true market economy.

Chapter 5
What to Do with the State-Owned Enterprises?

Dr. Ke [Clifford], the strategy you give us must be implementable!
—Words of the CCP party secretary of a large SOE
to the author in 2001 during a consulting project,
sharing his concern about the adaptability of
Western business practices to Chinese conditions.

Viewed superficially, it seemed to some that China was privatizing its largest state-owned enterprises (SOEs). Surely this would undermine the fundamentals of the "socialist" political order? The reality was that there was no inconsistency, since China's real intent was quite to the contrary. It was to breathe new life into the large SOEs in order to ensure their competitiveness and survival. It actually all fit together as part of *the China paradox*.

How is it that China's large SOEs, having signed up for the transparency and corporate governance required to get their stock market listings, pay scant attention to shareholders' rights and remain subservient to the vested interests in and around the CCP? At the end of the day, commitments made to improved SOE governance were little more than window dressing. The CCP's main goal was to use investors' money to reduce the burden of SOEs on the state.

The number one issue stemming from the legacy of the planned economy was what to do with the SOEs. This question dwarfed other legacy issues in size and complexity. The reform of China's SOEs can be divided into distinct phases.

Weaning the SOEs Off the State (1978–93)

The principal goal was to radically increase the SOEs autonomy, get them off the state payroll, off life support, and make them "responsible for profit and loss" (zifu yingkui), thus enhancing their productivity, responsiveness to the market, overall financial performance, and survivability.

Xue Muqiao, a leading Chinese economist, writing in 1981, defined the powers that needed to be given to the SOEs as part of the reform:

1. Retain a proportion of their revenue for their own use and "abolish the government's monopoly" over the SOEs' income and expenditures.
2. Give the SOEs control over their fixed assets and working capital so that they can acquire new equipment without government approvals.

DOI 10.1515/9781501507212-005

3. Give them the ability to hire and fire employees; "break down the iron rice bowl system" (guaranteed lifetime employment and benefits).
4. Give the factory manager greater authority. "The Party Committee should not exercise direct control over production and business operations."[1]

The first three of these reforms were implemented across China under the banner of "separation of government and enterprise" (zhengqi fenkai). Tellingly, the term for state firms changed from state-run (guoying) enterprises to state-owned (guoyou) enterprises.[2]

The fourth reform, requiring the CCP to take a back seat in the SOE and not to interfere in its day-to-day business, has been implemented to varying degrees. But the further extension of that reform, entailing the clear "separation of party and enterprise," (dangqi fenkai) remains highly sensitive and hardly foreseeable under the current political order.

For SOEs to take on the "responsibility for profit and loss," there had to be a standardized and appropriate accounting system. China moved quickly to reintroduce Western-style double-entry accounting, which had been used during the Republican period and then abandoned after 1949 in favor of the Soviet accounting system, which fit the centrally planned economy. Now, as the economic reforms gained momentum, China issued the Accounting Law (1985) and other related regulations.

SOEs were left to their own devices to struggle for survival. Smaller SOEs faced serious financial stress in the new environment as they were cut adrift from the mother ship of the state.

In 1994, I did due diligence on Beijing Jianzhong Machinery Company which dated back to 1953, when it was constructed with the help of Soviet engineers and loans and technically, still reported into the then Ministry of Electronics Industry. It was making a small post-tax profit but was in a downward spiral. Sales growth over the previous four years had not even kept up with inflation. As I noted at the time:

> "The overwhelming atmosphere ... is that of an old-style factory which is ill-equipped to survive in the new economic order.... [Its] premises are run down and decaying. Grass grows from the pathways between workshops. The fountain at the factory entrance does not function. The buildings, which mostly date from the 1950s and 1960s, are in a state of disrepair and greatly underutilized, with the current production activities in some cases only occupying small corners of the large workshops."[3]

Jianzhong suffered from a dismal lack of strategic focus. In the 130,000 square meters of the factory compound it produced a broad range of custom-made products, including vacuum furnaces, equipment for the semiconductor industry, mass flow controllers, and other products such as resistors, capacitors, and transformers. It had tried recently to diversify into consumer products such as washing machines and that had failed. It was still searching for new product areas for the underutilized factory. One new option under consideration was electronic ignitions and locks for automobiles.

It had 1,100 employees in the main factory and 300 more in subsidiaries. The largest of the subsidiaries had the task of seeking alternative employment for staff in excess of the factory's needs, essentially serving as an outplacement service. The factory also had 800 pensioners, which cost the firm RMB 3 MM a year.

The factory suffered from so-called "triangular debt," a backed-up chain of accounts receivable between Chinese suppliers and customers. The payment period for Jianzhong's receivables had increased from the normal 30 days to as long as one year, forcing it to take on large working capital loans.

Ultimately, the factory survived and moved into one of Beijing's science parks, where it now produces pressure valves. Today, the massive site of the old factory is part of the inner city, has been redeveloped for commercial real estate, and most of the workforce was let go with some compensation.

Another example of a small SOE that faced financial pressures was Xindu Brewery, located in the suburbs of Chengdu, Sichuan. In 1991, its parent, a chemical-fertilizer producer owned by the local government, had taken over the brewery, expanding it from 10,000 tpy (tons per year) capacity to 50,000 tpy. But that was still just half of what was deemed to be an economic scale. Those who have no interest whatsoever in accounting should probably fast forward past this anecdote. But for others it may serve as an interesting window into how things are not always what they seem.

The brewery shared with me the company accounts, which were set out according to China's new accounting standards. The beer business itself was booming. Over the previous four years, its production had grown three-fold while revenues had grown five-fold (in part fueled by inflation of about 25%). At the peak of the summer season, trucks queued up outside the brewery to get draft beer, which was highly prized by the consumer and in very short supply.

At first glance, the brewery seemed financially troubled. It was sinking under the burden of debt used both for fixed assets (equipment) and working capital. After payment of interest (equivalent to 10% of revenues), the pretax margin was 5% to 6%, a precipitous decline from 20% four years earlier. The brewery's financial leverage (that is Total Liabilities/Total Assets) was 93% and would typically rise to 100% as it built up inventory in preparation for the hot summer months. In other words, on paper, it was technically close to bankruptcy.

Looking more carefully at the brewery's accounts, it became apparent that its financial situation was poor, but certainly not disastrous. Though 80% of the loans were short term (not matching the long-term fixed assets they were financing), the bank debt (loans with a term of 3 or 6 months) was repeatedly rolled over at maturity, without objections from the bank lender.

Some of the other debt should have been reclassified as quasi-equity. Large beer distributors lent money to the brewery to ensure access to beer during the tight summer supply situation. Interest needed to be paid on these loans, but there was no pressure whatsoever to repay the principal.

Tax payable for consumption tax (paid on "luxuries" such as beer) and value-added tax, was another large item on the balance sheet but remained waived by the local government tax bureau.

While it was true that profitability was shrinking under a heavy debt burden, when the accounts were reconfigured and examined closely, the brewery in fact was not facing imminent collapse. As Xindu emphasized to me, it was in much better shape than the seriously loss-making Chengdu Brewery downtown, which had problems with beer quality and was facing the collapse of customer demand.

In the end, Xindu Brewery found a buyer, and today is part of China's largest brewing group. Beer production has been transferred to a new site with economies of scale, while on the old site, workers' apartments, which used to be part of the old SOE, are on the market for the equivalent of about US$ 63,000 per unit.

Central Planning Fades Away

As central planning was gradually unwound, ministries were merged or downgraded. Officials were retired or sent to work in government-sponsored industry associations. This was very traumatic for the bureaucrats who had been used to operating the economy down to the finest local level of detail.

Moreover, unraveling the old system also alarmed some reformers. In 1981, the reforming economist Xue Muqiao pushed back on the growing decentralization, expressing disdain for "the anarchy in production, typical of capitalism."

Chinese production of replacement orthopedic implants for hips and knees is an example of the kind of market "anarchy" he inveighed against. Under central planning, China's State Pharmaceutical Administration (SPA) not only regulated quality standards, but also controlled all factories producing medical equipment and pharmaceuticals. SPA had one factory in Shanghai and two in Tianjin producing hip and knee implants manufactured from materials such as titanium and cobalt alloys supplied from factories under the Ministry of Aeronautics Industry.

But by 1994, SPA's control over the sector had essentially melted away. New entities outside of SPA's orbit entered the market with their own implants. Among these were factories under the Ministry of Aeronautics Industry, using their materials expertise as the starting point for implant manufacture. Even a factory established by the Ministry of Education began producing implants. Some nonstate companies in Jiangsu had also jumped into the market.

The SPA found it impossible to supervise product quality, both the design and integrity of the implant itself and the sterile conditions in which it should be packed, leading to repeated incidents in which the implanted replacement joint broke after implantation or the entire joint became infected. One of these problems, the so-called "Tianjin Incident," was a milestone as one of China's first successful consumer lawsuits over medical malpractice. China's entire implant industry was backward and risky, something apparent to citizens and honest doctors alike. Poor quality in this critical area resulted in strong demand for foreign implants, permitting international firms such as Stryker, DePuy, and Zimmer to grow strong in China. China continues to be plagued by lax regulation and weak quality control, as was seen in the baby milk formula scandal.[4]

When the Chinese government finally abandoned central planning in 1993 and called for the establishment of a "socialist market economy," progress had been made in giving SOEs control over their destiny. But the major questions had yet to be addressed. As an OECD report put it:

"These measures [the first phase of SOE reforms] were limited in that they neither modified corporate governance nor significantly restructured business. As a result, the reformed SOEs remained intrinsically unchanged in their ownership and corporate structure."[5]

During the next phase, the pace of reform quickened and bold steps were taken to address these issues that held SOEs back.

Addressing Ownership and Governance (1993–2003)

After central planning was finally abandoned in 1993, China began a bold program whereby the largest SOEs were subjected to "restructuring and change of ownership" (<u>chongzu gaizhi</u>) (a diversification of ownership through stock listings but *not* outright privatization) with the goal of making them fit to compete in the mixed economy with local private firms and, most critically, with foreign entrants into the China market.

Meanwhile, many smaller nonstrategic or nonviable SOEs were completely privatized or sold off to Chinese or foreign interests. Others were simply closed down and their buildings demolished to make space for shopping malls, office blocks, or superhighways.

While the SOE sector had success stories, such as the well-run glass plant in Dalian discussed earlier, overall, it was falling behind and becoming a drain on the economy. The urgency for reform received a massive boost as a result of competition from the booming Chinese private sector, which was finding its feet, and the threat from foreign firms during the run-up to China's accession to the World Trade Organization in 2001.

Deng's push for SOE reforms was encapsulated in the slogan "Grasp the large and let go of the small," whereby several hundred large SOEs were restructured, followed in most cases by a stock market listing, while many small- to medium-sized SOEs, which we shall term the "dogs," were privatized or closed.

Selling off the "Dogs"

In 1995, the Chinese government began to openly seek private buyers of many thousands of small- to medium-sized SOEs, primarily owned at the province and city level or lower. These SOEs were in general subscale, inefficient, polluting, debt-burdened, and loss-making: classic "dogs," or firms that were past saving as independent entities. In 1998, I visited two breweries that the government was seeking to sell off.

Jiutai Brewery, located among sorghum and corn fields on the broad plain 40 km north of Changchun in Jilin Province, was on the block to be privatized. Market conditions favored the brewery. The Changchun area had a population of six million with annual beer demand of 350,000 to 400,000 tons. China's northeast had the nation's highest per capita beer consumption. Nearby Changchun Brewery (capacity 30,000 tpy) had recently closed down due to poor management, high costs, and pressure from lenders, leaving Jiutai as the only brewery of any size in the area. Beers from all over China were shipped into Changchun, and there was clearly a market vacuum to be filled.

But Jiutai was struggling. Its brewing capacity had been increased from 25,000 to 50,000 tons but the bottleneck, so to speak, came as a result of the existing two Romanian-built bottling lines that limited output to 35,000 tpy.

The brewery was subscale and fixed costs were too high. Its beer quality was unstable, often having a sulfurous smell, and it had to resort to price cutting to win market share. It lacked premium brands. It was facing a net loss of RMB 5 MM (million) on sales of RMB 28 MM. Bank loans totaled RMB 39 MM and almost all were short-term, leaving no financial flexibility. Brewery Director and CCP Secretary Sun explained to me that to complete expansion to 50,000 tpy, the brewery needed additional capital of RMB 20 MM for a new bottling line, as well as working capital. Jiutai was ultimately sold to a Guangdong-based group.

Three years earlier, in 1995, I visited the Xingcheng Juhuadao Brewery in Liaoning Province. As a first step toward privatization, it had already been transformed into a "share" company with factory staff holding 5% of the company and the city government the rest. The plant director was seeking capital to expand the capacity from 30,000 to 100,000 tpy. When I returned in 1998, the director told me that he had personally invested RMB 3-4 MM to become joint owner along with three other individuals.

He did not explain where his capital came from and I did not probe. But, while in Liaoning, I learned that local entrepreneurs linked to local officials had been able to acquire the state firms for a knock-down price. As a result, the central government became outraged and forced the privatization program in Jilin to be suspended for a time.

Among the factories of China's "light industry" sector, which produced consumer products ranging from bicycles to face cream and beer, there were numerous such "dogs." Many were sold to foreign companies seeking to create a manufacturing footprint across China. A classic example is Procter & Gamble, which formed detergent JVs with struggling Chinese firms at key regional points across China, from Guangdong to Chengdu, creating a network of satellite plants integrated into P&G China's operations. The same detergent powder manufacturing capacity grab was carried out by Unilever and to a lesser extent by Henkel.

Transforming the Large SOEs

When it came to large-scale SOEs, most were first restructured, followed by a stock market listing (initial public offering, or IPO), a process described by the Chinese government as "Restructuring and Change of Ownership." In contrast to the fate of the "dogs" discussed above, there was no intent to privatize these large SOEs.

The restructuring process corporatized the SOEs through establishing boards of directors and through making their subsidiaries clearly subordinate to the parent company. They were required to develop a market-oriented strategy with a clear business focus, which implied the disposal of nonviable parts of the business lines and the shedding of the heavy burden of surplus employees and social roles that they had inherited from the planned economy.

For the government, the key goal of the IPOs was to utilize "other people's money," that is to raise funds through selling a minority of shares (30% to 40%) to the public, which were to be used to recapitalize the ailing SOEs and reduce the burden on the state.

Although some foreign observers describe this as privatization, in reality it was far from that since the Chinese government (directly, through its residual shareholding) and the CCP (through its political role in every state firm) still called the shots.

Combining the restructuring with a stock market listing (IPO) also had the goal of utilizing market and shareholder pressure, as well as independent directors, to improve SOE corporate governance. Making SOEs conform to international stock market standards was intended to create momentum toward a degree of real and not just superficial change. As it turned out, such a check on SOE behavior proved to be pie-in-the-sky.

The SOE leaders themselves, as distinguished from the officials who oversaw them, described to me their stock listing as a way to create further distance between themselves and the government/CCP, thus giving them more control over business strategy, as well as over salaries and incentives. After a bright start, that vision has also not been fully realized so far. In fact, much of those benefits of increased autonomy resulting from the IPOs are being rolled back.

Management Consulting to the Rescue

In the West, management consulting is tolerated as a necessary evil. In China, it has been embraced as a vital catalyst for SOE change and has earned the respect of Chinese business and political leaders alike. International management consultants, hired for the restructuring and pre-IPO business plan, served as the hands-on change agents needed to push the SOE reform process forward. A handful of top (mainly US) strategy consulting firms took on this huge and daunting task. They worked alongside an array of other advisors, such investment banks, accounting firms, asset valuation firms, PR firms, and insurers.

Encouraged by the knowledge that Premier Zhu Rongji personally was highly supportive of bringing in foreign consulting firms for the restructuring/IPO projects, large SOEs reacted swiftly to select their consulting firm based on express criteria, such as specific sector knowledge, team size and composition, market reputation, and, of course, price. The project would last about three months and be staffed with 10 to 15 consultants.

The consultants provided fact-based analysis of the SOE to create consensus around a proposed direction. This was something that neither the government nor the SOE itself could do on its own. The consultants provided an initial diagnostic followed by comprehensive plans on business strategy, organization, and governance. Above all, the SOEs were keen to transfer international industry-specific best practices to the SOEs to enhance their competitiveness in the new domestic market environment and ultimately internationally.

While the SOEs were hungry for the transformation the consultants offered, they also felt an entirely justified anxiety that without the new business plan being tailored to fit objective Chinese conditions, it would be hard to deliver real change. One SOE CCP secretary waved his finger at me and stressed: "Dr. Ke [my Chinese name], the strategy you give us must be implementable!" The issue of creating a bridge between strategic recommendations and effective action is serious enough in the West, but it is infinitely more complex in the Chinese cultural and political context.

Keeping things on track was challenging. At one client site, the team members from the SOE side were happy to sit playing computer games rather than doing their allotted tasks. Another project came to a halt for at least a week while the SOE participated in a campaign to study CCP Chairman Jiang Zemin's "theory" on the "Three Represents."

But more often than not, the delays we faced on projects had to do with the need for the SOE management to build a consensus around a given proposed path of action. In the West, top management will typically work with the consultant until there is a relatively fully formed plan. But in Chinese SOEs, the fear of making mistakes and an aversion to risk-taking make it common for senior management to delay a choice from among a series of strategic options presented to them by the consultants. Instead they share half-formed plans with a broad raft of middle management to gain feedback. While this may be a smart way to uncover and deal with opposition or objections to the preferred option, and also provides the illusion of internal democracy at work, this tactic also leads to early and unnecessary concessions that can undermine the focus and coherence of the final plan.

Though it is tough working with SOEs, it has many redeeming features and is not all a hard grind. Senior SOE executives are often very accessible and typically embrace the presence of the consulting team. You can sit with the leaders in the canteen cafeteria at breakfast time. Or you can simply walk the corridor, knock on the door, and have an informal chat. That includes the CEO and the CCP secretary. Or they invite you to their senior offsite meeting at their retreat in the hills, often called an "activity center" but more like their own in-house club and spa.

Diagnosing the Problems

Before recommending a cure, we had to conduct a full diagnosis of the current situation. With Chinese SOEs, this is complex and time-consuming, taking our team weeks to analyze, pull apart, reorder, repair, and rework the firm's accounts to make sense of them, to strip out extraneous factors, and to uncover the true picture of the firm, overall and by business line.

Typical was a central-level large SOE that was highly fragmented with approximately 1,000 subsidiaries. Approximately is the right term. It included its "estimated" 400 local JVs or partnerships; 541 of the thousand were third-level subsidiaries, with little or no direct interaction with central management since, like all the subsidiaries, they were legally constituted as semi-autonomous entities. This patchwork quilt of entities made it impossible to standardize procedures or to provide a consistent network of services for customers across China.

Given this type of fragmented organization, there was often no consistent accounting across the subsidiaries from year-to-year. The consolidation of accounts was incomplete and there was no common, shared management information system (MIS). The SOE parent company had an urgent need to improve its financial reporting and control.

As the restructuring proceeded, it was often difficult to transform the local entities and integrate them under central corporate control since they were closely linked into their respective local governments, which relied on them for tax revenues. Even when the SOE forced these entities to change their ownership structure, the local authorities still did their utmost to block the SOEs attempts to consolidate the firm's finances. Without this consolidation of the subsidiaries' accounts, the SOE was unable to minimize its tax bill by pooling the results of all its subsidiaries and using losses from one entity to offset the profits from another.

Having created a true picture of the SOE's finances, it was common to find that the company's selling, general, and administrative (SG&A) expense was not allocated accurately to the specific lines of business, thus masking their true performance. The painstaking patching together of disparate information resulted in the SOE seeing for the first time with the utmost clarity what the issues were, where it was profitable, where it was bleeding money. Most critically, it could see how the firm, based on certain key metrics, measured up to competitors, in particular, global players. As we shared the results of the diagnostic phase, the eyes of client's management teams became riveted on the data revealed. There were expressions of surprise and consternation. It was a revelation, a critical moment of shock, truth, and enlightenment.

In one project, some of the lines of business were deeply in the red, with little prospect of turning the corner. Overall, the firm showed a small net profit of 2%. Net cash flow after capital investment had been negative. The prognosis was that with declining margins, growing competition, and a heavy cost structure, the firm would likely become loss-making in the near future unless there was fundamental change. We described a "self-reinforcing downward spiral within the company," starting with the "deterioration in service levels and competitiveness" and leading to cash shortages and "underinvestment in assets, skills, and IT."[6]

This type of shock treatment through fact-based analysis, and not on emotion or denial, showed a completely fresh and unexpected picture that was just what was needed to galvanize SOEs into action, to get them to embrace the restructuring and the strategic rethink. Through the clarity of our diagnosis, we also built the credibility to win further management support as we moved on to recommendations for the path forward, which often entailed tough choices and painful decisions.

What Do We Want to Be?

Smart business strategy starts with an outside-in approach, which first looks at the market and customer needs and then meshes those against the firm's capabilities and skills (or what could be acquired or built).

This holistic concept was quite revolutionary to SOE leaders brought up on Stalinist engineering and production-led approaches, which paid scant regard to what the customer really wanted. On top of that, as central planning was slowly unwound, SOEs delighted in their newfound freedom and jumped into new business areas that appeared to have profit potential. The absence of a clear business focus became a major issue.

Strategy-making typically entails framing a series of options that offer the potential of profitable and sustainable growth. It is about "options" since there is never just one correct road forward. The profiles of the options, in terms of risk and return, complexity, ease of execution, etc., will vary enormously. The company has to use its judgment to select one option (or perhaps maybe a hybrid version). At a certain point, a decision has to be made about the company's strategic focus, what it will offer in terms of products or services, how it can differentiate or position itself—essentially answering the fundamental question, "what do we want to be?" Without answering this basic question, it is difficult to address a series of other questions that logically follow—around required partnerships, processes, technology, organization, skills, funding, etc.

To help an SOE create a clear and differentiated business focus, the challenge often became building the case for de-emphasizing or completely exiting from business lines that did not fit the selected strategic option. Often, we had to deal with the sentimental attachment to a loss-making or ill-fitting existing business line built by one of the senior leaders of the firm.

When the strategic choices were developed for consideration by a Chinese SOE, we found that the criterion of profitability alone was rarely enough to trump the goal of maintaining jobs and social stability. But there were other ways to frame the choice. By adding the criterion of "attractiveness to investors" (that is, when it came to the stock market listing) we were able to win the day and arrive at management consensus within the SOE for a reasonably narrow focus involving significant cuts in the workforce.

As one SOE chairman argued with passion, without the successful raising of funds at the IPO, there was no prospect of dealing with the massive overhang of the SOE's social obligations. Of course, even after the focus was agreed on, there were continued rear-guard actions, ambushes, and pushback to reduce the scope of the restructuring.

Good Company, Bad Company

The SOE restructuring typically entailed adopting a "good company, bad company" approach. Globally, it is common for failing banks to be divided into two entities, the "good bank," which holds healthy assets and conducts new lending, and a "bad bank," where the nonperforming loans are parked, pending sale or write-off. A similar process was used to resolve the legacy burden of large Chinese SOEs. The SOE parent established a subsidiary company into which were injected the strong core assets and staff needed for the restructured business that was to be offered to investors at the IPO. The rest of the assets and staff remained in the parent holding company, pending resolution of some kind.

At the heart of the burden SOEs inherited from the planned economy was the "work-unit" system whereby each large enterprise was responsible for schooling, healthcare, and retirees. An extreme example of this model was the massive chemical works located in Jilin City in China's northeast near the North Korean border. When I visited Jilin City in the mid-1980s, this was the quintessential one-company town, with every element of social welfare for most of the city's citizens handled by the company itself (though, curiously, with the exception of the crematorium).

In 1994, Jilin Chemical went through a restructuring and the following year was listed in Hong Kong and New York. But rather than turning over a new leaf, it was unable to resolve the legacy SOE burden and sank into a financial crisis due to "heavy interest expenses, staff redundancy costs, and write-offs on receivables, inventory, and old equipment." Then in 2005, a series of explosions rocked one of its plants, sending a slick of carcinogens down the Songhua River into Heilongjiang and, ultimately, to the Amur River in Russia. In 2006, Jilin was delisted from the stock market and PetroChina took it over. The Jilin Chemical situation was an example of botched SOE reform. Fortunately, many other SOEs were more courageous in addressing the core issues.

In one SOE active across China, we found that prior to restructuring, once expenses were correctly reallocated to its provincial subsidiaries, eight provinces generated about 56% of total revenues and, of these, five generated 45% of the total net profit. These were all obviously candidates for inclusion in the to-be-listed part of the company. Meanwhile, 13 loss-making provincial entities were annually losing a combined RMB 77 MM. Looking at the balance sheet, two of the firm's ten business lines accounted for a whopping 95% of its long-term debt. Thus, the detailed fact-based analysis began to lay bare the strategic choices that could be made.

Excess staff was typically a tough issue to be resolved during a restructuring. There was a constant tension between making the firm attractive to public investors on the one hand and the risk of unemployment leading to social instability on the other.

One SOE I worked with had, prior to restructuring, about 70,000 employees. About 31% were "nonactive" but still on the payroll, including retirees, early retirees, and those laid off but still supported by the firm. The staff did not have the skills or training suited to the new company or the new market conditions. Less than 25% had received education above the upper middle school level. Also, the workforce was aging, with one-third in the 41–50-year age bracket. Due to the excessive layers of management, only about 60% of the staff were directly related to business activities.

About 45% of the active workforce was excess to the firm's needs. The cost of addressing the excess and nonactive employees was estimated to be up to RMB 2.8 BN, with the cost being highest if the excess employees were made redundant immediately rather than step by step.[7]

This SOE was listed in Hong Kong and has performed profitably ever since. To maximize the success of the IPO, the excess employees were left in the unlisted parent and not included in the listed entity. Although resolution of the excess employee issue was not included in the offering prospectus as one of the uses of funds from the IPO, given the poor state of Chinese SOE governance, it is likely that the parent company subsequently raided the funds of the listed entity to help resolve that redundancy issue in the unlisted part.

In some SOE IPOs, the redundant staff was included in the listed part of the company. This was the case of the refining and petrochemical company Sinopec, which raised more than US$ 5 BN through an IPO in Hong Kong in 2000. At listing, Sinopec had 511,800 workers, raising serious concerns among investors and analysts. A year later, Sinopec had to take an RMB 2.5 BN charge to dispose of 68,000 employees.

Who Actually Owns Us?

It may seem strange but one of the most common complaints from SOEs was, as one CEO put it, "We are not clear who our owner is." Even though the reforms gave SOEs a degree of management autonomy, they nonetheless belong to the "socialist" economy. In theory, the SOE is owned by the "whole people," but in practice that ownership is exercised by the state. That is where things become unclear and confusing.

Under central planning, things had been clearer. Each SOE belonged under and reported up to its "department-in-charge" (<u>zhuguan</u> <u>bumen</u>), usually a central ministry or one of its bureaus at the local level. But as the reforms gained momentum, many industrial ministries were simply abolished and "ownership" was transferred to the State Economic and Trade Commission (SETC) which is now merged into the NDRC (National Development and Reform Commission).

In one SOE, we identified seven ministries, commissions, and the CCP, which all shared responsibility for its destiny, resulting in confusion and often paralysis in decision-making.[8] The management of this SOE concluded that, given this array of stakeholders often with overlapping responsibilities, above them they essentially reported into a "vacuum." The result was a Kafkaesque labyrinth of bureaucracy which threw up massive barriers to getting things done.

In 2003, the government established the State-owned Assets Supervision and Administration Commission (SASAC) specifically to play the role of the state owner of the SOEs. This move was welcomed by SOE managers, but due to its shortage of staff and weakness in specialist industrial knowledge, SASAC lacks the clout or teeth needed to reign in SOE power. There has been talk of making SASAC more like Temasek, which supervises Singapore's state firms. This has not occurred. China's vested interests are unlikely to embrace the Singapore-style of SOE governance, which prides itself on transparency and even-handed treatment.

While the role of the government in SOEs is widely debated in China, there is no open discussion of the "800-pound gorilla in the room"—that is, the remaining role of the CCP in SOEs. Early in the reforms there had been calls for the "separation of party from enterprise," but this issue remains highly sensitive, unfinished business, since it goes to the heart of the endemic cronyism in China's SOE sector. While the government has pulled back from interference in the day-to-day operations of SOEs, the CCP has yet to do so.

The CCP still appoints the top management of the 50 or so largest SOEs, while a SASAC department (controlled by the CCP) handles appointment in the 60 or so other central SOEs, plus local ones. Within the SOE there is a CCP committee, the head (secretary) of which outranks the SOE chairman or CEO. He or she nominally takes a backseat role but can quickly spring into action. Also, with a permanent office in each SOE is a representative of the CCP's Central Commission for Discipline Inspection. A classic holdover from the paranoia of the Stalinist state, where nobody is trusted and where everybody watches each other, that person is intended to provide a check on corrupt practices in the SOE.

To what extent are we to believe that the listed parts of Chinese SOEs can adhere to the OECD Principles of Corporate Governance that they openly aspire to during IPOs—namely, fairness, transparency, accountability, and responsibility? Holding the management of publicly traded firms accountable to shareholders is tough enough in the West. In China, it is an impossible task. After the IPO, the government retains a controlling equity position and the views of minority interests cannot find a voice. Although Professor Wu Jinglian, credited as being the founder the Chinese "corporate governance movement," did successfully lobby to make independent directors obligatory in the listed Chinese firms, their effectiveness as a means to improve accountability and transparency remains to be seen. It is common for funds to be siphoned off from the listed entity to help support the unlisted parent.

But to be fair, the risk of government influence and poor governance is clearly spelled out in the typical IPO investor prospectus of a Chinese SOE. It is made abundantly clear that SOE success hangs on more than just a sound strategy and management team. Political patronage plays a key role in determining the value of the firm. Given China's market potential, investors, whether large fund managers or small retail investors, have been perfectly willing to take on the additional risks created by the lack of transparency.

Can SOE Culture Be Changed?

Does this mean that the strenuous efforts to help SOEs transform themselves were in vain? Far from it. Following a restructuring, most SOEs became more confident, better run, and more competitive. But legacy issues such as political control and corruption weigh heavily on them, slowing their progress and reinforcing their old culture.

Once the management consultants had crafted a detailed strategic plan and implementation path, at the end of the day, it was up to the SOE to execute the recommendations. For the SOE, transformation to be deep rooted and sustained required an additional ingredient, namely a radical shift toward a corporate culture that fits the emerging market-oriented economy. These changes may be summed up as follows:

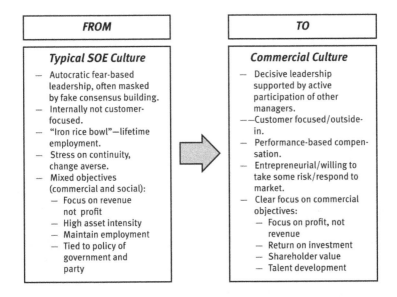

FROM	TO
Typical SOE Culture	**Commercial Culture**
— Autocratic fear-based leadership, often masked by fake consensus building.	— Decisive leadership supported by active participation of other managers.
— Internally not customer-focused.	——Customer focused/outside-in.
— "Iron rice bowl"—lifetime employment.	— Performance-based compensation.
— Stress on continuity, change averse.	— Entrepreneurial/willing to take some risk/respond to market.
— Mixed objectives (commercial and social):	— Clear focus on commercial objectives:
— Focus on revenue not profit	— Focus on profit, not revenue
— High asset intensity	— Return on investment
— Maintain employment	— Shareholder value
— Tied to policy of government and party	— Talent development

Notwithstanding the heavy influence of old ways of doing things, SOE management has been eager to embrace these changes to the corporate culture, focusing on profit, not just revenues, on quality and customer service, not just on volume.

It is also true that reform-minded SOE leaders often make concessions to social or political goals and water down what in the West might be a "rational" approach to enterprise reform, resulting in something short of what was originally recommended. But it is not for us to say that China shouldn't choose a cautious reform trajectory that can limit the social pain of such change.

Within large old-style SOEs, there is a strong, earthy camaraderie, not just within its "leadership group," but between them and the working level. But one also comes to see the dark side, a fear-based autocratic culture that still manifests itself in institutionalized psychological cruelty and brutality meted out to employees that would not be tolerated for one moment in a Western corporate setting. The SOE boss often feels he needs to assert his authority by publicly humiliating an employee, much as a Mafia leader would. This is, of course, part of the fundamental culture of China's ruling CCP. Although we are encouraged by a degree of social relaxation, the veil of civility and decency easily falls away, revealing a CCP faithful to its dismal tradition of violence. The leopard has not lost its spots.

Still, during the period 1993–2003, despite serious headwinds, many large SOEs successfully made radical changes to their strategy, organization, operations, and culture, thus putting them on a sounder financial footing and preparing them to face new competition.

Many reform-minded SOE managers look back at Zhu Rongji (Premier, 1998–2003) as a highly positive role model. Somewhat professorial in style and not a true CCP insider, he was given the risky task of turning the economy around after the initial period of gradual reform had failed to rejuvenate the state sector. He accepted what some say looked like a poison chalice.

He was impatient and often given to berating colleagues who did not share his urgency. He called for limited "managed" competition in state-dominated sectors, breaking up monopolies in telecoms, for instance. He not only radically transformed the large SOEs but also, at significant personal risk, pushed through China's accession to the WTO against widespread opposition. At a speech I heard him make in New York during the final stages of WTO accession negotiations, he said that when he returned to China he might well be regarded as a "traitor" (hanjian in Chinese).

That period was a peak of SOE reform, during which old-style SOEs made great strides toward a corporate transformation. The willingness of the CCP to embrace this change, and to use a light hand in that process, permitted the balance of forces within *the China paradox* to function smoothly. Unfortunately, that progress has not been sustained.

SOE Reform Falters (2003 Onward)

The reform of China's old-style SOEs ground to a halt and in some cases was pushed back. Today, Chinese SOEs are typically much larger than enterprises in the private sector. They own about 30% of industrial and commercial assets in China, but account for only 3% of the total number of enterprises.[9] Their sheer scale, coupled with their political connections and dominance in key sectors such as transportation, power generation, oil and gas, and telecoms, gives them a central and dominant role in the new mixed-economy.

The true picture of SOE health has been hidden from sight under subsidies and privileged treatment from the government. One nongovernment think tank in China reported that during the period 2001–2008, once you stripped out the effect of low-cost land and debt financing at an average annual interest rate of 1.5% that SOEs have enjoyed (compared to 5.4% for private firms!), many of them did not actually make a net profit.[10] Other analysts have estimated that, since the financial crisis of 2006–2007, the SOE's return-on-assets has been about 4.6% compared to 9.1% in China's private sector.[11]

Still, prognostications of the SOEs' coming demise proved to be way off the mark. One observer in 2001 wrote that [Chinese] "State-Owned Enterprises Are Dying."[12] Nothing of the sort has happened. Quite to the contrary, SOEs remain integral to the CCP's agenda for China and look set to be sustained come what may.

While Zhu Rongji had a sincere vision for a more market-oriented economy, his successors failed to push for further SOE reform and on the contrary provided privileged treatment for large old-style SOEs. This policy became commonly referred to as "*the state advances, the private retreats,*" a slogan created around 2008, when the Chinese government failed to assist a troubled private airline (named Okay) while at the same time it provided massive financial assistance to the three main state-owned airlines.

This cozy environment was not conducive to creating better, leaner, more efficient SOEs. On the contrary, it undermined financial discipline and created a polluting relationship between SOEs and the government/CCP. An example of this symbiosis is the way top government officials are regularly rotated in and out of the top jobs in China's telecom companies. Strong, informal relationships between the CCP and SOEs also feed the cronyism and corruption in China's SOE sector.

Just how beneficial this environment is for SOEs can be seen in the decision by a Chinese shipping firm around 2002 to change its key bank relationships. It cancelled the main syndicated loan facility it had with a group of foreign banks and refinanced with a facility from a group of Chinese banks. One reason for this move was quite simple. The shipping company was under significant financial stress. Chinese banks are less likely than foreign banks to strictly enforce loan covenants on balance sheet leverage (ratio of debt to equity) and call a default.

The RMB 4 trillion (US$ 586 BN) economic stimulus plan announced by the Chinese government in late 2008 to help reduce the impact of the global recession greatly reinforced the power of the SOEs, which benefited from funding directed through state banks into major infrastructure projects. Much of that funding was misappropriated or simply spent badly on unneeded or environmentally harmful projects.

Under the leadership of Hu Jintao (2003–13), large old-style state firms became fiefdoms under the control of CCP factions and an expression of cronyism on a grand scale. Once Hu's rule was over, people finally began to openly say what they had been thinking for long time. A top economist based at Peking University said to me:

> "The recent period has been [a] wasted ten years, where no reform took place. If there is no progress, then you fall back.... By standing still on reform, it gave opportunity for people like Bo Xilai [mayor of Chongqing, who was imprisoned on charges of corruption]. The previous government had no strategy, no vision."[13]

A senior executive in the listed part of a large central SOE echoed that message when he told me:

> "The last 10 years have been lost years. If there were positive achievements during that period, then it was due to the remaining legacy of [former Premier] Zhu Rongji. In the new period ... there will be the lingering negative effect of the last ten years."

The change of leadership with the arrival of Xi Jinping was accompanied by much hope that the deadening effect of the previous ten years would be replaced by revived energy to drive economic reforms forward. A CCP meeting pledged to "deepen" the reforms through improving the professionalism of SOEs and further reducing the role of government in their governance. It pushed for further diversification of SOE ownership, with additional private capital to be introduced into large SOEs. This cross-holding approach was ostensibly to improve SOE governance. But there is little chance of this since the CCP continues to have the final, decisive word. It invites the cynical view that this is the CCP using its muscle to siphon off funds from private firms.

To execute this policy, six central-level SOEs were selected for further experimentation in more diversified ownership, according the stated principle of "less controversial entities first." This was indeed the case, since these six firms merely included an agro-industrial conglomerate, a building materials specialist, and a ductile pipe producer! More token than real. Just baby steps and no bold move that could demonstrate true intent.

Still, the government has sought valiantly to address overcapacity in the bloated state sector. China's shipping lines, faced with global excessive tonnage and slumping freight rates, were forced to merge. To trim back the shipbuilding sector, where China has more than 5,000 shipyards accounting for around 40% of global capacity, China's banks resorted to refusing to issue *deposit refund guarantees*, without which it is impossible to win new shipbuilding contracts. In the aluminum and cement industries, the government has pushed hard to reduce massive overcapacity, while slowing growth in the demand for electricity is forcing the consolidation of coal mines. But these attempts to deal with the hangover from China's unbridled development binge often face bitter resistance at the local level. The government's forced mergers of large SOEs will struggle to achieve true consolidation and a reduction in capacity. The outcome may simply be larger bad companies.

It is not clear whether Xi Jinping's efforts to root out corruption in SOEs is simply to consolidate his political power or is the first step toward deepening SOE reform, but the anticorruption campaign against the SOEs has certainly given the CCP the opportunity to claw back power. While the CCP had never withdrawn from SOEs, since the reforms it has been forced to take more of a backseat. One SOE leader pointed out to me that under Xi the reforms are being rolled back:

> "Under the banner of anticorruption, the party is playing an increasingly strong role in the company."

For example, one of the key benefits he saw from the IPO was the freedom management gained over how it compensates employees. He complained that now the CCP was calling on the company to restrict bonuses, reducing its ability to recruit and motivate employees. He also criticized the decision to cancel Lunar New Year parties in SOEs: "This has greatly disappointed our employees. We are the wealth creators."

The reformed old-style SOEs certainly are a massive improvement. But the stronger interference in SOE governance does not bode well for China. There was hope that the old state sector could be radically transformed so that it could stand on its own feet. However, now it looks likely to be a continued burden, a drag on progress. Its sustainability hinges less on its own performance and more on the survival of its godfather, the CCP.

Still, the old-style SOEs do vary greatly in terms of management, strategy, products, and services, operations, or ethics. This often depends on the degree they have truly transformed their corporate culture and gone beyond a limited and token patching up or "packaging" of the firm, just sufficient enough to satisfy foreign investors during the IPO stage.

A New Type of SOE Shows the Way Forward

One bright aspect of the reforms is that they have permitted a new breed of highly successful SOEs to emerge, largely unencumbered by the legacy of central planning. Like China's private firms, although they survive by looking over their shoulder at the CCP and sacrificing some of their autonomy, they nonetheless have demonstrated the mettle to survive and flourish despite the political system.

Lenovo is an excellent example of this new breed of SOE. Later we will examine its extraordinary emergence to become the largest personal computer maker in the world with sales of US$ 46 BN. Here we highlight its hybrid ownership.

The company was established in 1984 by Liu Chuanzhi and other engineers from the Institute of Computing Technology with initial capital from the Chinese Academy of Sciences (CAS), to which it reported. Though the state maintains an equity share through the original CAS investment, its management draws a clear distinction between its ownership status and that of the old SOEs.

Lenovo CEO, Yang Yuanqing, revealed the need to avoid pigeonholing the ownership of these newly emerged state-sponsored companies:

> "Lenovo is a 100% market-oriented company. Some people have said we are a state-owned enterprise. It's 100% not true. In 1984, the Chinese Academy of Sciences only invested $25,000 in our company. The purpose ... to invest ... was that they wanted to commercialize their research results. The Chinese Academy of Sciences is a pure research entity in China, owned by the government. From this point, you could say we're different from state-owned enterprises."[14]

He stressed that even through the Chinese state has an equity interest in Lenovo, it is not treated like a traditional SOE.

> "This company is run totally by the founders and management team. The government has never been involved in our daily operation, in important decisions, strategic direction, nomination of the CEO and top executives and financial management. Everything is done by our management team."[15]

This is a key point. Based on government taking a backseat, Lenovo's governance is superior to that of old-style SOEs. This can help explain Lenovo's stellar track record and market reputation.

The Chinese firm Qingdao Haier is now the world's largest manufacturer of white goods (washing machines, refrigerators, air-conditioners, etc.). Unlike Lenovo, it is not a recent start-up. With its origins in the 1920s, it had become a local level SOE in 1949. Despite that, it belongs firmly among a new breed of SOEs in that its transformation into a modern enterprise was not part of ponderous restructuring instigated by the central government, but instead was the result of bottom-up entrepreneurial efforts within the firm, albeit supported strongly by local government.

In 1982, Haier's predecessor, Qingdao Refrigerator Factory, looked out-for-the-count, financially bankrupt but not yet closed down. The Qingdao government had the good sense to bring in Zhang Ruimin, a self-taught manager (he had not received a higher education due to the Cultural Revolution) to run the factory and today he remains CEO of Haier, which has global sales of US\$ 29 BN and 80,000 employees worldwide. In 2016, Haier acquired GE's household appliance business for US\$ 5.8 BN, adding about US\$8 BN of annual revenues and making it number one in the US market, ahead of Whirlpool and Electrolux.

Haier Group's ownership is a blend of state-owned and private, which allows a variety of stakeholders to benefit without too much scrutiny. It is described as a "collective enterprise," owned by its Employee Shareholding Committee. The Qingdao government will tell you that the state no longer has any residual shares in Haier, but that it still "supervises" the company.

The high degree of autonomy from the government enjoyed by Haier has allowed it to flourish and grow. Meanwhile, the Qingdao government reaps enormous fiscal revenues from Haier's success. Behind the scenes, Haier's top managers are given room to become wealthy through cozy tie-ins with suppliers or distributors, or through being awarded shares in Haier's listed companies. Key decisions throughout Haier are all taken at the Haier Group level. It does not suffer from the fragmented governance through multiple subsidiaries that old-style SOEs live with.

Zhang first set about creating a solid foundation in China. He rectified the firm's appalling quality problems, bringing in German technology, spending 4% of revenues on R&D (in-line with international norms), acquiring 18 local Qingdao firms, and thus quickly establishing the Haier brand, which became associated with high quality and excellent customer service.

In its rapid growth, Haier faced some challenges. It diversified into areas such as pharmaceuticals, logistics, tourism, computers, and handsets, struggling in some of them. In its core white-goods business, the degree of customization it offered to customers was higher than normally seen in global markets, undermining profitability.

But Haier was able to raise funds through listing subsidiaries in Hong Kong and Shanghai. It also was supported and nurtured by the Qingdao government, but without being subjected to the interference that centrally controlled SOEs typically face.

Around 1998, it began exporting, then started setting up overseas factories (Haier's South Carolina plant was the first Chinese factory in the US) and five R&D centers. It decided to take on the difficult task of penetrating the developed countries first and then, only with an established global brand, moved into emerging markets of the Middle East and Africa. In recent years, it has focused on creating a truly "borderless" networked enterprise with IT systems and business processes that permit a flow of information so that production can be fine-tuned to short-term shifts in market demand. It has embraced a consumer-centric approach rather than simply pushing products blindly out into inventory and the market.

Haier has made good use of foreign consultants. It is effective at publicly articulating its growth trajectory and business philosophy ("entrepreneurship and innovation"). It connects to the consumer through its website, where it invites the public to participate in a contest to create "a slogan that expresses the essence of Haier."

As you approach Haier's sprawling campus at One Haier Road in Qingdao's High Tech Zone in the clean, breezy sea air of the Laoshan District, you are looking at China's vision for its large firms. A helicopter rises from the firm's landing pad just in front of the main offices. The campus is spotlessly clean and tidy, with none of the litter or waste that is prevalent in areas just outside the gates of the company.

Working with Haier, it became clear that, putting aside the hype, Haier is representative of a powerful new breed of Chinese enterprises linked to the government but managed in a highly autonomous way. CEO Zhang Ruimin is concurrently also the firm's CCP secretary, thus permitting a unified approach. So far, the firm's success has been closely linked to his ability to perform a delicate balancing act in addressing the agendas of the multiple stakeholders while limiting the role the government and CCP to just a light touch.

In 1992, the enlightened Qingdao government had continued success in creating another new-style SOE, Hisense. Based on a tiny local electronics factory, Hisense has grown to be a global player in consumer electronics and white goods with sales of US$ 15 BN.

Other new SOEs have been established by the central government to play a more traditional SOE role, strongly plugged in to the government ministries. This occurred in the new but highly regulated area of mobile phone services, initially with China Mobile (spun off from China Telecom in 1999) and China Unicom (set up in 1994), established by the government to provide a duopoly in this sector. These kinds of new SOEs have more in common with the restructured old-style SOEs than with the Haiers of China. Despite having stock market-listed entities, these firms, in sectors regarded by the government as highly strategic, are held closely under the thumb of the CCP. They are subjected to forced mergers and divestment whenever the authorities choose to reshape the sector. Their top executives are changed at the whim of the CCP.

In looking at China's SOEs, a clear pattern emerges, a close correlation between their degree of separation from the government/CCP and the quality of the SOE. The greater the separation, the better the quality. The Qingdao government seems signed up to this concept but that is not the norm. Stuffed full of government patronage, most of the largest SOEs are able to sustain themselves and dominate the economy—but only as long as the current political order exists. If that order melted away, these firms would find themselves ill-equipped to compete.

Hopes have been dashed that the outcome might be a bright new revitalized state sector, part of a true hybrid economy run more like capitalism albeit under CCP autocracy. Earlier trends in that direction have been reversed. As one senior SOE leader put it to me, "the CCP has returned and now controls 100% of our strategic business decisions."

Fortunately, the private sector and the new-style SOEs are strong enough to maintain their trajectory and will underpin China's future growth, even if the political system begins to melt down. But most of the SOEs are fated to be part of the new experimental socialist order, their future resting precariously in the hands of the CCP.

The future of China's SOEs is inextricably linked to that of the ruling CCP. When you buy shares in a Chinese telephone company, you are placing your faith in the CCP. Assuming the CCP does not collapse or be overthrown, the large SOEs will be able to maintain their dominant position. But under current conditions, it looks highly unlikely that the CCP will choose to take SOE reform to the next level—that is, withdrawing from their governance. Therefore, the large SOEs, for example in telecoms, electricity, shipbuilding, and transportation, will likely survive but not flourish. On the world stage, we shall meet Chinese firms in shipping, aviation, and oil and gas; but they will be ponderous and flat-footed, lacking the agility that could make them major competitors. In the absence of deeper reform, backsliding will continue and the conservative legacy will drown out the forces of change and innovation, thus undermining *the China paradox.*

Were the CCP to melt away and China to experience regime change but under continued autocracy, the chances are the new rulers would doubledown on SOE dominance rather than break up the SOE oligopoly.

New-style SOEs such as Lenovo and Haier act more like private firms and, assuming there is no complete meltdown in China, they will continue to establish themselves in the world. Fortunately for China, their future does not depend so heavily on the CCP or a successor regime.

There are also some sectors where the Chinese government and SOEs are teaming up to take on the world. China has developed its own capability in high-speed rail and in Generation III nuclear power technology. This concerted effort to launch such technologies into global markets looks likely to pay off in the medium-term. We should not underestimate the CP's residual ability to make things happen when the stakes are high.

Chapter 6
The Private Economy Emerges Unannounced

Moving forward relying on one's own strengths.

—The declared guiding spirit of Wanxiang, one of China's leading private
companies, adopted in the absence of
state support.

As the economic reforms began in the early 1980s, anxious officials in Beijing with furrowed brows were embarking on the slow unwinding of central
planning and weighing the various options for reforming the SOEs, none
of which were painless or risk-free. Meanwhile, far from their gaze, the future private economy was emerging at the grass roots.

The intent here is not to prescribe private enterprise as the best solution for China. Private companies come in many forms and much depends
on how well they are regulated and, for that matter, on how much space
they are given to flourish. But in the Chinese context, the private economy
that has recently emerged stands out as, broadly speaking, more productive, innovative, and agile than the post-reform SOE economy. How then
do we reconcile the existence of such a vibrant private sector in China
alongside the dominant entrenched economic interests of the CCP?

First, the private sector in China survives only by diluting its independence through forging links to the CCP. Second, the CCP has learned not only
to live with, but also to appreciate, the private sector since it contributes so
much to the economy. This is part of the delicate equilibrium that underpins *the China paradox*. The CCP has shown remarkable pragmatism in permitting the private sector to take off, while always maintaining the dominant state sector as a counterbalance.

Will the private sector continue to be the poor relative within the Chinese economic order or will it, by dint of its own wealth and success, become more confident, assertive, and bolder to the extent that it can push
back against CCP power?

In the period 1978–1993, China's GDP grew at an average of 9%. But
the contribution of the SOEs to industrial output fell from 78% to 43%.[1] So
what was keeping China afloat? It was not foreign direct investment (it accounted for only 5% of investment in the 1990s) but the amazing growth of
township and village enterprises (TVEs), which occurred largely spontane-
ously. This stunning phenomenon, which occurred under the radar with

DOI 10.1515/9781501507212-006

limited support from the central government, ultimately turned out to be a key element that helped turn the national economy around during that difficult and risky transitional period. In turn, it became the foundation block of China's privately owned enterprises (POEs) once they became legally permitted. China's private sector today strongly outperforms the state sector both in profitability and in job creation.

TVEs—Engine for Growth as the Reforms Took Shape

One of Deng Xiaoping's first policy moves after gaining full power in 1978 was to abolish the People's Communes, rural units of 5,000 to 20,000 households, which since 1958 had combined collective farming with rural industry. Land use was given back to individual farmer households. Numerous small commune-based, collectively owned[2] factories and workshops began transforming themselves into TVEs. These rural factories are one of the enduring positive legacies of the Maoist period. As one Western academic wrote with foresight during the Cultural Revolution,

> "China is today developing a high-level of machine labor skills and factory discipline in previously non-industrialized areas, and a pool of experienced engineering and technical skills necessary to convert production techniques to local equipment and materials are gradually being developed."[3]

The author went on to describe the rural bearings repair workshops he had visited in 1971: "these enterprises are usually fairly small, with between 50 and a hundred workers" and predicted that:

> "A number of these enterprises will eventually develop into small specialized bearings factories.... Small bearings factories may be able to take over the production of a considerable proportion of intermediate size ranges where quality requirements are not so stringent. Some small enterprises are already able to manufacture bearings used for simple machine tools, electric motors and ... farm machinery."[4]

He added that some plants had even started to produce automobile bearings.[5]

This was spot on and highly prophetic. Fast forward to 1997 when I was working on China's bearings industry. About 200 of China's 500 bearings manufacturers were TVEs, accounting for 25% of output volume and 50% of export volume, primarily making miniature bearings used in consumer products such as electric fans. In the key product category of tapered roller bearings, TVEs had a 35% share in China's agricultural machinery sector.

TVEs were loosely owned by local governments and did not count as directly linked into the state sector. Nor were they POEs (they only became legal in 1988). This relationship between local government and TVEs was highly symbiotic and mutually supportive, quite unlike that between SOEs and government. Management was contracted out to entrepreneurs, and profits were shared. TVEs were a throwback to the late-Qing system of "*official supervision, merchant management.*"

The age of the TVEs in the 1980s and early 1990s was short but stunning in its impact. They were truly the "engine of growth."[6] Although the coastal provinces of Jiangsu and Zhejiang saw the most feverish TVE activity, it was a nationwide phenomenon.

The power of TVEs was brought home to me in the late 1980s when I was consulting to a US firm that wanted to set up a plant in China to produce medical consumables, such as lint, cotton, wool, and bandages. After the disbanding of collective farming, peasants could grow what they wished, and in North China, in some years, they switched away from cotton growing, leading to a serious shortage of raw cotton used by the SOE textile mills to produce cotton yarn, a vital raw material for my client.

I visited the northern city of Tianjin to see for myself. The large SOE textile mills, each employing thousands of workers, were indeed in dire straits, since, with no centrally planned procurement of cotton anymore, were at the mercy of the local farmers who switched crops depending on the market price. Although these large mills still had imported British spinning equipment dating back to the 1930s, they had to pay attention to work conditions, which, most importantly, had to be well-ventilated to take out cotton and dust particles that can do serious harm to workers' health.

The same day, I went 20 km out into the countryside. We bumped along narrow, tree-lined roads until we turned into a rundown-looking TVE textile mill owned by the local government. Inside, it was very hot and difficult to talk over the racket from the spinning machines. It was hard to breathe. The air was laden with dust and fibers from the production. The TVE management was fully confident of being able to supply the yarn, explaining that production was not threatened by any shortage of raw cotton since the mill had a captive supply from local farmers.

The vibrancy and energy of this TVE contrasted with the gloomy situation in the large SOE textile mill I had visited earlier in the day. But it was also obvious that the TVE's ability to compete was at least in part due to its backward and polluted working conditions. I saw this in many other TVEs. The TVE model played a key role for a time, but needed to evolve toward more modern and efficient production, as well as an ownership system less tied to local officials.

A TVE I visited in the mid-1990s had already successfully entered the export market. Originally part of a fishing commune located by the sea in Qingdao at the foot of the towering limestone Laoshan Peak, it harvested kelp (a type of seaweed), which its factory processed into sodium alginate (used as a thickener and stabilizer in food, including in the production of fake shark's fin!) and mannitol (used in pharmaceutical tablets).

The day we arrived there was a banquet at which the company went to great lengths to demonstrate its intimate relationship with the local government. Among those partaking of the meal of exquisite seafood were the head and party secretary of Qingdao's Hi-Tech Park, the county mayor, and a representative from the local branch of the Bank of China.

In the negotiations that took place the next day, its managers gave off an air of rural simplicity that belied their excellent business instincts. After lunch, Mr. Zhou, the general manager and CCP secretary, lay full-length on a bench beside the negotiating table, sleeping and snoring and then waking up with perfect timing to reinforce a key negotiating issue. They were a well-organized and smart negotiating team.

Despite its energy and earthy smartness, like many TVEs, this one had an Achilles heel, which was its environmental impact. After we conducted a survey, the areas of concern included leaking toxic chemicals (e.g., formaldehyde), unsafe installation of tanks for sulfuric acid, and discharge of untreated effluent into the sea.[7] There was little way the foreign company could invest with this TVE since it could not meet US Good Manufacturing Practices for the pharmaceutical industry or the foreign firm's own in-house standards.

Many TVEs were highly flawed and ultimately faded away or transformed themselves into private firms. The litany of common defects included subscale operations, out-of-date equipment, poor product quality, low levels of efficiency, shortage of capital, environmental pollution, and dangerous working conditions. They were given to short-term thinking, with abrupt shifts in business focus or excessive diversification, and were dependent on corrupt relationships with local government. Ultimately, cities were forced to bail out some TVEs and nudged others to broaden their ownership (including through stock market listings) or to go fully private.

Despite all their weaknesses, TVEs were a crucial transitional breed of Chinese enterprise that laid the foundation for the emergence of truly private enterprises.

In Guangdong's Shunde City, on the muddy west bank of the Pearl River, industry is almost entirely privately owned or TVEs. As early as 1990, Shunde had 19,540 TVEs, 38 of which contributed industrial output of RMB 3.3 BN. By 1998, its per capita GDP was already around US$ 3,000 and rose to more than US$ 14,000 by 2007, one of the highest in China.

Shunde is the home of Midea, founded in 1968 as a small repair shop it became a TVE and has grown to be a global supplier of home appliances and air conditioners, with sales of US$ 25 BN. Also based in Shunde is Galanz, which started life as a workshop making car dusters from poultry feathers and is now a world leader in microwave ovens.

POEs Flourish, Especially If Far from the Capital

Many TVEs were the forerunners of, or disguised as, private firms. After 1988, when regulations first permitted this, they began to show their true colors and transform themselves into full-fledged POEs. Between 1993 and 2002, the number of TVEs in China fell from 1.69 million to 730,000.[8] This trend from TVE to private enterprise was pronounced in Guangdong and also in Jiangsu.

In Zhejiang Province, POEs emerged fastest and often not through a TVE transition phase. Even before the law permitted POEs, Zhejiang entrepreneurs were operating essentially as POEs, without the need to share their profits with local officials. The Zhejiang city of Wenzhou was the "epicenter of private firm development,"[9] and the Wenzhou model was celebrated by free market advocates in China.

During the first 30 years of the PRC, Zhejiang had been neglected in terms of industrial development due in part to its location on the military front line close to the rebel province of Taiwan. Only Hangzhou had a significant population of large SOEs. Once the economic reforms started, Zhejiang benefited from its former isolation (Wenzhou was only connected to China's rail network in 2009) and relative freedom from central government interference. It was also less burdened by the SOE legacy than other parts of China. However, the Wenzhou model had serious limitations. Accumulated wealth was not ploughed back into the businesses but was dissipated in risky real estate investment.

In Zhejiang, the port of Ningbo, like Wenzhou, has played a leading role in the recent revival of private enterprise in China. Ningbo is famous for its successful traders and businessmen, and during the reforms there, it has seen a strong resurgence of that tradition. One milestone in the rise of private business in China was the US$ 150 MM purchase in 2003 of the Shanghai

Hilton Hotel by a Ningbo businessman who had made a fortune building expressways in Zhejiang. He sold it in 2012 for US$ 328 MM. Then in 2011, an-
other Ningbo businessman became the first Chinese entrepreneur to acquire
land-use rights of an island in China, off the coast of Zhejiang, with plans to
create a hunting park with wild boar and pheasants!

A striking aspect of Ningbo is the strong role permitted for private education, alongside the government schools. The city has 116 private primary and middle schools which receive government financial support and
whose teachers enjoy the same pensions and social benefits as those in
government schools. This is not to suggest that China is abandoning the
primacy of state-run schools. But it does illustrate how deeply rooted the
private economy can become in certain parts of China when there is a sympathetic local government.

The new entrepreneurial middle class is also becoming vocal on social
issues. The Ningbo government backed off a plan to expand a paraxylene
plant after residents demonstrated. Similar protests have also occurred in
the cities of Xiamen and Dalian, both places on the leading edge of market-
style reforms.

Wanxiang—A Pioneering Private Company Forges Its Own Path

Despite instances of a supportive local government, most POEs have been
forced to rely on their own strengths and resources. Hangzhou-based Wanxiang Group is an excellent example.

The story of Wanxiang's stellar rise began in 1969, when its current
leader, Lu Guanqiu, and six other farmers used capital equivalent to US$
500 to establish the Ningwei People's Commune Agricultural Machinery
Repair Factory. As Wanxiang explained to me, from the outset, the firm saw
itself as a private concern, but needed a "Red Hat" to survive. It was called
a collective enterprise, a TVE, and only later became a private enterprise.
Today, it is the world's largest producer of universal joint assemblies for
the auto industry with market shares of 65% in China and 10% globally.
Wanxiang has sales of US$ 24 BN. Lu's net worth is estimated at about US$
2 BN. It has more than 40 overseas factories and more than 10,000 of its
30,000 employees are outside China. It is a leader among Chinese firms
"going out into the world."

By 1979, after ten years of operation, Wanxiang had what for a commune workshop was substantial revenue of RMB 1MM to 2 MM. But Lu

Guanqiu, with his eyes set on more rapid growth, addressed the issue of product focus and decided to concentrate on auto components, in particular universal joints. (In Chinese, wanxiang is the universal in universal joint, hence the firm's name). Later, Wanxiang expanded into drive shafts, bearings, and steering assemblies, and more recently into electric vehicles and batteries.

In 1979, Wanxiang's key challenge was that, as a TVE, it lay outside the state sector and the planned economy. It lacked access to quotas of raw materials supplied under the plan, and it was forced to smelt and to heat-treat scrap metal. When it came to selling its finished products, it was barred from participating in sales planning meetings attended by SOEs. Even though Wanxiang took to waiting at the door outside such meetings, the SOEs were unwilling to give the company orders. After Lu lowered his prices and held low-profile meetings in his hotel room, sales began to take off since his product quality was comparable to that of imports, while SOE competitors could not reach that level.

Wanxiang found state-owned banks unwilling to lend, given the company's TVE status. Today, as a major private company, Wanxiang finds things easier. For instance, China Development Bank provides loans to Wanxiang. But, as Wanxiang explained to me, even today, the state banks will lend only for specific projects (for instance, to support its battery and electric vehicle development program as part of the state's high-tech Plan 863), but not for general working capital uses. To raise capital to fuel its growth, Wanxiang has listed on the Shenzhen Stock Exchange.

Reflecting its painful emergence, Wanxiang encapsulates its business philosophy in the traditional Chinese saying, "moving forward relying on one's own strengths" (liangli erxing).

Given the obstacles in the domestic market, Wanxiang made an early decision to enter export markets. Even exporting was complicated since the biannual government-sponsored trade fair in Guangzhou was only for SOEs. Wanxiang was forced to exhibit at other firms' booths at the fair.

A breakthrough came in 1984, when Wanxiang won its first order from the Ohio-based Zeller Corporation, then the largest US supplier of universal joints. Profits from the export business were low but through it, Wanxiang was able to learn quickly and upgrade product quality, ultimately helping the company sell domestically to the fast-developing Chinese auto industry.

Auto component suppliers benefit from moving up the value chain to a stage where, as a so-called *tier one* supplier, they can enjoy an intimate relationship with the car assembler. Although Wanxiang initially only made parts, it progressed to producing assemblies, then systems, and finally to supplying complete modules for installation by the car makers, thus gaining that valuable tier one status.

Wanxiang also addressed the needs of the geographically dispersed Chinese auto makers, which, anxious about overreliance on the nation's unreliable logistics, insisted on being supplied from nearby plants. Local government also called for local investment to create jobs. Foreign firms were willing to put in extra warehousing close to the car factory to ensure just-in-time (J-I-T) delivery, but were reluctant to set up multiple subscale inefficient plants in China. Wanxiang took on this challenge, establishing 41 factories in China with a total floor area of 6 square kilometers to produce parts, assemblies, and complete modules close to their customers in Shanghai, Changchun, Wuhan, Hefei, Haikou, and other cities.

While Wanxiang spurred on its technical development by embarking on export sales, it declined the opportunity to sell exclusively through Zeller and was able to build its own sales channels internationally and under its own brand. Wanxiang was not prepared to be just another outsourced supplier to foreign component firms.

The next big step was to become established overseas as one of China's earliest multinational corporations. Lu's son-in-law, who was studying for his Ph.D. in Kentucky, established Wanxiang USA in Chicago in 1995 with only US$ 20,000 of capital due to the restrictions on taking funds out of China. By 2011, Wanxiang USA had revenues of US$ 2.2 BN. American banks were keen to lend to the company. Now it has 18 overseas subsidiaries, in manufacturing and R&D. Recently, Wanxiang acquired a bankrupt battery company in the US, strengthening its technology portfolio for electric vehicles. It has also invested in a Chicago-based private equity firm.[10]

Wanxiang's success has been underpinned by the quality and continuity of Lu Guanqiu's exceptional leadership. He is planning for an orderly succession, bringing in his son as president.[11] His talented son-in-law, head of the US operations, has in turn successfully recruited US managers, such as a CFO who has been with the US subsidiary since its inception.

Lu quietly built his global firm with very little publicity. He also had the good fortune to be located in Zhejiang, which for decades has had a highly enlightened government not inclined to interfere in private entrepreneurship. But when successful POEs reach significant scale, they are driven both by pragmatic good sense (in autocratic China) and genuine patriotic feelings into a closer embrace with the government and CCP. To a degree, Wanxiang is certainly incorporated into "China, Inc." Lu is a delegate to the National People's Congress and also secretary of Wanxiang's CCP Committee (yes, private companies have them too!). However, in discussions I have had with Wanxiang's management, they argue convincingly that the influence of the CCP is not as intrusive as that in SOEs.

Huawei—A Private Firm as "National Champion"

In contrast to Wanxiang, some POEs, due to their strategic role in the economy, have received special attention from the government. This is the case with China's electronics giant, Huawei Technologies.

Huawei, based in Shenzhen and established in 1987 by Ren Zhengfei with registered capital of RMB 21,000, is one of China's most celebrated POEs. Ren came from a farming family in Hunan and had served in the Chinese army. Having started from manufacturing simple telecom equipment, Huawei is now a global giant in switches, routers, mobile telephone infrastructure, mobile handsets, HD video, and computers, with global sales in 2015 of US\$ 60 BN. On internet infrastructure, it competes globally against the likes of Cisco and Siemens. Nearly half of its 140,000 employees are engaged in R&D at centers in China and 12 other countries.

Much of the international commentary about Huawei has to do with its opaque ownership. Though it describes itself as a "private company wholly-owned by its employees," it is often suggested that, through Ren's army background, it has links to the Chinese military. Whether the connection to the army is true or not, that may be a red herring, since the crucial fact is that Huawei from the outset has enjoyed a close relationship with the government, but likely stopping short of direct ownership. Although Huawei refuses to reveal details of its ownership, thus precluding a stock listing or a private placement of stock, this has not held Huawei back, since capital to fuel its growth is readily available from state banks. Huawei's blend of private enterprise entrepreneurial behavior, coupled with strong but arms-length government support, has proven to be a powerful combination, allowing it to outpace, for instance, its Shenzhen SOE competitor ZTE, also a national champion.

In its early days, Huawei was a very useful, ostensibly nongovernment vehicle for China to sell telecom equipment discreetly to countries, such as Iran, that are regarded internationally as pariahs. But since then,

Huawei has grown into a mainstream global supplier of telecommunications equipment, though still attracting controversy.

In 2003, Cisco Systems sued Huawei for theft of intellectual property; the suit was settled out of court. Since then, Huawei has gone on to successfully develop its own technology, products, and services up to a global quality. More recently, the company has been largely excluded from the US telecommunications infrastructure business, a third of the world market, after Congress labeled Huawei a security risk. But it has managed elsewhere to sidestep such concerns and grow strongly. In international markets, Huawei has been savvy about hiring retired officials. In Britain, it has addressed the security concerns by setting up an "independent cybersecurity evaluation center" with the British government, which gave Huawei a clean bill of health.

A key factor in Huawei's success has been the strength of Ren Zhengfei's leadership, which I saw close up while I was consulting to Huawei. Ren is astute, with a fiercely independent frame of mind. In 2000, shortly before the dot-com bubble burst, he told us he was not impressed by competitor Cisco's stock market value of US\$ 269 BN and added with prescience that when the stock price fell, Cisco would find it hard to retain the talent that had been attracted by stock options. Shortly afterward, the bubble did indeed break: Cisco's market value fell 86% and today is still only about US\$ 130 BN less than half of its peak stock valuation. Cisco did survive the hubris of that period, but Ren called it correctly.

Back then, one of Huawei's biggest challenges was managing the firm's explosive growth in sales, which had reached around US\$ 2.6 BN. Huawei had been on a binge of hiring smart Chinese Ph.Ds., many of whom were appointed as "general managers" with little attention given to what or whom they were managing or whether there were overlapping roles. Step-by-step, we recommended an entirely new organizational structure. Ren added his input, which included an innovative approach whereby the CEO role rotated every six months to a different member of an eight-person executive management team. Ren built a strong team which has stood the test of time. Four of the top executives I worked with 15 years ago are still in place.

Government support for Huawei was there from the outset. In the late 1990s, Huawei and three other firms described as China's "four flowers" of the telecom equipment industry received financial support from the government. Today, the support continues. In emerging markets, Huawei plays a key role in China's geopolitical plays, supporting major infrastructure development programs from Africa to Latin America. China Development Bank provided Huawei with a US\$ 30 BN line of credit to support its international expansion through buyer credits. This underlines the fact that those large Chinese POEs in sectors deemed to be of national strategic value are inevitably intertwined with the interests of "China, Inc."

Private Firms Sustain the Economy

POEs account for 83% of the estimated 360 million people employed in urban areas and 90% of new job creation.[12] Chinese government data indicates that in 2014 the profits of larger industrial POEs are growing at double the rate of profit growth at state-owned industrial firms. POE profits now outstrip those of SOEs.[13] When we consider the smaller universe of firms that are listed on the stock market, there is a similar picture: private firms are outperforming SOEs in terms of higher profit margins, higher return on investment, and lower indebtedness.[14]

While the funds from the 2008 stimulus plan flowed mainly to SOEs and local government, POEs remained starved of capital. The inevitable result was the emergence of what is called "shadow banking," an informal banking system (estimated today at around one-third the size of official bank lending) which has filled the gap that the state banks were unwilling or unable to fill.

To be fair, the state banks have had good reasons for not lending to private small- and medium-sized enterprises. As one foreign banker explained it to me:

> "They didn't know how to lend to small companies without getting cheated. They look at the [borrower's] balance sheet, or take the security of pledged assets, but these are not reliable.[15]"

China's interest rate regime has also done little to encourage banks to diversify their lending toward POEs. The controls on interest rates have meant that there is a large spread between deposit rates (2% to 3 %) and lending rates (6% to 7%) Thus, "banks can earn easy money. They don't need to use technology to distinguish risk and to fund [the real needs].[16] Fortunately, China continues to relax controls over interest rates, which will force banks to compete for new business and begin lending to small POEs.

But even large and financially strong POEs can find funding an issue. One private Chinese real estate firm requested loans of RMB 3 BN from a Chinese state bank, which was able to offer only regular loans of RMB 50 MM. The remainder of the financing was provided through shadow banking.

So, China's private sector emerged largely by dint of its own efforts. Many reform-minded officials acknowledged the ability of the private sector to keep the economy afloat while the SOEs were being patched up and rebuilt. But it has and still does face opposition and discrimination from bureaucrats brought up on a diet of opposition to free market capitalism. The CCP shows an ambiguous attitude, stressing its "unwavering" commitment to the primacy at the SOEs while in a somewhat patronizing fashion stating that it will continue to "encourage, support and guide" the "healthy development" of the "nonstate" (private) sector.[17]

POEs continue to have this curious status. On the one hand they create jobs, innovation, profits, and tax revenues, while on the other hand, they live exposed and vulnerable, in the shadow of the formidable vested interests that rule the state sector. While planning their path forward, China's entrepreneurs are forced to look over their shoulder and stay vigilant of predatory, venal, and interfering government officials. The good news is that many of China's private enterprises have grown to a point where they can be more assertive and begin to dictate their own terms. As they (and the new-style SOEs, which operate like private firms) become full-fledged multinationals, they will be less easily intimidated within China.

It is true that some Chinese POEs have become sprawling conglomerates with a weak strategic focus. Loaded with bank debt, they have made risky forays into international business. The Chinese government, worried about capital flight and systemic financial risk has begun reigning in these firms, such as Anbang, Fosun, Wanda, and HNA, and their billionaire owners. But other POEs such Wanxiang and Huawei and quasi-POEs such as Lenovo and Haier with better corporate governance, are able to maintain a high degree of autonomy, without such overt government interference.

It is likely that the dramatic comeback of China's capitalist class, which was eradicated during Mao's rule, is irreversible, whether the CCP likes it or not. In the unlikely event that the CCP embraces further deeper economic reforms, then the private sector might just come to be accepted as the foundation of the economy, not the second-class citizen that it is today. But one way or another, the genie is out of the bottle.

Chapter 7
Magnet for Foreign Investment

1987: "If we say there are areas [of the Open Door implementation] that are inadequate, then it is that the door is not opened wide enough."

—Deng Xiaoping defending his policy, 1987[1]

2005: "Some 80% of AmCham survey respondents continue to view Chinese IPR enforcement as ineffective or totally ineffective."

—American Chamber of Commerce PRC, 2005[2]

2010: "Many [members] have begun questioning their long-term viability in China as they consider the obstacles presented by an increasingly difficult regulatory environment."

—American Chamber of Commerce PRC, 2010[3]

The CCP was acutely aware of the disastrous impact of China's isolation during the Mao years and acted quickly to reverse that mindset. Setting aside its narrowly nationalist and restrictive instincts, it launched the "Open Door" (<u>duiwai</u> <u>kaifang</u>) policy, which has enabled the massive flow of foreign direct investment (FDI) into China, but, it should be stressed, only to the extent that it served the party's goals of national revival.

FDI has been used to fill China's gaps in skills, technology, products, and services. The OpenDoor policy has been integral to China's "catch-up" approach. But once those goals are achieved, China is happy to scale back the welcome to FDI and put up new barriers. Even at its peak, the policy was nothing like a true open door. While many foreign firms have done well during this window of opportunity, they do not harbor any illusions that they will ever be treated like Chinese firms or that there will be a complete "opening up." On the contrary, they brace themselves for future restrictions once China feels confident enough to discard their erstwhile foreign partners and investors.

At the beginning of the reforms, Deng Xiaoping pushed back against colleagues who feared that FDI would threaten the monopolies enjoyed by SOEs or that encouraging entrepreneurial attitudes might lead to corrupt behavior. He took the view that FDI would help transform the state sector and encourage business innovation.

DOI 10.1515/9781501507212-007

From virtually zero in 1978, FDI grew only slowly during the 1980s, but expanded explosively in the early 1990s after Deng Xiaoping put new life into the reform process and created the surge in market demand. By the late 1990s, FDI was running at annual rates of around US$ 45 BN and today it is around US$ 100 BN (similar to the FDI the US attracts annually).

Though many foreign firms have found the process of investment in China to be painful and frustrating, they have typically accepted this punishment and gone on to achieve acceptable returns from their investments. A survey of a group of the largest US firms recently reported that 83% were profitable in China but with smaller margins than before, due to domestic competitors, rising costs, and discriminatory government policies.[4]

Nonetheless, there is a distinct air of disenchantment among foreign investors in China. With the emergence of home-grown Chinese firms that can deliver the quality needed, China's earlier massive hunger for foreign investment has largely been assuaged. The Chinese government surreptitiously creates an environment that benefits local firms and restricts foreign players.

Why Did China Welcome FDI?

Access to technology. China sought access to overseas technology and management skills to drive productivity, industrial upgrading, and innovation. Especially in the early days of FDI, there was the hope that, through engagement in JVs with foreign firms, technology and skills would be absorbed, "rub off" onto the Chinese side, be informally transferred to, or stolen by local firms. This has occurred but not to the extent envisaged.

Capital formation. At the beginning of the reform process in 1978–1979, China spent heavily on imports of capital equipment for industry, severely straining the economy. FDI, which encouraged foreign investors to pony up some of the investment, was rightly seen as a more sustainable route.

However, Chinese firms today have ready access to investment funds from the stock market or from state banks. It is hard today to get major Chinese firms interested in a JV. If they are willing to partner, then they will typically demand majority equity and operating control.

Jobs. FDI was important in creating jobs, in offsetting the impact of layoffs resulting from the restructuring or selling-off of SOEs, thus permitting a softer landing during the pain of unwinding the planned economy.

Getting rid of small SOEs. In the wake of the meltdown in the state sector, FDI offered China an opportunity to find investors or buyers for countless smaller SOEs that had little or no viable future. Typically, these firms brought nothing to the table in the way of products or skills. At best, they might provide some market access and product distribution. At the end of the day, their main value might be the land assets that could be cleared for a new factory, plus some residual connections to local officials.

For the foreign investor, taking over an old state factory was fraught with a range of issues, including poorly defined land ownership rights and the risk of having to remediate the land due to toxic chemicals. Many investors gravitated to the simpler solution of developing a greenfield site already laid out in a development zone.

Why Has China Been so Attractive to Foreign Investors?

Cheap labor. Much of the early FDI was in export-oriented industries attracted by China's low labor costs, and FDI still accounts for about half of China's exports.

But with rising salary levels and the RMB appreciation, China has become less attractive as the location for labor-intensive industry. Factory workers' pay in Suzhou, one of China's richest cities, is US\$ 600 per month compared to about US\$ 500 in Romania. Production is being switched to countries with lower labor rates, such as Cambodia or Bangladesh.

The size of the domestic China market. Even before China's GDP began to surge in the early 1990s, most major multinational firms had their eyes on the potential that China might represent and laid plans for market entry. Some went in too early, while others got the timing right. After China's phenomenal takeoff in the 1990s, for most major multinational firms, it became hard to argue against establishing a position in the China market.

New infrastructure coupled with financial incentives. China focused the initial opening up of the economy to FDI in a series of Special Economic Zones (SEZs) in South China, first in Shenzhen (1979), then in Zhuhai,

Shantou, Xiamen, and Hainan. These were at first mainly export-oriented. Then in 1984, industrial zones were established in 14 coastal cities, with an emphasis on domestic market-oriented FDI.

Today, there are around 400 central government-approved development zones in China, including high-tech zones and export-processing (duty-free) zones. One fifth of accumulated foreign direct investment is located in 210 of these zones, and this in turn accounts for one eighth of China's GDP.

When I first visited the Shenzhen SEZ in the early 80s, shortly after its establishment, it had a population of several hundred thousand compared to more than 10 million today. Explosions periodically shook the zone as dynamite leveled mountain tops, after which huge excavators and trucks brought the rocks to the sea for massive land reclamation. A pall of construction dust hung over the zone. Broad new roads, with scarcely a car on them, crisscrossed the landscape. Flying over the SEZ, you saw one enormous construction site with red bare soil where earlier there had been lychee orchards.

Today, Shenzhen is a bustling, tidy, and green city with an excellent subway system and enjoying much more space than nearby Hong Kong. It became the home of Chinese corporate giants such as the telecom equipment firms Huawei and ZTE. Shenzhen became a magnet for talent from all over China.

The success of Shenzhen and other SEZs was built on a number of factors. To make the economic experiment more acceptable to conservative elements in the CCP, it was conducted in South China, far from the capital, and there was, in effect, a border (called the "second line") with police and customs posts on all roads between it and the rest of China, limiting access for Chinese citizens. That way it could be claimed that the experiment would not impinge on the broader economy. Of course, once the successful role of the SEZs was fully validated, "opening up" was extended beyond this Trojan horse of Deng's reforms.

Processes in Shenzhen were streamlined. On economic matters, its government reported directly to the central government, bypassing the Guangdong province government. In contrast to other places in China where land ownership was often unclear and an impediment to forming new ventures, this issue was quickly clarified. Tax incentives for FDI were initially more generous than outside the zone and project approvals from the government were smoother and quicker.

China Has Its Cake and Gets to Eat It, Too

Due to the size and potential of its market, China was not only able to attract massive FDI, but was also able to do so on its own terms, with restrictions on what types of firms were invited into China, the timing of that entry, and under what conditions.

Having welcomed FDI only in oil exploration, China quickly expanded it into auto and other manufacturing. But it was slow to open up sectors such as the services industry, including logistics and retailing. Some areas, which are deemed to be highly strategic and sensitive from a security point of view, such as telecommunications and publishing, remain firmly closed to FDI.

Initially, foreign firms were only permitted to establish JVs with Chinese partners. Though the intent behind this was to enable the upgrading of the Chinese businesses through the transfer of technology and management skills, this proved more problematic than expected. It became apparent that many JVs were stymied by disputes between the foreign and Chinese partners, by ponderous decision-making, and by bloated workforces that the Chinese side sometimes insisted on contributing to the JV.

In the late 1980s, after ten years of forcing foreign investors to form JVs, the Chinese government finally legalized ventures that were 100% foreign-owned, and this mode quickly overtook JVs as the preferred vehicle for new investments. Enlightened officials,[5] whom I came to know and appreciate, openly accepted that firms fully owned by foreigners were more efficient and productive than JVs.

As part of its accession to the WTO in 2002, China agreed to further open up the economy, for instance, in logistics, banking, and insurance. But this loosening up was phased in over four years, allowing Chinese firms time to get ready for the new competition.

After WTO accession, China carefully implemented the further loosening up of FDI regulations it had agreed to. But, at the same time, it resorted to other tactics to limit foreign competition, requiring government agencies, for example, to procure only foreign technology that had been developed in China as "indigenous innovation." After outrage from foreign firms who saw this as a ploy to force them to transfer sensitive technology to China, these measures were officially abandoned. But the cat was out of the bag. The government's desire to foster local Chinese players had been clearly signaled to its procurement offices. Compounding this squeeze on foreign suppliers has been Chinese concern (reinforced by the Snowden revelations) that the security of foreign information technology has been compromised by the US government.

Based on my own experience, the following contrasting examples in the auto, logistics, and high-tech sectors illustrate how China has been highly selective in its approach to FDI.

Win-Win in the Auto Industry

Early in the reforms, China moved quickly to attract FDI in certain strategic manufacturing areas, such as automobiles. Auto assembly/OEMs (original equipment manufacturers) were opened up to foreigners but to this day their equity stake cannot exceed 50%.

The 50/50 JVs are problematic due to no clear equity control, often resulting in management friction and poor governance. But although foreign auto firms in China faced many serious challenges in the early years, the remarkable outcome has been that, against all the odds, these 50/50 auto JVs have for the most part worked smoothly to the benefit of both the foreign and Chinese sides. At the end of the day, there was a productive give-and-take between the partners, motivated by the enormous market opportunity they were sitting astride.

China's opening up of the auto sector to foreign firms had two goals. The first was to kick-start the industry, which under central planning had failed to keep up with world trends, to create a local supply of vehicles and to avoid further growth in auto imports. In this respect, the opening up has been a huge success. But the second goal, to help local Chinese producers learn the ropes and create strong local auto brands, had not been fully realized.

Early in the reform process, China formed a series of auto JVs with foreign firms: Volkswagen (VW) (Shanghai, 1984), American Motors (Beijing, 1984), and Peugeot (Guangzhou, 1985). They bore the full burden of being early pioneers. The volume market was not yet there, auto parts suppliers were absent, and Chinese red tape made it difficult to import kits for assembly. Meanwhile, the Japanese car makers stuck to exporting to China (China imported more than 350,000 cars in 1985, mainly complete fleets of Toyotas used as taxis). After the reforms were put back on track in 1992, consumer demand finally took off, permitting economies of scale and profitability. In due course, other auto makers, such as Toyota in 1993 and GM in 1997, made more timely entries into manufacturing in China.

The Starting Point

It is easy to see why China turned to foreign auto firms to help transform the industry. From the previous 30 years they had little to show for their efforts, despite help from the Soviets. As China began its reforms, representative local auto products (photos below) were:

Left: The "Liberation" (Jiefang) truck. First produced in 1956 by the First Auto Works, Changchun, it was a five-ton, medium-size, gasoline-powered vehicle, and a copy of a Soviet design. China lacked locally made heavy trucks needed for long-distance haulage.

Middle: The "Shanghai" Sedan. First produced in 1958 by Shanghai Auto had a Chinese body on a chassis derived from a World War II Benz. It was underpowered and with extremely poor handling. This living antique was phased out in the 1970s.

Right: The "Red Flag" limousine. First produced by the First Auto Works, Changchun, in 1963 was based on a 1955 Chrysler. Production ended in 1980. It was built in small numbers so that Chinese leaders and visiting dignitaries did not have to ride in Soviet-made ZIL limousines, which had been used in the 1950s.

Central planning yielded poor results in the auto sector.

Writing in 1989, I highlighted a series of constraints faced by China's auto industry, many of them related closely to the legacy of the planned economy:

Abysmally low productivity: In 1987, 470,000 vehicles were produced by an industry with 1.4 million employees and fixed assets of US$ 15 BN.

Absence of economies of scale: Auto production was dispersed among more than 100 factories. Only two had a capacity of 100,000 vehicles per year. One Chinese official, with a clear awareness of the challenges, described the industry to me as being composed of "fragmented or disconnected yet overlapping entities."

Unresponsive to market demand. As part of the Soviet heavy industry model, Chinese manufacturers focused not on passenger cars but on trucks. But even with trucks, they got it wrong. The Jiefang truck (shown above), although a reliable workhorse, could not satisfy demand for heavy trucks (10–15 tons), except, of course, by being dangerously overloaded.

Lack of investment funds. The government had ambitious plans but no real money had been allocated. My conclusion at that time was they would need to rely on foreign investors to foot part of the bill.

Shortage of raw materials and components. One GM executive, working on the firm's potential entry into the China market, stated to me in 1988:

> "There is not enough steel, gas, rubber, or roads, there are bottlenecks for every component, and they don't have the money to develop anything."[6]

GM delayed its China entry until 1997.

In 1988, China's Second Auto Works (SAW) in Shiyan, Hubei, which made trucks, had to close for ten days due to their state supply of steel being cut by more than 25%.

Shortage of foreign exchange. Initially, foreign investors such as VW and American Motors, given the absence of suitable local components and the low production volumes, began assembly through importing SKD or CKD* kits. Their expansion of production was constrained by government restrictions on foreign exchange to pay for the kits.

Volkswagen: An Early Entrant Pays Its Dues

The early foreign investors in China's auto industry (VW, American Motors, and Peugeot) had to sweat it out with slow growth, compounded by issues around the local supply of components and foreign exchange controls.

---

* SKD is semi-knocked down, CKD is completely knocked down.

My visit to Shanghai VW (SVW) in 1989 highlighted the tough conditions this early entrant had to contend with. Output of VW Santanas had been 15,000 in 1988 and were projected to be just 20,000 in 1989. At that time, VW's component suppliers had not yet followed them into China, and they were dependent on the import of kits for local assembly. In China, the foreign exchange, needed to pay for the kits, was a scarce resource. SVW hoped unrealistically to get around this massive bottleneck by generating its own foreign exchange through the export of engines and a few finished cars.

On the plus side, SVW told me they had reached a quality level superior to that achieved in Brazil, Mexico, and South Africa and were confident of reaching or exceeding the quality levels achieved in Germany. Productivity at SVW Shanghai was also improving rapidly. The amount of direct worker time on the line needed to complete a vehicle had fallen from 20 hours in 1985 to 6.6 hours at the end of 1988. Further productivity gains were to be achieved through the introduction of spot-welding robots in the body shop. Although SVW was still importing the high value, heavyweight "short block"—a sub-assembly including the cast engine block—it was constructing a new engine facility in Shanghai to manufacture 100% of the engine.

The shortage of foreign exchange limited SVW's growth and created friction with the Shanghai government. On top of that, VW was working on a separate JV with the First Auto Works (FAW) in Changchun. VW urged the Shanghai government to have the Shanghai JV join forces with the new one in order to bring economies-of-scale and efficiency in a shared component supply technology platform. The Shanghai government demurred, suggesting that VW focus on growing SVW's production. Shanghai Mayor Zhu Rongji (later to be China's premier) quietly threatened VW that Shanghai might consider bringing other foreign manufacturers into Shanghai. VW went ahead with the JV with FAW (signed in 1991). While the realities of Chinese provincialism or "localism" prevented the two centers of VW production in China from merging, later some limited synergy was created between the two entities by VW's China Holding Company, which owned 10% of each JV's equity.

VW paid its dues and survived to become dominant in China. The VW Group, which includes VW, Audi, Skoda, Porsche, and Bentley brands, sold 3.55 million vehicles in China in 2015, making it number two in that market, just a fraction behind GM. VW's profitable growth in China has served to counterbalance poor results elsewhere in the world. Even with the cooling of the Chinese economy, China remains critical to VW's global business.

The Foreign Component Suppliers Arrive

From the late 1980s onward, a wide range of auto component suppliers established factories in China. I personally consulted on projects for auto glass and auto paint, piston rings, starters and generators, auto electronics/engine management systems, bearings, auto air-conditioning compressors, catalytic converters, bonding agents for radial tires, and more. For these investors in the auto component sector, the choice of location and partner was often strictly dictated by the Chinese side in the OEM JVs and the local government that manipulated them. This pressure was most pronounced in Shanghai.

In 1985, VW pledged that the minimum local content of materials, parts, and so on in their Shanghai vehicles (measured by value) would reach 85% by 1991, but by year-end 1988 they had reached just 25%. To turn this around, SVW set up the Shanghai Santana Localization Community comprising 120 manufacturers and research institutes, mainly from Shanghai, while the Shanghai government also set up its Santana Local Content Office. Potential component suppliers were invited to meetings where they were addressed by SVW leaders and the Shanghai Planning Commission. When Shanghai referred to "localization," it went beyond just location in China; it meant *in* Shanghai (or close by). Foreign suppliers who were bold enough to locate elsewhere were threatened with being shut out of Shanghai.

This pattern of "localism" was repeated in other cities. A manufacturer of auto air conditioning was told bluntly by the Chongqing government that to supply the Ford plant in that city, deep in the interior of Western China 1400 km from the coast, it would have to form a JV, rather than simply put up a warehouse. The Chongqing government won the day. A full manufacturing JV with a local company was formed, even though from a simple commercial market point of view, it would have been more efficient to be located elsewhere.

General Motors Benefits from a Late Entry

GM reaped the benefits of a later market entry. My discussions with GM in the 1980s centered on the question of whether it should follow VW into the China market immediately and before there was a significant local supply of high quality components, or whether GM should wait until the local supply infrastructure was more complete. GM chose to wait.

In 1997, after years of negotiations with multiple partners in China, GM pressed the button and established its JV in Shanghai (SGM, Shanghai General Motors). Today, China is GM's largest market where in 2015 it sold 3.7 million vehicles, making it number one in that market. It is investing US$ 11 BN to achieve further growth.

By waiting to become a late entrant, GM benefited in several ways. It resisted government pressure to establish a JV with Second Auto Works in Hubei province far into the interior. Then when it came to building the plant in Shanghai, there was a viable infrastructure of foreign auto-component suppliers around Shanghai and more broadly in China.

Once established, the GM management in Shanghai forged an excellent working relationship with the JV Chairman Hu Maoyuan (from the Chinese side), demonstrating a successful approach to the complexity of a 50/50 JV. SGM's complete redesign of the cockpit of the Buick Regal for the China market won praise from consumers.

GM did face problems when its Chinese partner SAIC (Shanghai Automotive Industry Corp.), for instance, illegally transferred technology from GM's Daewoo subsidiary to the Chinese firm, Chery. When I asked a senior GM manager in Shanghai whom they saw as their main competitor, he responded "our partner!"

GM's success in China is closely related to the impeccable timing of its entry, whether by design or partly by luck. In 1997, consumer demand for cars in China was at an inflection point, taking off, in stark contrast to the late 1980s. Ford entered much later and probably missed the perfect timing, resulting in a China market share of only 4%, compared to GM and VW, each with 15%.

In terms of creating a domestic supply of vehicles that can satisfy the nation's needs (barring some imports of very high-end vehicles such as Ferrari and Porsche), the introduction of FDI achieved its goals. The Chinese auto market is now the largest in the world, having grown annually at 24% for ten years, reaching 24.6 million new vehicle sales in 2015. The growth is likely to continue but will not be so stellar. The growth in sales fell to 4.7% in 2015, due to the economic cooling, restrictions on ownership, and increased maturity of the market, with used cars now an alternative to new cars. Auto makers in China have in some cases trimmed production. Profit margins in China, which have accounted for one-half of VW and 40% of GM global profits respectively, are under pressure. Even though the era of high growth and fat profits in China compared to the developed markets may be over, China remains central to the plans of global auto firms.

Local Auto Firms Fail to Impress

While the opening up of China's auto industry should be deemed a resounding success in terms of satisfying market demand, the goal of sparking the emergence of globally competitive Chinese automakers simply has not been realized. Chinese auto brands produced by 171 companies reached a peak China market share of 49% in 2010 in part due to US$ 1 BN of government subsidies. This government support was abandoned and the market share of Chinese brands declined to around 40%. Chinese-branded vehicles have a place at the low end of the market, but find it hard to command consumer loyalty.

Given the ready availability of auto components, many of the barriers to entry into auto manufacture and assembly have fallen away globally. Most component suppliers have established production in China. Moreover, there is plenty of capital to fund Chinese start-ups. So how do we explain China's poor showing in this area?

Foreign automakers have perfected the art of efficient, lean, high-volume manufacturing while Chinese home-grown vehicles suffer from poor product quality and unreliable after-sales service. But at the heart of the challenge facing Chinese players is the fact that the global auto industry has become less about engineering and more about design that provides an enhanced experience to the consumer. This involves not just the vehicle's look but its instrumentation, ride, and handling, all of which is fine-tuned for specific market segments. In turn, this design and customer appeal is reflected in the brand positioning. So far, auto design, software (in the broadest sense), and branding, as opposed to the hardware (components), is where China lags behind.

So, it is not at all surprising that the first China-built vehicles to arrive in the US are all manufactured by foreign firms which are able to achieve global standards in quality, safety, and design. GM and Volvo (albeit owned by Chinese firm Geely, but still run by the Swedish management) have already shipped vehicles from China to the US and this trend is underlined by Ford's decision to base its global production of its Focus car in China.[7]

China's Auto Industry Growth Is Unsustainable

Nobody should imagine for one moment that auto sales in China can sustain double-digit annual growth rates. The auto market is cooling and it needs to. Vehicle emissions in China are having a devastating impact on public health. China's leaders have "declared war" on pollution, which has become a major source of dissent especially among the emerging new middle class. A decade ago, I would regularly hear China's officials and economists embracing "auto-centric development," much like the old US model, whereby auto production has a knock-on effect across the economy. Some officials even regarded the growing pollution as a badge of honor in that it demonstrated that China was moving forward. You will not hear that view in China today.

In each major city, quotas have been placed on new vehicle registration, and registration fees have been increased. In some cases, these fees are higher than the cheapest cars, resulting in local auto brands retreating from megacities like Beijing.

China is plowing funds into the development of electric vehicles (EVs), including battery technology. The prospect exists that China may well leapfrog the rest of the world both in the design and production of EVs and in their widespread adoption to reduce pollution.

Why Did China Neglect Logistics and Resist Its "Opening Up" to FDI?

At the beginning of the reforms, China's logistics industry was in very poor condition, just like the auto industry. The highly centralized state-planned distribution system had melted away, leaving logistics in a primitive, fragmented, and highly inefficient condition, quite unsuited to the requirements of a modern economy.

Logistics may not be the most glamorous or eye-catching subject and is unlikely to be an attention grabber at a dinner party. But the importance of modern logistics cannot be underestimated since it is the lubricant that keeps industry and commerce running smoothly. Sadly, China delayed addressing its backward logistics resulting in serious bottlenecks that have held back the integration of the national economy.

First, what do we mean by modern logistics? Once, logistics often referred to the military supply system. More recently, as logistics has become a buzzword, even small trucking companies have taken to labeling their companies as logistics firms. For the sake of clarity, we define modern logistics as follows: It is increasingly an outsourced service (thus the commonly used term "third party logistics," or 3PL) in contrast to logistics handled in-house by the shipper (that is, the manufacturer). It is an integrated, seamless solution including transportation, warehousing, freight forwarding, customs clearance, and certain value-added services (break shipment, repackaging). While with more basic logistics there is a spot market (you switch logistics providers regularly), contracts between the modern 3PL and the shipper are usually long-term or multiyear.

At the heart of the entire process is sophisticated computer software that enables time-specific delivery, tracking of shipments, electronic links to the IT systems of customers and officials (e.g., Customs at the port), in effect creating a digital supply chain. The 3PL is focused on the integrated solution and may choose to adopt an asset-light approach, itself outsourcing trucking and warehousing.

The Woeful State of China's Logistics

With the dissolution of the centrally planned economy, the Ministry of Domestic Trade (successor to the Ministry of Materials) was abolished. Some of its staff stayed on to manage the government-run China Federation of Logistics and Purchasing (CFLP). In 2002, I was bestowed with the honor of being the only non-Chinese to be elected an executive director of CFLP. Professor Ding Junfa, my good friend and vice chairman of CFLP, published a book in which he set out in no-uncertain terms the drastic backwardness of China's logistics.

China's logistics costs accounted for 20% of GDP compared to only 9.9% in the US. Huge quantities of working capital were tied up in raw materials inventory, which was held an average of 30 days, far from a J-I-T (just-in-time) approach. Logistics costs represented 30% to 40% of product cost—"unimaginable in developed, market-oriented economies," he added. Finished product inventory periods in China totaled 80 days (45 days in the factory warehouse and 35 days in the retail store), compared to 12 days in the US. Many enterprises had set up their own transportation fleets and warehousing, which was costly, underutilized, and inefficient. Seventy percent of truck haulage was done by factories themselves. Empty backhauls represented 37% of the transportation. Average truck speeds were 50 km/hour.[8] This was a stark indictment of the weakness of China's logistics capability.

China's truck fleet was dominated by locally built, five-ton (medium-size) vehicles that were unsuitable for long-haul goods transport and even today are often covered by a tarpaulin, rather than a secure, waterproof box car. It is common for trucks to be seriously overloaded, which creates hazards and quickly wears out the roads. Things are improving, in part since foreign heavy truck firms such as Daimler Benz and Freightliner have established production sites in China.

China's road infrastructure has also been transformed. In the space of about 20 years, some 85,000 km of superhighways were built, making it the largest such network in the world. But other factors hold China back from using this network effectively. Road tolls are too high. There is also a widespread practice of local governments levying their own illegal tolls.

China's rail freight system has proven to be a major bottleneck. Back in 1993, Shanghai People's Printing Factory No. 8, then China's leader in packaging printing, told me it relied on rail freight and explained with pride that a key government relationship was one it cultivated with the local goods railway station, where someone was permanently posted to ensure products got loaded onto the wagons. It had to pay "fees" or bribes to facilitate matters.[9]

China's rail freight system still lags behind the world. Its intermodal system (that is, containers carried by rail with short haul by truck at both ends) remains seriously underdeveloped. Although the height of rail tunnels is being increased to accommodate double-stacked container trains, containerization of railway goods traffic is still at an extremely low rate of 5% to 6%.

When in 2001 we conducted a comprehensive survey of China's 3PL market, we found Chinese manufacturers highly reluctant to outsource their logistics, since post-reforms they had already built their own in-house logistics capability and in any case had no confidence in the service levels of 3PL providers. More than ten years later, in 2012, another survey revealed a continuing resistance to contract logistics (3PL) with only one in four respondents saying they outsourced this service.[10]

So why did China not embrace foreign investment to drive change in logistics in the way it did in the auto industry? There are a number of possible explanations.

First, domestic transportation, logistics, and domestic trade were regarded as having high strategic and security importance to the nation and, therefore, should not be exposed to foreign investment and control.

Second, as a legacy of the Stalinist planning mentality, China's leaders were engineering-oriented (that is, hardware- or product-oriented) and heavily focused on manufacturing. They undervalued the critical role played by service industries, such as logistics.

Third, they wanted to provide local service industries with time to find their feet before opening things up to foreign competition. This applied not only to logistics, but also to the service industry more broadly, including the retail sector and department stores, where foreign investment initially was also highly restricted.

Beginning with its WTO accession in 2001, China began slowly opening up logistics to foreign investment. It took until December 2005, four years later, for regulations to permit 100% foreign-owned freight forwarding/logistics companies. Foreign firms such as DB Schenker, Ryder, Kerry, and Schneider National entered the market, focusing largely on their multinational customers in China and the cross-border logistics they require. Beyond that, there is the need for ever more complex supply chains as their customers penetrate China's interior, including the remote western areas.

To this day, the China logistics market remains bifurcated. Foreign 3PLs typically serve the multi-national corporations (MNCs) who have entered the China market. A handful of China logistics players, such as China Merchants/Sinotrans and Cosco Logistics, have reached high levels of modern logistics service that permit them to win long-term contracts from foreign firms in China. But most Chinese logistics firms focus more on Chinese manufacturers, a market segment that remains fragmented, with low levels of service and highly price-conscious customers.

There is an urgent need for world-class logistics services. But it will also require a shift in the mentality of Chinese manufacturers. While many have made great progress in understanding the impact of logistics on their cost structure, for others there is a long way to go before they rate the quality of logistics service (safety, reliability, transparency, tracking, etc.) as highly as the price of the service. Serious efforts are required from central government to reign in the illegal tolls imposed by local government. National operating licenses for 3PLs should not have to be supplemented by local provincial operating licenses.

The Motorola Breakthrough

Chicago-based Motorola, which started as a manufacturer of car radios, grew rapidly during World War II as a producer of two-way radios for the military. Based on its radio technology, it went on to be a pioneer in pagers and cellular phones (it invented the first mobile phone in 1973), both the handsets and the infrastructure. It also designed and made semiconductors to drive these and other devices.

In the mid-1980s, Motorola CEO Bob Galvin, son of founder Paul Galvin, had the vision to see the potential that China represented. But he stated adamantly that, "I do not want to form a joint venture [in China]." Looking around the Chinese semiconductor industry at that time, it was perfectly obvious that there was no potential Chinese partner that could bring any benefits to the table, except government connections. One major concern was protecting the firm's leading-edge technology and skills. Motorola wanted to create a "center of excellence in China" without the impediments and risks implied by taking on a Chinese partner. That sounded reasonable but flew in the face of what some Beijing bureaucrats, stage-managing this sector, wanted.

The Chinese government, then as now, is not monolithic on policy issues, with different views reflecting different stakeholder interests. Just as with the auto industry, many officials of the state-owned semiconductor industry had a distinct preference for forcing foreign entrants into JVs. Firms such as Philips, Alcatel, and NEC agreed to form JVs in which the Chinese side typically had a majority equity position. But Motorola stuck to its guns and would not entertain putting its first and primary China investment into a JV.

Meanwhile, there were other Chinese officials who had the foresight to encourage top-flight foreign firms to enter the market on a very different basis. In 1986, China published the first regulations permitting 100% foreign firms (wholly foreign-owned enterprises, or WFOE). Initially, they were restricted to businesses that were export-oriented or high technology. Motorola naturally was able to cross the high-tech hurdle. In 1986, Bob Galvin visited Li Tieying, who headed the Ministry of Electronics Industry (MEI) and the next year presented the Chinese government with what he called the Track B Proposal ("B" was the vision of a wholly Motorola-owned venture in China, in contrast to the JV route).

Some aspects of the Track B proposal were already possible, at least in principle, under the new WFOE law. But given it was such a strategic area, the government had a free hand to frustrate a foreign entrant if it so wished. The Galvin proposal set out its wish list: WFOE as the investment vehicle, domestic market access, full operating control, ability to deal directly with employees, and no union interference (Galvin had initially objected to having a trade union but when it was explained that it was just a tool of the CCP, his concerns were allayed!).

Motorola worked assiduously at different levels of the Chinese government arguing the case for this bold experiment.

Winning central government support. Minister Li Tieying, with whom Galvin worked closely, was a very senior figure, since he concurrently served as vice director of the State Council's Leading Group for the Invigoration of the Electronics Industry and, most significantly, as a member of the CCP's Politburo. Motorola also worked with the MEI Vice Minister Zeng Peiyan, who warmed to the idea of Motorola's China proposal being a trial project, in line with China's practice of introducing reforms experimentally. He validated Motorola's strategy of working with the government just a few steps ahead of what the evolving regulatory environment technically permitted—or, so to speak, riding the wave of regulatory change in China. Risky but rewarding, if you get it right.

The then Ministry of Foreign Economic Relations and Trade (MOFERT) and Ms. Ma Xiuhong, head of its department that handled foreign investment approvals (she later become vice minister), was reform-minded and strongly supported the Motorola project. But given the project size and the features that lay beyond what the law permitted, coupled with the strategic nature of the semiconductor business, the proposal needed to be referred up to China's State Council, which had the authority to issue a "special approval." This approval would make the deal fully legal, even though it was some steps ahead of the regulatory change.

Tianjin government acts decisively. Motorola's hand in selecting the site of the venture was to a great extent guided by the Chinese government, which recommended either Xiamen (in Fujian in South China) or Tianjin (close to Beijing). Both cities predictably promised Motorola impressive support.

Xiamen's mayor praised Motorola's choice of a WFOE investment vehicle, stating that "our biggest problem is management" and adding that they had done an investigation of 200 foreign enterprises in Xiamen and found that WFOEs were better managed than JVs. "That is why we encourage WFOEs," he concluded. The mayor also addressed Motorola's anxiety over its ability to decide employee issues. Motorola would, he said, be "fully free in all areas, including recruitment, salaries, and firing." That may not seem so astounding today in China, but at that time, it was extremely hard to make changes to the workforce, even if the foreign investor ostensibly had full operating control.

Motorola's choice of location was ultimately Tianjin, on the coast of the Bohai Gulf in North China, not far from Beijing but separated enough from the capital so as not to be overburdened by the central government bureaucracy. The Tianjin Economic-Technological Development Area (TEDA) was a fast mover in attracting FDI and actively urged investors to form WFOEs rather than JVs. TEDA was also hungry for a major anchor investment and believed that winning the Motorola project would be a breakthrough for the zone as it competed with other cities, such as Dalian and Shanghai.

The president of TEDA's commercial arm was Ye Disheng, a Cantonese electronics engineer who had worked for ten years in the MEI under Li Tieying. Chairman of TEDA's government arm, its administrative commission, was Zhang Wei, then still in his 30s and described by his colleagues at TEDA as a "rising political star." Zhang had been a delegate to the CCP National Congress in 1987 and was close to Hu Qiuli, a reformist member of the Politburo's Standing Committee (the highest level of the CCP). He also had good contacts with Li Lanqing, who had previously been Tianjin mayor and at that time was vice minister of MOFERT, which handled foreign investments.

Zhang Wei and TEDA worked extremely closely with Tianjin Mayor Li Ruihuan, another CCP moderate who had been responsible for pulling Tianjin out of a 40-year slumber, building a new road system and putting the city back on the map. Mayor Li was also concurrently Tianjin CCP secretary and a member of the CCP's Politburo.

In the middle of 1988, Zhang Wei and his colleagues engineered a round of golf in Tianjin for Mayor Li and CCP General Secretary Zhao Ziyang (China's top leader) at which an agreement was reached on moving forward on Motorola's Tianjin deal, the "Plan B."

Some may shrug their shoulders and say this was just another case of using relationships (<u>guanxi</u>) in China to get early mover advantage. In fact, it went far beyond that model of doing business and was an important milestone in history when reformist leaders were in ascendancy and strongly motivated to push out the boundaries of how foreign firms operated in China.

The next year, in June 1989, the Tiananmen Square Massacre occurred. Zhao Ziyang, who had supported the deal with Motorola, was dismissed and held under house arrest in a Beijing hutong (alley) until his death in 2005. Zhang Wei, by then promoted to head of foreign trade in Tianjin, took the courageous step of resigning in protest at the imposition of martial law (that was *before* the actual massacre). He was then held under house arrest and ultimately left China and went into exile. Conservative elements took advantage of the political chill to try to recentralize the economy and put a brake on further reforms.

While many companies pulled back from China, Motorola continued its efforts, culminating in March 1992 with the official approval of its Tianjin WFOE, which was licensed to produce the full range of Motorola products: pagers, cellular phones, cellular infrastructure, two-way radios, auto electronics, and semiconductors. Motorola minimized its risk through pledging to install a full semiconductor wafer fab (fabrication plant) *only* when "market conditions permitted." This permitted wiggle room, and it took a number of years before the Motorola venture in Tianjin started its semiconductor production, first with "assembly and test," then investing in a full wafer fab in 1995.

Tianjin rightly perceived the Motorola project to be the linchpin of its strategy to attract major foreign investors. Its persistence in pushing the project forward, even while cold winds were blowing in the post-Tiananmen Square Massacre period, was rewarded. Other major firms followed Motorola into TEDA, including Samsung, which located a major manufacturing complex there.

Having established itself, Motorola enjoyed a long period of fast growth and profitability in China. It used China profits to pay several hundred million US$ of cash for its new office in Beijing. It first dominated the pager market, then the mobile phone market, until Chinese and South Korean competitors arrived on the scene. In the 1990s, Motorola was regarded by aspiring Chinese professionals as one of the most admired foreign-invested firms. Later, Motorola's global disarray and dismemberment led to the decline of the Tianjin venture and the rest of Motorola's business in China. But that is another story.

Why FDI Will Stick with China

Although FDI remains at a high level and the regulatory process has been greatly simplified, the Chinese side's hunger and enthusiasm for it that we saw in the 1980s and 1990s has waned. FDI is simply not as significant to the economy as before and, reflecting that, most of the preferential tax treatment accorded to FDI in the early days has been discontinued.

Chinese firms now have alternative sources of investment capital, including the stock market. They have acquired new management skills and show a newfound confidence. Though they may engage with a foreign partner in a learning process, their eyes are firmly fixed on becoming a global force themselves and so they are unwilling to form JVs in which equity and management are ceded to the foreign party. Foreign investors should take note that any JV arrangement runs the risk of being short term—a marriage of convenience until the Chinese side is ready to go it alone. Moreover, the Chinese government has proven to be perfectly willing to step in to block potential "national champions" from being taken over by foreign investors, such as private equity funds.

While China remains an investment magnet, the foreign investors in many sectors are more sanguine about the possibility of establishing a long-term, profitable business in China. Many have been disappointed by the lackluster performance of JVs and since as early as the year 2000, the WFOE overtook the JV as the most popular foreign investment vehicle. Most investments now entail entirely new facilities built on greenfield sites, without the burden of preexisting operations and the legacy of a bloated workforce with skills ill-suited to the new business.

China still has an "open door" to FDI since, quite apart from its WTO obligations, it sees merit in having foreign companies competing in the domestic market. This not only keeps local firms on their toes but also permits access to foreign technology and business processes. Foreign firms in China are an excellent training ground for managers and engineers that eventually move on to Chinese competitors.

In some sectors, foreign investors have been relatively free to grow in line with China's economy. This has been the case with manufacturers of fast-moving consumer goods, such as P&G and Unilever; with fast-food chains, such as KFC and McDonald's; and with the auto industry. It is true that foreign firms are singled out and held to higher standards than local firms with regard to issues such as product quality, environmental compliance, and employee working conditions. Some foreign firms have been fined under China's anti-monopoly law for rigging prices. FDI represents a high profile punching bag.

Some foreign investors quietly accept that the market will increasingly be rigged by the Chinese government in favor of local players. This feeling is most acute in information and communication technology (ICT), where the government has control over most procurement. It is fair to assume that the Chinese government at the level of the State Council's Leading Groups, using data fed from the ministries below them, carefully and painstakingly monitor the entire China operations of the largest foreign ICT firms, such as IBM and HP, and manipulate the market. On the one hand, foreign firms are permitted to have a limited market share and a degree of profitability within a range that sustains their interest in China, while on the other hand China is able to put boundaries on their growth so that they do not pose an excessive threat to the designated Chinese national champions, such as Huawei.

Though all this is troublesome and frustrating, most foreign investors will grin and bear it. They will stick with the China market. For the time being, the door remains open or at least ajar. Those foreign firms with strongly differentiated products or services can still profit from China's growth.

Looking further out, the role of FDI looks more uncertain. Over recent decades, the CCP has smartly engineered an uneasy but productive balance between FDI and Chinese interests, something that has been a key plank of *the China paradox*. While the government has used all kinds of red tape to control and guide the flow of FDI into China, at the same time early on in the reforms, it showed a strong hunger for FDI and at times displayed a cap-in-hand, almost subservient posture to foreign firms.

That posture certainly belongs to the past, and there are signs that China is swinging much further in the other direction, going beyond just self-confidence and more toward dangerous hubris. Feeling that it has sucked all it can out of foreign firms, it may ultimately abandon any belief it ever had in a true "open door." Rather than relying on inbound FDI, China is increasingly looking to overseas acquisitions as an alternative way to acquire technology.

If China is in a sense declaring victory in its utilization of FDI, this would be an enormous mistake. Given the speed of technology change, China would also be poorly served by making China less attractive to FDI. FDI brings vital skills and management techniques. China needs to remain connected to the global knowledge economy if it is to break through into the big league of advanced nations. The less welcoming attitude to FDI may threaten to cut China off from world trends and be debilitating to China's rise. This is just one more data point that suggests that *the China paradox* is fading away, and that the sun is setting on what was an extraordinary period of reform during which an enlightened and pragmatic CCP permitted foreign businesses to contribute to China's rejuvenation.

Chapter 8
Business Models at the Heart of China's Emergence

We've been trying to exchange market access for technology, but we've barely gotten hold of any key technologies in the past 30 years.[1]

—A leader of a Chinese car maker
bemoaning the fact that the
"learn and catch up" business model
has failed to create a competitive
indigenous Chinese auto industry.

The significant scientific and engineering obstacles and the resulting high cost of developing thorium-powered reactors may require the sort of long-term commitment and resources that only another world power, like China, can provide.[2]

—A foreign commentator expressing the
hope that China will achieve
"novel product" innovation
through developing power
generation using molten
salt reactors.

Are we going to permit a company to VIOLATE our water resources because we received/have been promised aid by the government of the People's Republic of China? Is this part of a "pay back package" for the National Stadium...?[3]

—Outrage from a citizen of the Caribbean country
of Grenada at the destruction of an aquifer by a
Chinese investor.

The following four business models highlight different ways in which Chinese firms have grasped the opportunities created by the reforms that contributed to China's meteoric rise.

Model 1. Learn and Catch Up

After Mao died, China found itself in a developmental dead end, lagging far behind the industrialized countries. Although we may concede that catch-up from such a low base was bound to be impressive, still it is fair to say that China, using the "learn and catch-up" model, has achieved stunning results beyond what had been anticipated.

DOI 10.1515/9781501507212-008

China's use of this model is not without its critics and detractors. Some observers do not equate this model with innovation, preferring to give that accolade to the development of purely novel products or technologies. But as a leading US economist told me, "China has developed a marvelous system for extracting value for business training and playing catch-up in technology. This is significant innovation."[4] Based on analysis of China's IT industry, it is argued that:

> "China shines by keeping its industrial production and service industries in perfect tandem with the technological frontier.... It runs as fast as possible in order to remain at the cusp of the global technology frontier without actually advancing the frontier itself."[5]

This model is also more complex than some would suggest, involving participation in multiple elements of the value chain (the entire process through which goods and services are delivered). China, through taking advantage of the way globalization has fragmented the production steps, has created:

> ". . .a formidable competitive capacity to innovate in different segments of the research, development and production chain.... China's innovation capability is not just process (or incremental) innovation, but also in the organization of production, manufacturing techniques, and technologies, delivery, design, and second-generation innovation. Those capabilities enable China to move quickly into new niches once they have proved profitable by the original innovator."[6]

However, in some instances, China's zeal for acquiring foreign technology has extended IPR theft. China with impunity stole the float glass technology developed by the UK firm Pilkington. We shall see below how a Chinese firm brazenly ripped off GM's auto technology. I recall in the 1980s having to physically pull down Chinese business visitors at a chemical plant in Pennsylvania who were clambering up access ladders at the plant to take measurements of valves that gave vital clues to the proprietary technology.

But we should also give credit to China's efforts at further developing technology, also known as *re-innovation*, even though it may at times enter a grey area close to theft.

The Chinese desire to create its own propriety technology bears some resemblance to the path taken by South Korea. In 1986, I helped Samsung to do an audit of its consumer electronics technology, our findings showed that Japanese ownership of the technology meant that virtually nothing could be freely transferred into ventures that Samsung might establish in China. But within ten years Samsung had developed its own proprietary

VCRs and other products, including the semiconductors that powered them, all of which could be deployed in China. Taiwan went through a similar process as South Korea. China now follows suit.

China's large domestic market and its resulting ability to attract foreign direct investment stand out as key advantages in gaining access to foreign technology. China has been willing to share some of its large domestic market with foreign players since in that process foreign technology is transferred into China. The Chinese side in JVs with foreigners can absorb and in some cases further develop, tweak, and improve the technology—the so-called "re-innovation."

While some skeptics doubt whether this model is sustainable, arguing that it is running "out of steam," or has outlived its usefulness due to flagging interest in China from foreign investors, there is ample evidence that foreign firms, such as those in semiconductors, are still willing to deploy their technology in China.

Few foreign investors have deluded themselves about the risk of technology theft they were exposing themselves to. Most subscribe to the principle of "use it or lose it." If you do not participate with the Chinese, then Chinese firms will sooner or later reverse-engineer the technology, absorb it from one of your competitors, or, more to the point today, acquire the foreign company and its intellectual property outright. At the end of the day, the best protection for technology rights is to ceaselessly innovate to keep ahead of competitors, be they Chinese or others.

Disappointment in Auto and Semiconductor

In these sectors, this model fell frustratingly short of the key goals of propelling China up the technology ladder. China became a manufacturer but not the product innovator.

We saw above how China attracted massive FDI into its auto industry. But although China is now the largest auto market in the world, the 50/50 JVs that legally remain the only market entry route for foreign players have not directly achieved China's goal of spawning its own indigenous auto industry and successful national brands.[7]

The JVs have, of course, indirectly contributed to China's local auto sector. First, they have provided the Chinese partners with huge piles of cash used to establish their own separate auto plants. But the results have been unimpressive. Today only about 10% of the profits of these Chinese partners come from their own brands, while the rest is still easily earned money from the JVs.

Second, with the foreign entrants to the Chinese auto industry came the establishment in China of a comprehensive locally based supply chain of auto-components manufacturers—some foreign, some Chinese. This has dramatically lowered the technological barriers for a new breed of local Chinese entrants, such as the SOE Chery and private firms Geely and BYD.

But despite these advantages and the process of learning (and theft), China has failed to create its own strong indigenous auto industry. Why do Chinese auto brands today remain confined mainly to the low end of the Chinese market and have a declining 40% market share?

The focus of global auto makers is increasingly not just on the underlying technology, but also on design and consumer appeal. This aesthetic aspect is an area where Chinese players struggle to impress Chinese consumers, even as quality and functionality continue to improve. Some Chinese firms have brought in foreign designers who have formerly worked for Ferrari or Pininfarina, while Shanghai Auto purchased the brand and designs from Rover of the UK.

The lack of strong design capability, let alone flair, is not the only reason why Chinese auto makers have failed to make the grade. The key competency of foreign auto firms includes how to establish dealer networks, after-sales service, and auto financing. A study I conducted in 2003 on the Chinese auto industry found sales and service to be chaotic and in their infancy.[8] Chinese players focused mainly on getting cars made and sold, rather than on providing service for the life of the vehicle. They treated their products more like a microwave oven than a car. We anticipated that foreign entrants could use their refined skills in the area of auto service to outpace emerging Chinese auto makers. This is exactly what happened.

Given the failure of this "learn and catch-up" model to propel China's indigenous auto industry forward, China is predictably migrating toward taking holdings in or acquiring foreign auto firms. In 2010, private Chinese auto maker Geely acquired Volvo. In 2014, China's SOE car firm Dongfeng acquired an equity stake in its partner's ailing French parent company Groupe PSA (maker of Peugeot and Citroen), permitting Dongfeng's participation in PSA's R&D process, including the soft art of product design.

Despite the poor showing of Chinese auto brands, we can expect the Chinese to export vehicles into developed markets and not just emerging markets of Asia and Africa. The foreign acquisitions will help in this respect. Volvo has already begun exporting certain China-built models to the

US. Chinese auto makers, when ordering parts from the US for delivery three years out, are beginning to specify that they should meet US and European regulatory standards.[9] There is also the potential that China will sidestep the tough challenge of improving the traditional car and will leapfrog into dominance in electric vehicles.

The limitations of the "learn and catch up" model can also be seen in China's semiconductor industry. In the 1990s, China was successful in enticing Taiwan, Japan, and US chip manufacturers to establish plants in China. But such is the pace of technology development that China has fallen behind and today can supply only 10% of its semiconductor needs. China annually spends as much as US$ 200 BN on semiconductor imports, equivalent to a year of oil imports. As a key part of China's ten-year "Made in China 2025" plan, a National Industry Investment Fund has been established which is plowing US$ 20 BN into the semiconductor industry.

As an indication that China is still able to trade market access in return for technology, foreign semiconductor firms are continuing to invest in China. Qualcomm has formed a JV to design and produce chips used in servers, while Intel has invested US$ 1.5 BN in a commercial spin-off from Qinghua University, which owns two chip design companies.[10] On top of this, Intel is converting its existing facility in Dalian to produce memory chips and has pledged overall to invest US$ 5.5 BN in China.[11] China has a strong bargaining position. Intel has only 10% of the equity in its new JV while Qualcomm has only 46% of its JV.

The government has selected Wuhan firm XMC to lead the establishment of a plant to produce memory chips (including DRAM). US$ 24 BN will be raised to finance this massive 87-acre facility, which will ultimately have a capacity of 300,000 wafer starts per month.[12,13]

At the same time, on orders from the government, China's semiconductor industry is seeking to gain access to core semiconductor design technology through a buying spree, scouring the global market for foreign semiconductor design firms it can acquire.[14] Several deals have already been done and others are in the pipeline. This is part of China's transitioning from the "partner, learn" model to one that involves "going out into the world" to acquire the technology and skills needed.

The Model Works Well—In Consumer Products, High-Speed Rail, and Nuclear Power

This model is not confined to absorbing manufacturing technology or product design. Shanghai Jahwa, a producer of fast-moving consumer products, was able to suck valuable marketing and sales skills out of its foreign partner. Jahwa's roots go back to 1889 as a cosmetic company established in Hong Kong. In the 1930s, it established a factory in Shanghai and, in 1949, as part of the forced nationalization, it was merged with other factories in Shanghai into an SOE. In 1987, the Shanghai government instructed it to form a JV with the US firm S.C. Johnson (also known as Johnson Wax) into which Jahwa contributed its main brands and key personnel.

The JV marriage, which was foisted upon Jahwa, turned out to be far from ideal. First, S.C. Johnson's emphasis on household cleaning products did not mesh that well with Jahwa's cosmetic brands, which, once subsumed into the JV, lost market share against foreign brands. Friction developed between Jahwa's charismatic leader Ge Wenyao and S.C. Johnson. The JV was dissolved in 1994.

As part of the dissolution of the JV, Jahwa got its brands back at no cost and, moreover, S.C. Johnson had to pay Jahwa significant compensation associated with the costs of about 1,000 employees being taken back by Jahwa from the JV. Furthermore, Jahwa managers explained to me just how assiduous and systematic they had been in learning S.C. Johnson's state-of-the-art marketing and sales knowledge and systems, including brand management, organizational structure, and distribution channels. Jahwa successfully absorbed this intellectual capital and took it with them when the JV was dissolved.

Next, let's discuss how China tweaked high-speed rail (HSR) technology. Under central planning, China's Ministry of Railways (MOR) controlled the entire rail sector, responsible for policy, regulation, operations, rolling-stock manufacturing, and railway construction. During the early period of the economic reforms, the MOR remained a perfect fossil of Soviet-style planning and fought tooth and nail against efforts, notably by Premier Zhu Rongji, to break it up. The first achievement in these efforts to reform the MOR came with the spin-off in 1986 of the MOR's rolling-stock manufacturing factories into a new commercial entity, followed 14 years later, with that entity being split into two new companies, CNR, comprising factories in North China, and CSR, comprising those in South China.

The rationale of forming these two companies was twofold. First, it created a duopoly, achieving Zhu's goal of limited or "managed" competition in strategic sectors. Second, it offered two Chinese partnership options for foreign rolling stock and locomotive manufacturers who wished to enter the China market, but were forced to do so through JVs. The foreign firms could tell their top management that the technology they were to transfer into the JV would be kept separate from that deployed by other foreign firms in another JV. But in reality, behind the scenes at CNR and CSR, things converged at the Chinese government level.

China's massive domestic demand for railway equipment proved to be irresistible to the world's HSR suppliers, who piled into the China market through JVs. Bombardier and Kawasaki partnered with entities under CSR, while Alstom and Siemens partnered with factories under CNR. Under the JV agreements, the foreign firms' proprietary HSR technology was transferred to the JV but with the restriction that it was only for use within China.

In the space of 15 years, China built 12,000 km of HSR in China, and this is expected to rise to 18,000 km. That bold program has left many issues in its wake. The MOR and related companies amassed enormous debts. One rail construction firm has debts of US$ 88 BN. An HSR accident in China left 40 dead. Although it was due to faulty signaling and the train was not traveling at high speed at the time, it nevertheless cast doubt over the future of the entire program. Even worse, the program was riddled with bribery and corruption. The MOR minister received a suspended death sentence and other senior MOR officials were also imprisoned.

Despite these problems, China has emerged as a powerful force in railway technology. The Chinese side of the JVs took the foreign technology and, in their words, "redesigned" key components that permitted the HSR to run at 350 to 380 kph compared to the original maximum of 250 kph. Warning signals went off when the Chinese began registering patents on this supposedly new technology in developed countries in preparation for export. Kawasaki threatened to sue for IPR infringement on its bullet-train technology. The Chinese government stressed that it had "absorbed foreign [rail] technology but also innovated it" and that they owned the "independent intellectual property rights."

The Chinese elaborated on the "innovation" they had made to permit the higher speeds of this "new generation" of HSR: new bogies, low derailment factor, new welding techniques for the lightweight aluminum body, and a redesigned nose with 5% less drag than that of Kawasaki. The Chinese bragged that their "new generation" of HSR was hugely different in "speed, comfort, and technology." Kawasaki later backed off of its threat of legal action, while the other foreign players avoided direct confrontation since they still hoped to sustain their sales in China and purchase China-made components for their international business.

China is already strong in international non-HSR projects. It is constructing a railway connecting China with Thailand via Laos. It has rail construction contracts with Nigeria and Sudan, and is supplying electric locomotives and rolling stock to the Boston subway, India, Malaysia, Turkey, and Brazil.

On the HSR-side, China is well positioned since the engineering costs of China-developed HSR are only one-third of those at comparable foreign companies.[15]

China is exploring HSR projects in California, the UK, Kazakhstan, Argentina, Qatar, and is holding discussions with 17 countries about an HSR linking China with Europe through central Asia. We shall likely see China winning major HSR projects in which it not only supplies rolling stock, but also undertakes the complete construction. In some cases, China will partner with local firms. But the bulk of the work will go to China.

Meanwhile, the Chinese government has re-merged CSR and CNR with the stated goal of avoiding a price war with each other in international projects. We may also add that now that foreign technology has been sucked into China, the purpose of having those two firms has run its course. The focus is now on combining forces for the deployment of the "re-innovated" rail technology that has been so cleverly absorbed and tweaked by China.

Next, the case of Generation III nuclear power. The pattern is similar to what we have seen in the rail sector. A large domestic market attracts foreign players willing to share their technology, after which China further develops the technology, which in its new form is now China's own property, ready to be deployed on the world market. But the main difference with the rail business is that the foreign suppliers of the nuclear power technology were fully complicit in the Chinese "re-innovation" of the technology and looked to have achieved a remarkable win-win with China.

China currently has 22 nuclear reactors in operation and 26 under construction. Nuclear accounts for only about 2% of China's electricity generation. But after a lengthy suspension of new nuclear projects following the Fukushima nuclear accident, China has now resumed its nuclear program, aiming to triple capacity to 58 gigawatts (GWe) by 2020 and 150 GWe by 2030.

The growth of nuclear power is of strategic importance to the nation as it seeks to reduce its reliance on coal-fueled generation, which contributes heavily to pollution.

China's original nuclear reactors were supplied by France, Russia, and Canada. Then in 2006–2007, China purchased the Generation III nuclear reactor technology, which, unlike the Fukushima-type PWR (pressurized water) reactor, has a "passive" safety system, with gravity-driven cooling that does not require electric pumps and can function even during a power cut. China signed Generation III contracts with Westinghouse (a US firm, owned by Toshiba of Japan) and with Areva (a French firm). For Westinghouse, the China deal was make or break. The US had stopped new nuclear plant building, and Westinghouse's AP 1000 Generation III technology was ready to go but untested. In return for a contract worth about US$ 8 BN to build four reactors, Westinghouse signed not only the standard contracts for the construction of the nuclear island and for nuclear fuel, but also a third nonstandard "comprehensive technology transfer contract" under which it provided the Chinese side with "technical information, design analysis, and other supporting information so that they have everything that they need to go ahead and build AP 1000s themselves in China in the future."[16]

Westinghouse formed a technical JV with its Chinese customer to qualify Chinese equipment suppliers and to enable them to produce all the components, including those highly critical to the safety of the reactor. The stated goal of the JV was not only to create a supply chain for Chinese reactors (with local content rising from 30% to 100% by 2015), but also to facilitate the export of critical nuclear components from China. Until then, Westinghouse had used South Korean suppliers for these key components.

Westinghouse handed over 75,000 documents to China that have been used to create a Chinese version of the AP 1000. But China has also developed 1200 megawatts (MWe) and 1400 MWe versions of the Generation III technology for which China owns the "independent" property rights and can therefore license to its global customers. Areva has been through a similar process of transferring its technology to China in return for market access.

China is set to remain the world's largest market for nuclear power technology, with plans for 101 new reactors at a cost of US$ 196 BN during the period 2015–2030. China has already approved the design of its own 1000 MWe reactor (Hualong One), based on foreign design, for which foreign technology suppliers will receive license fees. Further down the road,

China will be ready to launch the larger of the Generation III reactors, the intellectual property rights for which it will own.

Westinghouse had bet heavily on working with the Chinese and was hopeful it could continue to enjoy a share of China domestic sales. But when it came to a further eight AP 1000 reactors, on top of the four agreed in 2006, it was outbid by Chinese firms. Notwithstanding this disappointment, the international market has been stacking up to be a China-foreign win-win. Both sides rely heavily on each other.

In 2006 and 2007, when it first agreed to supply Generation III technology, Westinghouse had not yet built one of these reactors, and Areva was facing serious challenges with a first project in Finland. China took a risk in signing up for this technology, but in turn drove a hard bargain in terms of technology transfer. For the two foreign suppliers, the China projects were the perfect opportunity to showcase their technology and lay to rest market concerns over their attractive but at that time totally untested technology.

Building on the successful Generation III launch in China, these two firms are now out in the global market competing for new projects.

A French consortium of EDF, Areva, and the Chinese is close to signing a deal in the UK for the Hinkley Point project with a price tag of US$ 24 BN. While China would be a junior partner in this project (contributing one third of the equity), as well as in another with Westinghouse still undergoing technology vetting in the UK, it has extracted a commitment from the UK government that, by investing in the first two projects, it will get to play the prime role in the a third one in the UK. Initially, China's:

> "main involvement will be in the supply chain, providing some components.... [They] see Hinkley ... as the first step towards their goal of building a nuclear station using Chinese technology in the U.K. and as a stepping stone to starting a plant-export business to rival the Russians, the Japanese, and the French."[17]

The March 2017 announcement that Westinghouse had filed for Chapter 11 bankruptcy protection suggests that the new wave of nuclear power construction might be faltering. Concerns about safety, cost overruns, and the disposal of nuclear waste, coupled with the falling costs of renewables, are undermining public confidence in nuclear power. But the prospects are that China will pick up the pieces and come to dominate in those remaining parts of the global market that still choose to invest in nuclear power.

In the short term, China will still rely on foreign partners in nuclear engineering. The China projects led by Areva and Westinghouse, despite the financial headwinds and technical delays, will likely be completed. The foreign partners will continue to shoehorn China into developed overseas markets.

China is playing a long game. Using its financial muscle and its domestic nuclear power market as a test bed for its own technology, China will ultimately outgrow its partnerships with foreign firms, which it had earlier relied on to acquire technology and to allay concerns in overseas markets. The difficulties faced by Areva and Westinghouse have served to accelerate China's emergence as a dominant force in this sector. The win-win from the China-foreign link-up in nuclear power will have been shorter lived and less lucrative than had been anticipated by the foreign firms that placed such heavy bets.

Model 2. Picking off Underperforming Overseas Assets

China's outbound direct investment (ODI), the flow of investment capital out of China into specific businesses, has shown a sharp upward inflection and has now overtaken FDI into China. China is now a net exporter of investment capital.

While earlier Chinese overseas acquisitions were focused on natural resources such as oil, iron ore, copper, and lumber, more recently there has been a strong appetite for acquiring real estate, hotels, tourist resorts, and manufacturing.

The manufacturing acquisitions, ranging from agro-industry to cars and semiconductors are strategically driven by the desire to gain access to technology, skills, brands, and distribution channels. These acquisitions enjoy government support since it helps create "national champions" in key sectors while driving improvement in corporate governance through exposing Chinese firms to more rigorous regulatory environments overseas.

China's burst of activity in ODI is large and sudden, but is still not a surprise, given China's economic status, stage of development, and national ambitions. Alarm bells have rung in some quarters. Is that justified? Even if the trajectory of Chinese ODI is sharply upward, it seems invidious to argue that China does not have the right to invest overseas and enter our markets. Globalization is, after all, a two-way street. Moreover, the world remains dominated by extremely strong non-Chinese multi-national corporations (MNCs), typically with two dominating in each sector.[18]

Obstacles to China ODI

Chinese companies seeking to "go out into the world" face a host of obstacles in China, such as government approvals for capital transfers out of the country. A Chinese government think tank stated bluntly that the red tape leaves Chinese firms less nimble and entrepreneurial in their bidding for foreign acquisitions.[19] The government issued a new directive to simplify the ODI process, allowing Chinese firms making a deal under US$ 1 BN, in industries or countries not deemed to be "sensitive," to simply register the deal with the central government without the need for a government approval. Although it is, of course, the government that decides what is "sensitive," this is a step toward reducing the bureaucratic burden.

When it comes to overseas jurisdictions, a Chinese ODI also faces challenges. In 2005, China's CNOOC (offshore oil firm) pulled out of its US$ 18.5 BN bid for Unocal, after objections from US politicians. The US-firm Fairchild Semiconductor rejected a Chinese acquisition bid on the grounds that the Committee on Foreign Investment in the US (CFIUS), which reviews potential investments for their national security implications, might oppose the deal.

But many of the problems faced by Chinese firms overseas clearly result from their own lack of experience and local knowledge. Still, the examples of China ODI set out below demonstrate how Chinese firms have confounded the skeptics and defied the odds by acquiring and turning around underperforming businesses.

How Lenovo Mastered the Art of Turning Around a Troubled US Business

---

Lenovo, as one of a new breed of SOEs runs much like a private firm, is a successful Chinese multinational firm. It is the world's number one maker of personal computers and tablets, with sales of US$ 46 BN in 160 countries. At the heart of this remarkable story is how Lenovo acquired IBM's PC business, turned it around, and created sustained and profitable growth.

The early years. Lenovo was founded by Liu Chuanzhi and other electronics engineers at a research institute under the government-owned Chinese Academy of Sciences, which provided them with the RMB equivalent of US$ 25,000 of seed capital.

Initially, Lenovo served simply as an importer and distributor in China for foreign electronics manufacturers such as Toshiba and IBM. This was a low margin business and would become vulnerable as foreign computer firms established themselves in China and took control of their own distribution. Lenovo began the first of many "reinventions" of itself, anticipating market transitions and seeking more profitable opportunities. By the mid-1990s, only 28% of its profits came from its original business (distribution/agency and components), while 82% came from new activities, much of it higher margin—PC manufacturing, systems integration, and software.

Lenovo innovated through developing a motherboard for typing China characters on a computer that was first used in imported PCs and then later on their own PCs. It learned from Dell's lower cost direct sales approach, complementing the relationship selling ("pull approach") it had learned from IBM. CEO Liu also westernized the firm by requiring employees, for instance, to address superiors by their given names, rather than in the traditional manner of using the surname plus a job title (e.g., General Manager Wang, Chinese: <u>wangzong</u>).[20]

Having for a period protected its local computer industry from foreign competition, the Chinese government in 1992 began to open up China's computer market by reducing import tariffs and abolishing import quotas. Lenovo was soon to overtake then market leader Great Wall Computer through its leaner manufacturing operations and superior quality. Great Wall was slow to respond to the market changes.

Lenovo's dominance of the China market gave it economies of scale, as well as access to low-cost manufacturing. It was the perfect launching pad. But the China market was also attracting foreign competitors, such as Dell, which established a manufacturing base in Fujian province. Lenovo's leaders responded by entering the international market. Its foreign name was changed from Legend to Lenovo in 2003. Management consultants were hired to develop the "going out strategy."

IBM's PC division was up for sale and in 2004 Lenovo moved to acquire it, taking a massive and risky step into the unknown. The Chinese press described it as the "snake that swallowed the elephant." Here was Lenovo acquiring a loss-making foreign business many times its own size. One year after the acquisition its total revenues had grown from US$ 2.9 BN to US$ 13.3 BN.

IBM played a continuing role. So the deal was done. Lenovo purchased IBM's PC division for US$ 1.75 BN, of which, US$ 500 MM was assumed debt; a strong indicator of the poor shape the IBM business was in.

A further US$600 MM of the payment was in Lenovo shares, giving IBM nearly 19% of Lenovo. This teed things up for IBM to continue to support the PC business. For the next five years, Lenovo could use the IBM brand and sales and service support outside of China. This continued role for IBM helped Lenovo pass the hurdle of US government approvals.

Successful post-merger integration (PMI). The PMI of two companies is always complex and risky. It is commonly botched or poorly executed. In the case of Lenovo, there was the added dimension of China-US cultural integration. Against all the odds, Lenovo's PMI proved to be successful. But that does not mean that the process was easy or smooth.

PMI is an art, not an exact science. Lenovo chose to take it gradually, step-by-step, reassuring the former IBM executives and workers that things would not change too fast.

Lenovo's head office was first moved from Beijing to Armonk, New York (IBM headquarters), and then to North Carolina, the site of the IBM's manufacturing facility. Today, Lenovo has dual head offices in Beijing and North Carolina. US and global workforces were retained. English was adopted as Lenovo's official language. Multiple former IBM executives took key roles in Lenovo, including the head of IBM's PC division, who stayed on through the transition as CEO of Lenovo. From competitor Dell, Lenovo recruited its chief diversity officer, an African-American woman who is credited with helping Lenovo cope with the tough issues that arose during the PMI. Serious tensions did arise because of what was described as a "toxic" environment, with a "pervading sense of distrust"[21] between senior and working levels. It is said that at meetings Chinese employees would simply get tired of how much their US counterparts talked, even when they had nothing to contribute!

Lenovo is justifiably proud of how it somehow achieved an extraordinary melding of Western and Chinese skills and culture.

Complementary businesses fit together. The IBM PC business was loss-making. There was a major market shift from desktop to laptop. IBM did have its own notebook (ThinkPad) but was heavily focused on the high-end large enterprise segment. Moreover, it was suffering from "value migration" whereby profit was moving away from the equipment manufacturer/assembler (IBM) to those firms supplying the PC's operating system (Microsoft), microprocessors (Intel), and hard drives (Seagate). Despite the excellence of its PCs, for IBM it was an unsustainable business and a poor strategic fit. But for Lenovo it was quite the opposite. The IBM PC business was hugely complementary to that of Lenovo.

Lenovo dominated the China market and was highly focused on the consumer segment. IBM's business, in contrast, offered Lenovo access to global markets, strong distribution channels, and untapped potential in the small business area. IBM's ThinkPad notebook and its strong brand identity brought credibility and a quality image to Lenovo, of special value in dealing with large enterprise customers.

The large Chinese market provided economies of scale and profits. Though Lenovo is the leader in global PC markets, the Chinese market is the only one where, with a 35% market share, it has total dominance, and that, since the acquisition, has consistently accounted for around 40% of Lenovo's revenues. The Chinese market also provided a buffer during the last recession. While Lenovo suffered its one and only loss-making year due to a slump in large enterprise sales globally, it was the Chinese market that permitted Lenovo to recover.[22] During the recession, Lenovo also benefited from the Chinese government's stimulus spending that was channeled into rural areas and small- and medium-size businesses (SMBs).

Consumer electronics globally is a fairly low-margin business that can be compensated for by large volumes. Globally, Lenovo's operating margin is 2.7% compared to HP's 3.5%. But in China, Lenovo enjoys an operating margin of 5.4%, compared to only 0.8% in the US. This strength in China has permitted Lenovo to live with smaller margins in mature markets. In the US, Lenovo fought its way onto the shelves of Best Buy by accepting "razor-thin margins and potential losses for the first year or two."[23]

How the Chinese government helped. It is apparent from its fleet-footed management style and the absence of typical SOE culture that Lenovo operates pretty much like a private company. Still, the fact remains that the government-owned Chinese Academy of Sciences holds a 36% share in its parent, Legend Holdings, which in turn hold 32% of Lenovo's shares. Therefore, behind the scenes Lenovo does track back to "China, Inc."

Though Lenovo behaves as if removed from its government roots, at the same time it enjoys benefits from its hybrid status and its enormous significance to the Chinese economy. This implies that its financial stability is largely underwritten by the government and that it would not be allowed to fail. As a Chinese firm, it can enjoy healthy sales from Chinese government procurement.

A balanced product portfolio. Not only is the global PC business plagued by skinny margins, major market changes are also occurring. The shift away from desktops to notebooks/laptops continues. But these market transitions are gradual, leaving room for an efficient player like Lenovo to make money.

Lenovo pursued two strategic tracks, "protect and attack." It continues to "protect" its core desktop and notebook business, overtaking HP in part by its success in selling through the mass market Best Buy stores in the US. Success is based not just on price, but also on consumer appreciation of Lenovo products' sleek looks.[24] On the "attack" side, Lenovo stresses its laptops, tablets, mobile phones, cloud services, and low-end servers, which enjoy both fast growth and better profit margins.

Improving operational efficiency. Lenovo has been astute in hiring senior executives. Mary Ma (Ma Xuezheng) was brought in as chief financial officer. A Chinese woman who had studied in the UK, she was able to bridge the cultural divide, helping the interaction with the external world of finance. She put energy into streamlining processes, reducing procurement and manufacturing costs, and improving performance in the supply chain. Foreign logistics experts were hired. Lenovo trimmed the number of products it inherited from IBM. Travel expenses were reduced. An overall cost-reduction target of US$ 150 MM in 18 months was achieved well ahead of plan.

Financial stability and growth. The loss-making IBM business, many times larger than Lenovo, was absorbed and turned around financially with consistent double-digit revenue growth since the acquisition. The bottom line (post-tax profit) performance has shown more volatility. In 2009,[25] it suffered a loss of more than US$ 200MM, due to sagging demand in mature markets during the recession. After the subsequent global economic recovery, Lenovo, coupling new products with cost cutting, restored the bottom line, which in 2012 grew by 34%

In 2015, profit growth shrank to only 1%, due to the tough China smartphone market. But, Lenovo remains financially disciplined, maintaining low levels of bank debt, strong cash reserves, and easy access to the equity, bond, and loan markets, with financial flexibility to sustain its path of acquisitions.[26]

Further growth through overseas acquisitions. In 2014, Lenovo returned to the acquisition trail, announcing its purchase of IBM's low-end x86 server business for US$ 2.3 BN and of Motorola Mobility (smart phones) from Google for US$ 2.9 BN. The 2005 acquisition of the IBM PC division received US government (CFIUS) approval ahead of the statutory deadlines in part because IBM would continue to provide the division technical and sales support for five years. In the case of the IBM server business, there is a similar five-year arrangement, which allayed US concerns, and the deal was approved swiftly. The Motorola Mobility deal was also approved by CFIUS. Although Lenovo assumed 2,000 patents, the most sensitive patents stayed with Google.

While these businesses had been troubled and poor fits with their original parent companies, in Lenovo's hands they presented significant upside. As one observer put it, "one company's reject is another's potential gold mine."[27]

The margins of the low-end server business were low by IBM's standards, but for Lenovo they are superior to those of the PC business. Moreover, the business helps to fill out Lenovo's product offerings to the enterprise market. IBM had wanted as much as US$ 6 BN for this business, but settled for less than half that, partly in stock. While IBM's sales had been badly hit by Chinese reaction to the Snowden whistle-blowing, Lenovo, being Chinese, is not vulnerable to this issue.

The Motorola Mobility deal reveals a similar pattern. For Google, the sale of its Motorola handset business has been described as "offloading a doomed business." But Lenovo, in acquiring the business, saw things quite differently.

Today, Lenovo ships about 80 MM smartphones per year (accounting now for about 15% of its total revenues). Lenovo branded phones are selling strongly in emerging markets, while its Motorola phones are doing well in the low-end market in Europe and the US. Less encouraging is the fact that both globally and in China, Lenovo's smartphone market share has fallen to number five, in part due to challenges it faces in the transition from 3G to 4G. But Lenovo also points out that the "hypergrowth" in China handsets is at an end.[28] Lenovo sees a consolidation coming in the China handset industry, but argues that it will be one of the survivors.

The Lenovo case is striking in that it demonstrates how a Chinese firm can succeed at the daunting task of acquiring, merging with, and turning around a foreign manufacturing business. It is good example of how a hybrid quasi-private Chinese firm not only benefited from government support and the advantages of the large Chinese market, but also wholeheartedly embraced Western business principles.

Examples of Chinese firms successfully acquiring underperforming foreign firms also exist in the auto industry. In 2010, the loss-making Volvo car business was offloaded from Ford to the private Hangzhou-based Chinese auto maker Geely for US$ 1.8 BN. Once again, the snake eats the elephant. At that time, Geely had sales of around US$ 2 BN, compared to Volvo's US$ 12 BN. But Geely was profitable and able to borrow to support the acquisition.

Volvo strongly complemented Geely's capability. Volvo was a global firm established in the premium market with a strong brand and a reputation for safety innovation. Geely was number 10 in the China market, at the low-price, low-quality end, and unknown globally.[29]

Geely used a light hand in integrating the acquisition. The Volvo team was left in place. The head office remained in Gothenburg, Sweden, while its two plants, in Sweden and Belgium, were untouched. Meanwhile, Geely is expanding the Volvo production capacity in China and introducing new models. Since the acquisition, Volvo sales in China have expanded rapidly, more than making up for its poor performance in the US market. It is already exporting China-built Volvos to the US. It also has begun construction of a 100,000 vehicle facility in South Carolina. The intention is to double Volvo's global sales to 800,000 units by 2020.[30]

Another close parallel is the case of Wanxiang, a private manufacturer of auto components based in Zhejiang. As discussed above, it made its first overseas acquisition in 1995 in Chicago and by 2011 had US revenue of US$ 2.2 BN. Today it has 18 subsidiaries worldwide.

In the auto industry, because of shipping costs and the need for timely delivery, it is typical for parts suppliers to be located fairly close to the OEMs (the assembler of the final vehicle). In order to enter the US market, Wanxiang acquired a series of poorly performing parts producers in the US, gaining not only local manufacturing capacity and proprietary technology, but also sales and distribution channels and relationships with OEMs. In the US, Wanxiang created a strong local team recruited from the auto industry. It continues to be highly acquisitive and in 2013 bought a bankrupt US company that produces batteries for electric cars, winning against a joint bid from Johnson Controls and NEC.[31]

Chinese management teams have demonstrated unanticipated wisdom and subtlety in maintaining the best of the acquired firm and creating a cultural hybrid, while at the same time moving it toward profitability. Meanwhile, the global consumer does not automatically link the Lenovo and Volvo brands to China, any more than Acer Computer is linked to Taiwan or Jaguar/Land Rover is associated with India.

A common pattern among firms such as Lenovo, Geely, and Wanxiang is that they have put distance between themselves and the debilitating interference of government and the CCP, permitting them to move with agility, responding to customer needs and market transitions. The overseas experience gained by those bold and well-run Chinese firms is implanted back into the China market, sharpening China's overall competitiveness and quality of business management.

Model 3. "China, Inc." in Emerging Markets

The China, Inc. model works through three key sets of players—the government/CCP, financial institutions, and companies operating in lockstep to reap benefits from political relationships with emerging markets. This is controversial since China is widely perceived as playing a neocolonial role.

In many cases, the trend also is creating tensions between China and the recipient nations.

The Government/CCP

At the heart of the model, the Chinese government and CCP take the lead, forging relationships with the country in question, while other players in the model sit under the umbrella of government-to-government agreements.

China has some history of providing aid to Africa. In the period 1970–76, China paid for, constructed, and equipped the 1,860-km-long Tan-Zam Railway linking landlocked Zambia with Tanzania's port Dar es Salaam, thus avoiding Zambia having to ship its goods through Rhodesia (now called Zimbabwe), then run by a white minority regime. About 25,000 Chinese toiled to construct the railway. Zambians and Tanzanians were trained in railway engineering in Beijing. After being handed over to the two local governments, the railway fell into disrepair and financial insolvency, while congestion at the port also slowed the throughput of goods. China, in its current more business-like mode, has recently returned, providing an interest-free loan to revive the railway.

The rationale for China's engagement with emerging countries starts with the laudable goals of providing development aid. China publishes very few statistics on overseas aid and much of the effort is fudged with more commercial activities. In fact, the overseas development assistance (ODA) offered by China differs in certain key ways from that provided by other countries.[32]

China's ODA largely is comprised of concessional loans (low-interest, long-term) and government-sponsored investment. Grant aid and debt cancellation account for only about 5% of the total provided. Many of the loans are also repaid in kind (minerals, cotton, etc.).

As was observed in the 1970s, "'Aid' has never been an unconditional transfer of resources,"[33] and in this new age, strings are predictably still attached. China as a donor is no exception, but does not bother to go through the hypocrisy of pretending that the aid has an essentially ethical foundation. China's aid comes without caveats concerning human rights or national debt levels in the recipient countries. China's politically backed economic presence in many countries has become dominant, serving as a source of corruption and engendering civil dissent. There are accusations that China's actions are stifling job creation and economic growth in Africa by taking natural resources and shipping back finished products, in other words, behaving like a neocolonial power. While China does not back up its political presence with direct military threats or action, it does provide military funding, assistance, and weapons for client states.

China's political initiative can be driven by a single issue. For instance, in 2005, China got the tiny Caribbean nation of Grenada to recognize China and break with Taiwan, and in return provided US$ 60 MM to build a new cricket stadium, a national stadium, and a port.[34]

Typically, the Chinese leader and the leader of the recipient country sign broad-based agreements focusing on economic development needed by that nation, but which also serves Chinese economic interests—for instance, roads, railways, and ports that can facilitate the export of mineral resources the Chinese firms extract. During these same state visits, leaders of China's banks sign loan agreements with their counterparts, while key Chinese firms attend receptions where they are introduced into the commercial arrangements.

Financial Institutions

Three Chinese government financial institutions provide the finance at the heart of this business model.

The Export-Import Bank of China (China Exim Bank) is the only Chinese bank with the power to offer government concessional loans and preferential buyer credits (loans to purchasers of Chinese goods or services). China Exim Bank's loans to Africa during the period 2001–10 were US$ 67 BN, compared to US$ 55BN from the World Bank. As an example of the projects it finances, China Exim Bank provided two major loans to the Ivory Coast, one of US$ 500 MM for a hydroelectric plant to be constructed by the Chinese firm Sinohydro and another of US$ 875 MM to construct a second container terminal in Abidjan, with advisory services provided by a Beijing-based firm.

China Exim Bank does not have it all its own way. In 2012, it was forced by Niger to revise its US$ 980 MM loan so that the interest rate would not exceed 2%.

China Development Bank Corporation (CDB), though officially transformed into a commercial bank in 2008, remains, for all intents and purposes, a government policy bank.[35] At the end of 2013, CDB's total assets (that is, mainly loans) stood at US$ 1.14 trillion, of which 82% was in the domestic China market. The remaining, 18% or US$ 260 BN, were overseas loans, mainly in emerging markets. CDB, through its funding by sovereign risk-rated bonds, makes it the only commercial bank in China that can make loans beyond five years, suitable for long-term infrastructure projects.

CDB has also established a series of private equity funds. Its China-Africa Development Fund (CADFund) was established in 2007 with initial capital of US$ 5 BN and with the mandate to take equity stakes in investments alongside Chinese firms "going out into the world."

As with most "aid" offered by other countries, China's aid is closely linked to benefiting its own national companies. So, when in 2010 CDB lent the Zambian government US$ 1 BN for a hydro-electric power station, the CDB vice governor made the strings attached quite clear, stating: "[the Chinese firm] Sinohydro Corporation …, which has expressed an interest in developing the … power station, could bring valuable experience to the project." In project after project, arranged by China with local governments, it is typical for Chinese firms to be shoehorned into the projects without a competitive bidding process.

Figure 8.1 provides an example of how CDB plays its role in government-to-government-initiated deals by inserting itself into the financing at multiple stages. This particular story began in 2005 when China signed a memorandum to fund the refurbishment and upgrade of Zimbabwe's radio/TV network. US$ 90 MM was lent to Zimbabwe, US$ 63 MM of which was spent on equipment supplied by the private Chinese firm Star Communications. But given its dire financial condition, Zimbabwe was forced to fund the repayment through a JV chrome processing project formed with Star. Zimbabwe has very high-quality chrome ore deposits. Its reserves are second only to those in South Africa, though in terms of production it is only sixth in the world. CDB financed Star's equity share in the project, which processes chrome ore into ferro-chrome for export. The revenues from the chrome project received by the state-owned Zimbabwe mining firm partnering with Star are then remitted to CDB to pay back the radio/TV loan.

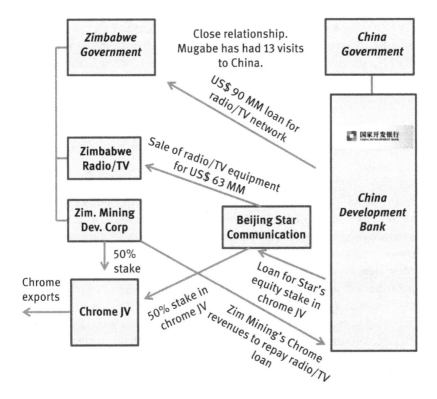

Figure 8.1: Figure 8.1. China/Zimbabwe chrome for telecom equipment deal.

The history of this new phase in the Zimbabwe-China political/economic embrace dates back to the early 2000s, when Zimbabwe launched its "Look East Policy," aimed at attracting Chinese investment to fill the gap left by departing Western firms. Even though he is a global pariah, Zimbabwe's President Mugabe, as China's "old friend," has been able to sustain his crumbling economy with Chinese money. Other foreign banks would not have touched the convoluted deal described above.

Although China has taken on some financial complexity and risk, it has created not only immediate value for Chinese firms, but also obtained longer-term strategic access to chrome. This exemplifies the view that "aid is trade" and demonstrates how Zimbabwe is mortgaging its future wealth to China. Moreover, any wealth generated by such mineral extraction (as described in the diamonds case below) is siphoned off by Mugabe and used to ensure the loyalty of the military.

China Export & Credit Insurance Corporation (Sinosure) is the third Chinese financial institution standing behind transactions in the emerging markets. It provides political, commercial, and credit risk insurance to Chinese firms.

Chinese Firms

The arrival of Chinese firms on the world stage was initially in natural resources. Due to the scale of its appetite for natural resources, manufacturing-heavy China has been a key driver of world commodity prices. Despite its slowing growth, China remains heavily dependent on overseas supplies of minerals. Only in rare earths—critical to the electronics industry—is China self-sufficient. Despite the advantages in world trade that come from its sheer buying power, China has adopted a variety of means to further assure its access to strategic commodities. Since 2007, CDB has lent Venezuela well over US$ 40 BN for a variety of purposes, but all to be repaid in oil, which has turned out to be a very risky proposition given oil price volatility. This pattern of loans being paid back in kind (natural resources) is a key characteristic of this business model.

In absolute terms, China's natural resource investments have been described as "tiny" or "peripheral," in comparison with the mining or oil giants of the West. But China's investments in natural resources have nonetheless had very large dollar numbers and, given China's scant interest in the ethical issues associated with these investments, many have provoked outrage in the world community; for example, the Chinese oil firm CNPC's investment in Sudan's oil.

The second type of Chinese firms participating in this model are construction companies. On the back of Chinese government funding, they win contracts to build basic infrastructure—roads, bridges, railways, power stations, cement plants, airports, mobile phone networks. The sector is highly orchestrated by the government-run China International Contractors Association (CHINCA), which Chinese construction firms are required to join in order to be able to operate overseas, and which provide a range of assistance, including seminars on foreign project risk management, to its 1,300 members.

Infrastructure construction by Chinese firms typically also include labor contracts under which large numbers of Chinese workers are imported. There is often serious friction with the local communities in Africa since the Chinese workers are seen as taking away local jobs. There have even been accusations that China is deploying prison labor. Though the Chinese workers wear uniforms and are subjected to heavy discipline within heavily guarded fenced-in compounds, there is, so far, no convincing evidence that they are indeed convicts. Chinese firms argue that local labor does not have the Chinese work ethic and some African observers concede that point.

Tied in with the construction contracts is the supply of process equipment for cement plants and off-road construction machinery. Chinese manufacturers have supplied South Africa, Thailand, UAE, Indonesia, and Belarus with world-scale 10,000 tons per day (tpd) cement plants.

The next phase of this China, Inc. model of overseas expansion is Chinese factories located in emerging markets. Chinese auto companies, such as Great Wall Auto, Geely, Changan, and Chery, already export into emerging markets, where product certification is easier than in developed countries. China's homegrown autos have a poor reputation in Africa, and are described as "rubbish quality, appalling design, and having a disturbing smell of glue." Chinese products in general are characterized by Africans as falling apart quickly, attracting the nickname "Fong Kong" in South Africa, while in Zimbabwe they are called "Zhing Zhong."[36] But China autos fill a market gap for low-end vehicles and, as sales volumes grow, Chinese firms are establishing local manufacturing facilities initially using imported kits. Chinese truck maker Foton has a plant in Kenya, Changan Auto is building one for cars in Nigeria and, in South Africa, China's FAW is setting up a facility to assemble light trucks.

In China, the textile industry is facing rising wages and cotton costs. Much of the textile and garment production, except at the very high end, is being moved from China to Africa and Southeast Asia. A Zhejiang firm has 40% of its production located in Nigeria, Ghana, and Tanzania, employing 2,600 African workers. It recently acquired a cotton plantation in Mali which will supply its African textile mills and reduce raw material costs by 50%.[37] Two Qingdao-based textile firms have invested in a textile mill in Zambia.

A Little-Known Firm from Anhui Grows in Africa

To illustrate the diversity of China's activity in emerging markets, it is instructive to look at the extraordinary development of a low-profile Chinese construction firm, Anhui Foreign Economic Construction Group (AFECC), based in Hefei, Anhui province. AFECC was established in 1992 as a vehicle for China's "going out" policy and enjoys close relationships with China's top leaders, as well as with those of emerging countries. Today it has subsidiaries across Africa, the Caribbean, and Asia, and staff in 30 countries. It has diversified into hotel ownership, supermarkets, and, most recently, into mining in Africa.

Hefei natives are proud that the celebrated late-Qing official Li Hongzhang and the current Premier Li Keqiang, were both born there. But to be honest, landlocked Hefei is the unremarkable capital of the undistinguished province of Anhui, overshadowed by the neighboring, much wealthier coastal provinces of Jiangsu and Zhejiang. Anhui has a flourishing cement industry, which coats much of the rural landscape with a fine dust, as well as a steel plant and its own homegrown car firm (Chery). Within Anhui, there is a big gap between its industrialized regions and its poorer agricultural areas, and it is not surprising that Anhui is a major source of itinerant unskilled labor for the rest of China, and for AFECC's overseas construction projects.

AFECC's headquarters building dates back to 1992, when the company was established. The 30-floor block dominates the largely low-rise southern suburbs of Hefei. The building is dated and tired looking. Space inside is cramped, with small desks and paneling of heavily varnished pine, all very humble and understated. The staff is young, friendly, and well-informed on project engineering issues. Many have traveled widely through Africa.

When you ask AFECC about its ownership, the answer is that it is state-owned and comes under Anhui Province's Bureau of Construction. In fact, that is just how things started out in 1992. The situation today is a classic example of how ownership in such firms more recently has been diversified to form an entity that straddles or fudges the state-owned/private divide. Further research revealed that the bureau now owns only 9.72% of the firm. AFECC's chairman and 13 other individuals control 46% of the equity, while the AFECC workers' union owns 38.36%, and a local building materials firm the remaining 5.92%.[38]

AFECC is not a very large firm. But its declared revenue rose rapidly from about US$ 600 MM in 2010 to about US$ 1 BN in 2013. As its new mining activities come on line, we can expect its revenues to grow even faster. A Chinese ratings agency, while noting AFECC's rising debt leverage, provided an overall highly positive assessment of AFECC, citing central government support for overseas construction contracting and the low risk that AFECC would not get paid for its work due to the fact that it is focused on aid projects financed directly by the government or through China Exim Bank.[39]

AFECC started out doing overseas construction projects supported by Chinese government concessional loans: sports stadiums (Grenada), airports (including Maputo, Mozambique), hospitals (Zambia), conference centers (Myanmar), universities (Malawi), government buildings (Mozambique), and military buildings (Ghana).

On the back of those construction projects, it also traded in building materials and then branched out into investing in its own hotel chain (the Golden Peacock Hotels in Malawi, Grenada, Mozambique, Madagascar, and Zambia) and supermarkets.

Then in 2009, AFECC made a bold move to diversify into mineral resources, which today include diamonds (Zimbabwe and Democratic Republic of the Congo), gold, emeralds, titanium-zirconium (Mozambique), and copper. CDB has provided loans to support these projects.

Except for its diamond business, most of AFECC's activities are routed through SOGECOA, its Paris-based subsidiary (see Figure 8.2). AFECC does not seek to disguise its relationship with SOGECOA, but the use of this structure nonetheless does provide a smoke-screen and dilutes the potentially negative impact of being seen as a Chinese firm.

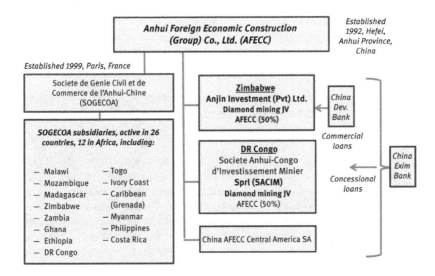

Figure 8.2: Figure 8.2. AFECC Organization Chart

As mentioned above, China got Grenada to switch diplomatic allegiance from Taiwan to the PRC by building a new cricket stadium. Through China Exim Bank, China has also provided financing for a new national stadium, bridges, and a port expansion. AFECC successfully completed these projects using imported Chinese labor.

Grenada is a small Caribbean nation with a population of 110,000 and a GDP of less than US$ 1BN. For good reason, the IMF advised Grenada against taking on significant debt from China Exim Bank, since it is out of proportion with the national economy. But this wise counsel fell on deaf ears. It was agreed that the bank would finance a new airport in Grenada. China and Grenada also agreed a mutual waiving of visa requirements, thus facilitating Chinese tourism into the island.

Although AFECC's stated corporate values are "sincerity, innovation, and pragmatism" reality indicates otherwise. In Grenada, AFECC owns the Sogecoa International Hotel, which has created controversy. Initially, the Grenada government halted the hotel's construction, alleging that AFECC was illegally importing furniture for the hotel, using containers supposedly holding building materials for the stadium. The hotel was completed, but a leading local critic of the government wrote an open letter to the government:

> "Consider the Sogecoa International Hotel and Restaurant, located in Woodlands on an AQUIFER from which NAWASA distributes water to the South. How in the world was this company permitted to build on this area, much less build a hotel and restaurant??!! What happened to our planning authorities? What happened to our water authority? Are we going to permit a company to VIOLATE our water resources because we received/have been promised aid by the government of the People's Republic of China? Is this part of a "pay back package" for the National Stadium.?"[40]

AFECC has a major presence in Mozambique, having built the new airport in Maputo, as well as a series of government buildings. Alongside its business activities, it also participates in China's exercise of soft power.

> "Corporations like AFECG [that is AFECC] often appear as state actors, and their corporate managers like to have their pictures taken with government officials. Photo-ops also arise when agreements are signed, for instance when a Chinese communist party delegation visited in 2011 to found a Confucius Institute in Maputo and to provide antimalaria medications. Spreading goodwill and generating soft power in Mozambique are an ongoing effort. Soft loans or outright bribes to officials are common."[41]

Commenting on an AFECC charitable program called "Journey to Brightness" which is providing free cataract operations in Mozambique, the same commentator stated:

> "Efforts like this one serve as a glossy veneer to distract from hard-core business moves that take place in a darker and shadier place, one without cameras and without a presence on the internet. What we see here are parts of a well-coordinated strategy by the Chinese government and its dependent corporations to become a dominant force in the economy of Mozambique and to exert greater influence over its government."[42]

In Mozambique, despite its charitable work, AFECC has not been immune to problems with the recipient country. In 2012, 60 of its Chinese workforce in Mozambique were arrested for not having legal work papers. In Malawi, where AFECC built the new parliament building, its efforts to diversify into minerals and obtain a license to drill for oil in Lake Malawi (Lake Nyasa) have met resistance due to allegations that it bribed a government minister during the bidding process. In 2013, in Zambia, AFECC's local subsidiary was charged with bribing the previous government by providing 10 campaign vehicles. In Zimbabwe, AFECC was known for paying its local construction workers US$ 4/day, far below the minimum wage.

Where AFECC's role becomes most problematic is in its diamond investments in Zimbabwe and in the Democratic Republic of the Congo. In Zimbabwe, it invested, jointly with its local partners, an initial US$ 310 MM to form Anjin Investment (Pvt) Ltd. (see Figure 8.2) in Zimbabwe's Marange diamond fields. To finance Phase 2 of the project, AFECC borrowed more than US$ 600 MM from CDB. By 2011, the JV had become the world largest producer of rough diamonds (industrial diamonds). Moreover, it received approval to sell on the open market from the Kimberley Process Certification Scheme, which was established to stop the sale of "conflict" diamonds, but has been largely ineffective. Anjin's sales were approved against the strong objections of a participating NGO, which then resigned from the Scheme.

AFECC's environmental record in Zimbabwe's diamond fields is not impressive. The Zimbabwe Environment Law Association and villagers have taken AFECC to court for polluting three rivers with sewage, chemicals, and mineral deposits. In a letter, AFECC accepted some responsibility: "It happened one or two times. Pumps broke down and little recycled water was not pumped away in time, resulting in the overflow of the water from the ponds...."[43]

But the biggest issue with the Anjin JV has been its vital role in keeping Mugabe in power. AFECC has 50% of Anjin's equity, while the government-owned Zimbabwe Mining Development Corporation holds 10%. The remaining 40% of the equity is held by a company under Zimbabwe's Ministry of Defense.[44] Anjin does not pay any taxes to the government and the revenues due to the Zimbabwe side are sucked out to provide off-budget financing for the country's military forces. Meanwhile, Zimbabwe has a GDP of around US$ 13 BN and government's international debt is US$ 7–8 BN. Interest payments on that debt have not been paid since 2000.

For Anjin, however, things in Zimbabwe have not been smooth sailing. In 2012, it fired 1,500 local workers for striking for higher wages. In 2013, it had to lay off 190 of the remaining 845 workers due to falling diamond prices and the cost of shifting from open cast to underground mining.

But AFECC continues its investment in African diamonds. In 2013, in the DR Congo, AFECC partnered with local interests to form a JV which took over two diamond exploration permits with access to reserves of 158 MM carats and a target output of 6 MM carats by 2016. As part of the deal, AFECC agreed to build a hydropower plant and an office for the "diamond regulator" at Kinshasa airport, and to help arrange a loan for an additional hydropower project.

AFECC is a vivid example of how the Chinese government and Chinese businesses collaborate for shared national goals. AFECC is a quintessential vehicle for Chinese government policy in emerging markets. But in a distinctly Chinese style, it is permitted to evolve in new, more commercial directions to the benefit of both management and local Chinese bureaucrats behind the scenes.

Transportation, Mines, and Downstream Industry

Since 2007, China has invested more than US$ 20 BN in Peru's copper mines, giving it a position in about one-third of Peru's copper industry and making Peru the second largest copper producer after Chile. In 2014, China invested a further US$ 6 BN for a stake in a Peruvian copper mine.

Likewise in Zambia, copper is the key attraction for China. In 1998, when Zambia privatized its copper industry, China Nonferrous Metal Mining Corporation (CNMC) took an 85% stake in the Chambishi copper mine.

Other projects and investment supported by China have followed: hydropower, roads, railways, farms, textile mills, industrial parks, and even a factory producing ammunition and uniforms.

Infrastructure improvement such as the revitalized Tan-Zam Railway and a new port in Tanzania facilitate the copper operations. The new port being built just north of Dar es Salaam will have a capacity of 20 million containers, plus a development zone, at a cost of US$ 10 BN to be financed by China Exim Bank. The Tan-Zam railway will be extended to this new port, massively assisting Zambia's export of copper and other goods.

China is also financing and constructing Lamu port in Kenya, with work on three berths under way out of a total planned 32 berths. It will be linked by an oil pipeline to South Sudan and by railway to Ethiopia and Uganda, greatly enhancing those countries' ability to export. There is a pattern to China's activities across many countries. Using its massive financial clout, it can build infrastructure that benefits the recipient country, Chinese construction companies, and equipment manufacturers, while providing long-term access to strategic minerals.

In buying into Zambia's Chambishi, which at that time was a "shell," a "dead mine," China to its credit was taking on significant risk which other firms were not willing to accept. CNMC is to build a copper smelter at Chambishi, investing US$ 220 MM and creating 1,436 jobs. Its annual capacity is currently for processing 300,000 tons of copper concentrate, and ultimately this volume is set to double. This is important to the Zambian economy.

But on the negative side, the Chinese have also offered the worst employment terms among the Zambia's mines, with lower wages, poor healthcare, and a proclivity for union bashing.[45] Fifty-one workers died from an explosion at a Chinese-run explosives factory related to the mining.

For good reason, China has met strong pushback from the Zambian citizens and the political opposition. There were riots at the Chambishi copper mine, and a strike at the smelter and at a coal mine. On several occasions, the Chinese owners panicked—shooting and killing local workers. Chinese managers have also been attacked and killed by local people.

The outrage over China's presence led the Zambian opposition to call the relationship with China one of "slave and master" and threatened to break diplomatic relations and revert to recognizing the rebel government in Taiwan. As it turns out, once the opposition leader got into power, on his first visit to Beijing in 2013 he was entirely acquiescent to China.[46] Money talks!

How to Assess the China, Inc. Business Model in Emerging Markets?

In the absence of other nations or companies willing to get involved so deeply, recipient countries appreciate the growth and wealth that Chinese money and investment can foster. But they also bristle at and sometimes (but rarely) resist what they see as overbearing, neocolonial behavior by China. The world also wrings its hands at what it sees as China's growing control of global natural resources, though in fact China remains a peripheral player in resources ownership (though in terms of its buying power in world trading it can hold sway).

China's track record over the past decade of expansion into emerging markets is rightly criticized for its breaches of universal ethical standards; whether in terms of environmental despoliation, labor abuses, or corrupt collusion with recipient governments that prop up tyrannical regimes while mortgaging future mineral resources to China. Many emerging countries are taking on China debt with little regard to the consequences. For instance, in 2012, Laos' GDP was US\$ 9.4 BN. But despite international disquiet, its rubber stamp parliament in the same year approved a US\$ 6.8 BN loan from China Exim Bank, secured not just by the railway assets, but also by two mining properties. The pattern continues.

China, Inc. in emerging markets is a bleak and disturbing business model. China has not only quickly learned tricks from the old colonial powers, but also has further refined that approach through substituting old-style military occupation with the power that finance can bring. China has even done away with the neocolonial niceties of development aid and human rights, which often mask economic domination. It is perfectly happy to work with any ruling group willing to comply with its economic demands.

Chinese leaders will tell you that they are mindful of the way the Chinese presence in a given country can become a political hot potato for the local government. They want to avoid disturbances and disruption that undermine the commercial effectiveness and profitability of the model. So in emerging markets we shall likely see more deals done on what seems to be a commercial basis with competitive bidding, rather than being mainly fixed at the government-to-government level. This would provide a veneer of due process and legitimacy, but would leave the fundamental workings of the model intact.

Notwithstanding moral outrage over how this model operates, the evidence does not support the view that this model is inherently unsustainable, at least in the short to medium term. Of course, anger and pushback in recipient countries will surely continue, as will international protests. But the model is likely to be around for some time, as long as China is in ascendancy and there are willing recipient nations.

Model 4. Novel Product or Technology Breakthrough

Globally, truly novel product or technology breakthroughs are few and far between. Long ago, there was bronze and the long bow. Then more recently there has been longitudinal navigation, steel, the spinning jenny, the steam engine, aircraft, antibiotics, the internal combustion engine, the cathode ray tube (TV), biotech, the computer, semiconductors and the internet. Although China also has a history of inventions—the compass, papermaking, printing (block and movable type), gunpowder, complex water control systems—in recent centuries that innovative spirit has stalled out, and we cannot point to major advances that have originated in China. The forces of traditional conservatism, a culture that looked back to a golden age rather than seeking to create change, a steady-state economy in which agriculture was prized and commerce looked down upon all canceled out, or rendered inoperable, ideas on industrialization, whether homegrown or imported.

China has demonstrated the ability to innovate, to adopt, and to develop existing technologies. But for any nation, the holy grail is the novel product or technology breakthrough. Such events are rare, across nations and across history.

While China's research and development (R&D) has received government resources, it has remained hostage to the vagaries of policy shifts, of stop-and-go reform, acceleration followed by temporary retrenchment, all of which have bred a cautious approach to R&D, deterring innovation.

> "This ever-changing environment of extreme uncertainty, with high risks and high gains, has a far-reaching effect on the behavior of the actors. Rational actors opted to focus on securing short-term gains while trying to minimize risk. Since industrial R&D, especially novel-product development, is both long term and high risk, the particularities of Chinese reform have kept actors from engaging in it."[47]

But as China emerges as a world-class scientific and industrial power, expectations are high that China can ultimately achieve its own breakthroughs. China enjoys significant advantages as it pushes the boundaries of science, such as strong domestic demand for environmentally sound technologies, massive financial muscle, a well-trained scientific establishment (including returnees from abroad), and, most critically, a determined and highly supportive government.

On the minus side, as discussed in Chapter 9, research and development is focused in government research institutes and traditionally separated from the industry that can commercialize the new technology. There are also cultural factors that stifle out-of-the-box thinking and risk-taking. The impact of government money for science and technology is dissipated by bureaucracy, waste, and corruption.

China today is pursuing R&D in areas where there are prospects of novel technology breakthroughs, in batteries for electric vehicles, for instance, or in utilizing metadata on gene sequencing to develop new medical treatments. But perhaps the most tantalizing of all the efforts going on in China has to do with molten salt reactors (MSRs) whereby thorium is used to generate electricity.

The concept of MSR technology has been around for decades, but to date has promised much but delivered nothing, with failed or abandoned projects across the globe. In 2011, China took up the challenge and, building upon technology acquired legitimately from the US Oak Ridge National Laboratory, launched its Thorium Molten Salt Reactor Project. The project is being run by the Shanghai Institute of Applied Physics (SINAP) under the leadership of Dr. Jiang Mianheng, who studied at Drexel University and happens to be the son of former Chinese leader Jiang Zemin. The project is receiving government funding of US$ 350 MM over five years with a team that started out with 140 PhDs, with plans to reach 750 scientists.

Why then go down this road, which so far has yielded no results? How does this technology compare to the new, safer Generation III light water reactors (LWR)? From China's point of view there are four advantages to MSRs—raw material supply, location of reactors, nuclear proliferation, and waste disposal.

Thorium, a rare earth, is plentiful in China. It is not a fissile material and, though it needs to be combined with uranium or plutonium to achieve the nuclear reaction, the uranium or plutonium used is reprocessed spent fuel from LWRs and so would greatly reduce China's dependence on uranium imports. Another potential benefit is that due to the high temperature in the reactor, hydrogen can also be combined with CO_2 to form methanol. Furthermore, the vision of project leader Jiang Mianheng includes using MSRs as a heat source for the liquefaction of coal into oil, which would reduce environmental damage from coal.

China also has massive and growing electricity needs in its interior that cannot be easily addressed by LWRs, which are water cooled and need to be located on the coast. MSRs use 95% to 97% less water than LWRs and thus can be located in the interior.

Waste products from MSRs have extremely high gamma radiation, rendering them highly trackable and fundamentally unattractive for those bent on nuclear proliferation for weapons use. The radioactivity of waste from MSRs has a much shorter half-life than that of waste from conventional LWRs, making disposal far less of a burden on the economics of nuclear power.

SINAP's initial target of building an operating experimental commercial-scale MSR within 25 years (by 2035) has been reset to ten years from 2014 (that is, by 2024). In the short term, SINAP is focusing on building two small MSRs, both 2 megawatts (MW): one molten salt-cooled high temperature reactor, commonly known as a fluoride salt-cooled high-temperature reactor (FHR) using solid fuel; and one pure thorium molten salt reactor (TMSR) using liquid thorium. The plan calls for subsequent experimental versions of 10 MW, then 100 MW, up to full size 1000 MW reactors.

For the US, having decided decades ago not to pursue this technology, it is somewhat embarrassing to find itself now providing support for the Chinese program. The US Department of Energy is working closely with the Chinese and providing funds for some of the research being done in the US, even though ultimately the technology would be owned by the Chinese.

The challenges facing China in these endeavors are enormous. In addition to SINAP, other institutes in Shanghai, Changchun, and Shenyang are working on various aspects. Efforts elsewhere in the world to make thorium power work have been stymied by the extremely high temperatures the technology operates at and the corrosive effect of the fluoride in the molten salts. China is working on high temperature salt pumps for the molten salt loops and new types of nickel alloys and other materials, such as silicon carbide.

There has been intense global interest in China's MSR program. When first launched, it received gushing praise:

"It may mark the passage of strategic leadership in energy policy from an inert and status quo West to a rising technological power willing to break the mold. If China's dash for thorium power succeeds, it will vastly alter the global energy landscape and may avert a calamitous conflict over resources as Asia's industrial revolutions clash head-on with the West's entrenched consumption."[48]

The safety aspects of thorium were lauded:

"... thorium must be bombarded with neutrons to drive the fission process. There is no chain reaction. Fission dies the moment you switch off the photon beam. There are not enough neutrons for it to continue of its own accord."[48]

However, based on the "bad history" of thorium nuclear technology, some experts, while acknowledging that on paper the design for MSRs may look "elegant," have expressed "deep skepticism that such an exotic technology will get built."[49]

Countering this, supporters of thorium stress that the thorium route was originally abandoned since there was abundant uranium from the weapons program for use in power generation and pointed out that experts in the UK, US, and France at that time all believed a thorium reactor could be built. Moreover, in the ensuing years, there have been major advances in materials science that can help make thorium a practical option. They also add that much of the opposition to thorium comes from proponents of competing LWRs.[50]

Given the potential longshot rewards, it makes perfect sense for the Chinese government to invest the modest sum of US$ 70 MM a year into the SINAP program. As one of China's multiple tracks towards energy security, the thorium program is an "extremely sensible and rational strategy."[51]

Discussing the US failure to sustain its thorium research, a commentator points out that the program requires "the sort of long-term commitment and resources that only another world power, like China, can provide".[52]

Even given the significant challenges along the path to a breakthrough in thorium power, China's deep resources and tenacity (the team in Shanghai is said to be working under "warlike" pressure),[53] coupled with China's urgent need for new energy sources, should give us some optimism that China may succeed where others have failed. China would own the technology that it can sell around the world. The effort being put into China's MSR program will also yield broader, knock-on innovation in materials science, for instance.

Implications for the Emergence of Chinese Firms on the Global Stage?

Without detracting from the energy of Chinese firms in embracing Western technology and management skills—and in some case further innovating—in all the models discussed we can see the hand of the Chinese government and the CCP, sometimes a light touch and at other times calling the shots. It is no exaggeration to say that the CCP's willingness to lead the reform process is central to the auspicious balance of forces that have animated China's recent rise. The CCP, unburdened of earlier hubris and motivated by the need to prop up its rule, has been at the heart of what we term *the China paradox.*

But the nature of China's hybrid economy is that business independence can ultimately be trumped by the power of the autocratic CCP. Any sizable Chinese firm, whether private or state-owned, that you may deal with can be leaned upon by the CCP, which exercises its power from behind the curtain. If the deal is of any national significance, then you are probably dealing with China, Inc. Behind the scenes, information is upstreamed to government or CCP "working groups" sitting in the shadows.

Understanding China, Inc.'s agenda and then aligning with it is often the path to a win-win transaction. But China plays a very long game. It shows flexibility in the short term to suck foreign investment and technology into China, while keeping its sights on the longer-term national advantage. The same is true in foreign markets where it operates with distant time horizons others could not contemplate.

Though *the China paradox,* and the role of the CCP in it, has proven hugely enabling for Chinese business, there is a cost to it. Given the CCP's power in the shadows, Chinese firms may not be as fleet-footed as their international competitors and may not achieve their true potential. Thus, foreign firms may rightly be cautious about accepting a bid to be acquired by a Chinese company, given the risk that the deal may be second guessed by higher powers in China who never appear at the negotiating table.

While in the big picture there is no doubt that the CCP rules the roost across the economy, we should not paint too simplistic a picture. Chinese firms across the state-owned/private divide are neither simple pawns of government policy nor passive subjects of the CCP Puppeteer-in-Chief. Chinese companies have gone through a crash course in how to run a business and feel pressure to perform. They face fierce competition at home and abroad.

Even in recent decades, when the CCP showed remarkable restraint in using a light hand as it influenced and guided Chinese firms, there was a constant effort by Chinese firms to assert their autonomy and to get the CCP out of their hair. The CCP under Xi Jinping shows a trend toward great autocracy and claw back of power and authority within Chinese firms, especially SOEs. This, coupled with anticorruption efforts, undermines the entrepreneurial spirit and is harming business decision-making. Chinese firms are riled at this apparent backsliding on the reforms, but are at present powerless to push back. The powerful dynamic between the CCP and the economy that fueled development is looking threatened. The smooth functioning of *the China paradox* is threatened and may evaporate.

In the short term, we may expect Chinese firms, whether operating in China or overseas, to feel the heavy burden of CCP influence. Foreign firms working with them need to be cognizant of this. As the CCP struggles to "readjust" the economy, there will be continued forced, bureaucratically driven mergers. Chinese investments overseas will be increasingly vetted by the CCP, which is mindful of capital flight, including that of funds put at risk by the anticorruption campaign.

But longer term, as China's modern-style firms, private or state-owned, grow and innovate, relying less on government patronage and creating their own profitable path, they will go beyond their current mutterings of dissent and increasingly be unwilling to accept interference from the CCP. These firms, bolstered by their own autonomous commercial success, will be harder to coerce than old-style SOEs and will increasingly break free.

As the CCP hunkers down, its relevance to the economy will come under scrutiny. Firms that have hitherto participated in these recent business models built on the symbiotic relationship between business and government will stride in innovative ways. While this may imply the end of the brief four decades of flourishing of *the China paradox*, there is also a positive side. Even if the CCP were to stumble seriously or fade toward irrelevance, these modern-style Chinese firms will still be able to persist and grow, taking their place on the world stage. Those seeking to forge business relationships with Chinese firms are well advised to determine whether their future partner is part of that new breed.

Chapter 9
What Could Disrupt or Sustain the China Paradox?

China's current problem is that the government-dominated economic structure has led to the collusion of public power and capital.

— Chinese economist, addressing a
conference at the New York Stock Exchange, 2013.

The China paradox has emerged as a complex, fragile, yet highly effective equilibrium between forces that on the face of it might seem inimical, but in this specific historical context have proven to share common ground. China's pragmatic CCP rulers energetically embraced foreign business ideas resulting in China's extraordinary revitalization without abandoning its fundamental modus operandi. The reforms have been critical to shoring up the autocratic political order.

The China paradox has been a highly successful construct that has served China well and confounded many naysayers. But it is also unsettling to observe just how shaky this edifice is. As we examine the factors underlying *the China paradox*, we shall throw light on how sustainable it is. Do the growing social, political, and economic fissures opening up in China imply that the Chinese model of recent decades will unravel unless fuller and broader reform is on the agenda?

Peace, Stability and the CCP

It is obvious that social order, peace (the absence of disruptive internal conflict or external wars), and stability[1] are fundamental to China's rise. While the conventional wisdom in developed Western countries is that the economy holds sway over politics, in China the opposite is the case. Politics weigh heavily as a factor determining the economic outcome. The CCP's role at the heart of China's governance is without doubt the most fundamental and troubling question facing China. In the language of scenario planning, it stands out as the "critical uncertainty."

DOI 10.1515/9781501507212-009

The CCP Has Survived and Adapted

While 1949 did bring national unity to China, it can hardly be said that, during the 27 years before the economic reforms began, the CCP presided over a peaceful China. Externally China was sucked into the Korean War. Domestically the CCP force-marched the population down a political and economic dead end, was responsible for a huge man-made famine, and brutally attacked the nation's intellectuals. After Mao launched the Cultural Revolution, which came close to civil war, a Western academic wrote that the CCP Congress held in 1969 "pronounced the last rites for the national organization that had brought the revolutionary movement to victory in 1949...."[2] As it turned out, the CCP was rebuilt and regained its position of authority. The CCP "teetered on the verge of self-destruction numerous times,"[3] but survived repeated errors and crimes.

In assessing social order in contemporary China, it is common to seek analogies from history, to compare the PRC with past imperial dynasties and regimes. Was the Maoist period a short dynasty that laid the foundations for a longer flourishing, as the Qin dynasty did for the Han dynasty and as the Sui did for the Tang? Alternatively, is the current reforming regime more like a brief dynastic revival before the ultimate demise of the dynasty, or will it see a fate similar that of the Nationalist government (1911–49) which, having reunified the nation, then collapsed under the weight of cronyism and corruption?[4]

In the post-Mao era, the CCP "has so far proved to be a sinuous, cynical and adaptive beast in the face of multiple challenges,"[5] shedding dogma and embracing change, while sustaining its hold on power. Having led the complex and risky reform process, the CCP is justifiably credited with this success by a grateful population. The CCP's credibility no longer lies in ideological leadership or its revolutionary achievements (though it still harkens back to these), but in its role of delivering economic growth year-in and year-out. The CCP openly discusses the risk to social stability (code for its hold on power) were the rate of economic growth to decline too far. While it may seem ironic that the People's Government fears its own people, we should also add that this anxiety is shared widely in society. As one senior Chinese business figure put it to me recently, "the Chinese themselves fear the Chinese people." Given the history of destructive social upheavals in China, the CCP is regarded by many as the only institution that can keep the lid on the Chinese pressure cooker.

Effective though the CCP has proven to be during the reforms so far, the question is whether it will be able to take China to the next level, to permit it to ascend the developmental ladder toward the "knowledge economy."

In contrast to the red terror that lay at the heart of Mao's system, the post-reform system also relies heavily on the "seduction," the co-opting of the population through economic progress, but still backed up by a more sparing use of terror.[6] The past four decades have, by the standards of modern Chinese history, been largely peaceful, thus creating the conditions for economic take-off.

That said, terror is still used against courageous individuals who have the temerity to speak out. To name just a few, there was Wei Jingsheng (1978, democracy activist who called for the "Fifth Modernization"—democracy), Wang Dan (1989, a leader of the democracy movement before the Tiananmen Square Massacre), Liu Xiaobo (1990, writer and human rights activist, Nobel Peace Prize Laureate), Gao Yaojie (who in 2001 blew the whistle on HIV-contaminated blood in Henan), Jiang Yanyong (2003, the medical doctor who exposed the extent of SARS cases in Beijing), and Ai Weiwei (2008, the artist who exposed substandard schools that collapsed during the Wenchuan earthquake).

The Tiananmen Square Massacre underscored the priority the CCP places on its survival. But although at that time some predicted the break-up of China into regional entities, the nation and the CCP passed a severe stress test.

> "Most of what I and so many others thought was true and inevitable at that time turned out to be wrong. There was no civil war, no fracturing of the country, and no return to Maoism."[7]

How Well Is the CCP Functioning Today?

There are many conflicting views on this. The CCP exhibits two apparently contradictory characteristics. At times it looks flat-footed, incompetent, systemically corrupt, out of touch with the needs of the age, and increasingly irrelevant. The other side is that the CCP is still able to lead strongly when absolutely needed. While it has exhibited a degree of atrophy or ossification such as that seen in the Soviet Union, it has also battled that through a powerful adaptability since Deng launched the reforms that helped strengthen its survivability.[8]

Though riddled with problems, the CCP is not weak or effete. It remains an effective organization and does not yet resemble the tired, isolated, and discredited regime it overthrew in 1949. Today, it has nearly 90 million members, plus the Communist Youth League serves as a funnel for new CCP recruits.

In the early years of the PRC, the CCP ruled with an iron fist and could implement policy swiftly at every level of society. No village, factory, school, family, or individual was untouched. Everybody was required to be an "activist" in support of CCP policy or face punishment. It had the power to determine every facet of people's lives. Today, the CCP is willing to leave the people to run their own lives and pursue wealth, just as long they are not engaged in public opposition.

Administratively, the reforms brought a massive decentralization of power down to the major cities, and the CCP at the center finds it hard to prevent problems from arising. Even if it does see a problem, it has to weigh whether it merits the full use of its authority to override or coerce local authorities who have stepped out of line. The center has to use its limited political capital very sparingly. On top of this, the loyalties of the CCP at the local level are often closely aligned with local interests. Information does not get transmitted up through the CCP structure to the center, leaving the CCP leaders blindsided.

The CCP's ability to anticipate or prevent problems has been hugely diminished. Due to weak control and pervasive corruption, man-made disasters—such as the huge explosion at a warehouse in Tianjin or the landslide in Shenzhen—occur with painful regularity. But when such events do occur, it has the muscle and determination to fix things and reassure the population, to dig itself out and salvage its credibility. When a massive problem does arise, the CCP is forced to pull its levers of power and make sure they work.

This is vividly illustrated by the CCP's reaction to natural disasters. During the outbreak of Severe Acute Respiratory Syndrome (SARS) in 2002–03, the CCP initially chose to lie to the people about the outbreak's scale until a courageous physician served as a whistle-blower. This undermined confidence in the CCP's ability to handle a crisis. But once the CCP changed its stance, fired the Minister of Public Health, and began an inquest into what had transpired, valuable reforms were implemented in the monitoring of infectious diseases. All local governments had to establish Medical Information Centers, which were linked by the internet to the central government. This was a massive innovation that has proven valuable in permitting a speedier response to subsequent disease outbreaks and has greatly reduced the ability of local government to hide the facts.

Initially, after the massive Sichuan earthquake in 2008, the lack of helicopters hampered an effective rescue of survivors in the remote affected areas. Moreover, many schoolchildren had perished when poorly constructed schools collapsed while neighboring buildings were left standing. But through its role in the subsequent rescue and recovery operations, the CCP was able to claw back its reputation. Working on establishing healthcare networks in Sichuan as part of the reconstruction, I saw close up how effective and well led the CCP can be. Temporary housing sprung up almost overnight. Each of China's provinces was allocated a Sichuan county to support during the recovery. Huge convoys of military vehicles brought in troops and materiel to support the efforts. This war-scale mobilization was stunning and impressive. Less impressive, of course, was the CCP's frantic but successful efforts to silence parents of dead schoolchildren who were calling for an investigation into why the schools had collapsed.

Post-reforms, China's looser governance, with much of the power residing at the local level, has meant that the CCP will continue to be set back on its heels and forced to be reactive. When things fall apart, it is forced to reflect hard before using its residual power. But when it does scramble to intervene, the CCP does certainly deliver and, in that respect, cannot be regarded as a broken institution close to collapse.

Still this pattern of late intervention is a symptom of the CCP's less than complete control and inevitably casts doubt over the CCP's longer-term relevance and survivability. Not surprisingly, the CCP is riddled with anxiety over its future and acutely mindful of how history has unkindly treated other ruling communist parties once they have lost their legitimacy.

The CCP Is Embedded in Businesses

Despite its softer touch, the CCP remains inserted into the fabric of Chinese society, whether through the ubiquitous "street committees," which keep watch on citizens, or in universities and businesses. Faithful to its Leninist roots, the CCP presence is a political insurance policy, a sleeper cell to be activated in a crisis." The CCP aims to "have an activist and advocate inside every significant institution in the whole country," so that it can intervene in the event of a crisis.[9]

The CCP has some kind of presence within all businesses once they reach a significant scale. The most formal presence is to be found in the large SOEs. The CEO is appointed by a CCP group at the central level. The secretary of the firm's CCP Committee sits on the board and outranks the CEO. In large SOEs there is also a representative of the CCP Disciplinary Commission who is supposed to deter or catch any bad practices in the firm, but is usually too close to the firm to play a useful role.

The clout of the CCP secretary in a SOE, in practice, depends very much on the guidance and signals emanating from the CCP's top leaders. At the height of the reforms under Zhu Rongji, the priority CCP leaders set was for bold restructuring with a focus on profitability and shareholder value, as China listed its large firms on the stock market and prepared for the foreign competition that would enter the market after accession to the WTO. I witnessed how a feisty and charismatic CEO pushed through a radical agenda that included drastically slashing the workforce, winning the argument against the firm's CCP Committee, which preferred a much more gradual, less painful but less effective restructuring process.

In large SOEs, the CCP Committee plays a key role in shaping the corporate culture. It uses notice boards on each floor to share information on the firm's CCP elections and member awards, CCP campaigns, and its leaders and congresses. It determines what political "study materials" members should focus on. I have seen business activities halted for several days to permit political meetings to drive home CCP policy. It also organizes the firm's social activities and celebrations.

There is a CCP Committee in most large Chinese POEs, but in the absence of state ownership, it is unable to throw its weight around as it does in SOEs. It is common for the founder or CEO of the private firm to also be its party secretary. CCP meetings at the firm are typically not permitted to interfere with business activities.

When it comes to foreign-invested enterprises (FIEs), there is normally just an unpublicized CCP cell in the firm, not a formal CCP Committee. All FIEs are required to have a trade union, not a free union but one controlled by the CCP. In a Sino-foreign JV, the human resources director is typically selected from the Chinese side of the JV and runs the trade union and, by implication, the CCP cell. In a 100% foreign-owned enterprise there is also a trade union, likewise controlled by the firm's undercover CCP cell. Although the role of the CCP in FIEs and their trade unions is generally benign, I have witnessed local authorities mobilize the FIE's trade union to shut down production as a negotiating ploy during heated negotiations with the foreign side. Also, the presence of the CCP in FIEs is taken into consideration when the foreign owner weighs the risks of transferring sensitive proprietary technology to the venture.

China's Fault Lines and Tensions

There are abundant threats to stability that need to be built into a risk assessment of China. Wealth inequality is massive and the gap continues to grow. Each year there are tens of thousands of officially recorded civil disturbances, many of them related to land-use rights. Religion of all kinds flourishes, much of it independently of the officially controlled churches. Ethnic tensions are close to boiling point with Tibetans and Xinjiang Uighurs defying Han-Chinese authority. In Hong Kong, pro-democracy sentiment has extended to calls for self-determination.

China's burgeoning new middle class is increasingly militant about environmental threats to their families. It is also anxious to defend its newfound wealth. Anger over China's stock market performance has spilled over into blaming the government. Were the people's savings to be lost through widespread Ponzi schemes (one already has been brought to light) or a real estate market collapse, things could get out of hand. The new middle class might turn on the CCP it has supported until now.

On top of the domestic tensions, we should add the risk of regional conflicts (for example, with Taiwan, Korea, Japan, and the Philippines) that might arise whether by design or sparked by an unintended event, thereby derailing economic growth and heightening the risk of domestic strife. Were regional tensions to reach a boiling point, it is easy to envisage container ships stopping their services to Chinese ports, cutting off access between China and its global markets.

The CCP and China's Future

The future role of the CCP is a thorny and highly sensitive issue. China's leaders today are well-versed in the conventional Marxist theory that the "economic base" plays the decisive role in determining the social system and that if the social-political "superstructure" gets out of kilter with or becomes unresponsive to economic change, then it has to transform itself or face social friction and worse.

Is China's unreformed, rigid one-party system—the type conceived of by Lenin and Stalin—appropriate for the China of tomorrow? Is it a living fossil that has outlived its usefulness? Will its proven tenacity and adaptability ultimately be outweighed by its own limitations and by the constraints it imposes on China's progress?

There are two fundamental and linked aspects that do not bode well for the CCP's future role: the tightening of its autocratic rule and the implications that may have for China's bid to move up the global economic ladder.

It is unsurprising that the CCP has absolutely no intention of giving up or diluting its monopoly on political power. Having shaped itself and China through violence and brutality over the last 60-plus years, the CCP is mindful of blood debts that have yet to be settled and of citizens (albeit a tiny minority) who can never forgive or forget. The CCP knows that, having ruled by the sword, it would likely die by the sword. The example of Gorbachev and the fate of the Soviet Union and its satellite countries remain seared into the brains of the CCP leadership. It is haunted by the specter of the final brutal moments of Romania's dictator Ceausescu and his wife. It stands resolute against anything that might undermine one-party rule. Though it may have become savvy in communicating its message, in hiring public relations firms and dressing its leaders in smart suits, the iron fist is always there ready to be used as needed.

But while during the early decades of the reforms there was a distinct political relaxation, we are now seeing a steady tightening of the CCP's authoritarian grip. On the economic front, the mood in SOEs has changed dramatically. Take the case of a mild-mannered CEO of a major SOE, whom I have known and appreciated for many years, who was recently forced to resign for his handling of a merger. A CCP official responsible for investigating CCP "discipline" denounced him, stating "the [merger] plan doesn't have a single word about how to strengthen the leadership of the party committees and party organizations. Not a single word. What kind of reform is this?"[10]

On the political front, a cold wind is blowing. Under Xi Jinping, power is concentrated in one man's hands to a greater extent than at any time since Mao. A personality cult around Xi is being constructed. Journalists are required to swear total obedience to the CCP. Newspaper headlines cry out, "Love the Party, protect the Party." Although Xi may only be "using Mao's methods to walk Deng's path,"[11] the call for total loyalty and tighter controls on the freedom of expression go far beyond the strict limits set by previous leaders. The new hyper-autocratic tone has faced opposition from influential individuals who hitherto have worked within the system.[12]

Indicating its deep anxiety (not paranoia, since it may be fully justified), the CCP issued an internal CCP document listing "7 topics not to be discussed" (qibujiang) since they "challenge" or "undermine" the CCP. The forbidden topics include "Western constitutional democracy" and anything that "negates the historical inevitability of China choosing the socialist path, and argues that the wrong path was mistakenly taken."[13,14] Uncompromising words from a hardline party.

The CCP faces the challenge of having a weak ideological underpinning and legitimacy. Given the vacuum created by its fading Marxist-Leninist credentials in the wake of Deng's ultra-pragmatism, Xi has gone further than other recent leaders in promoting the value of ancient Chinese philosophy—not just Confucianism but also Legalism. Confucianism stresses the innate virtue of humans while Legalism holds that only draconian laws can ensure stability. Although the two schools appear incompatible, the Confucianism that emerged during the Han Dynasty (206 B.C. – 220 A.D.) incorporated plenty of Legalist principles, creating a hybrid statecraft that looked gentlemanly on the surface but was hard and cruel on the inside. Today, this is echoed in one of the CCP's guiding principles: "externally relaxed, internally tense."

Xi has put energy into tackling the issue of corruption. In a "measured and calculating" manner[15] he has taken on independent power bases in the security services, the army, and in key sectors of the economy. In so doing he has not only consolidated his own personal power but also reasserted the absolute authority of a Leninist party, which was undermined by factionalism during the previous Hu administration.[16]

The anticorruption campaign has been welcomed by many, especially by the man-in-the-street. Moreover, since corruption is the life blood of the vested interests, it can be argued that taking on corruption is a prerequisite for any potential deepening of SOE reform.

But as Xi pushes pledges to sustain the campaign long term, he runs the risk of undermining the CCP's own credibility as more court trials of its leaders take place. It is apparent that the CCP has not resolved the vexing question of how to smoothly handle political succession. Xi has talked about dealing with "political plot activities" that sought "to wreck and split the party," language that comes close to describing a potential coup d'état.[17] Though we should not bet against Xi seeing out his current five-year term or enjoying a second term, the concentration of power in his hands heightens the risk that he will be made the fall guy.

One consequence of the CCP's autocratic rule is a stifling intellectual environment resulting from what is popularly called the "Policy to keep the People ignorant" (yumin zhengce), which is directly in conflict with China's goal of entering the "knowledge economy."

China has spent the past 150 or so years finding ways to selectively import certain aspects of Western society while at the same time steadfastly avoiding social contamination by Western ideas. We saw how in the late 19th century the Self Strengthening Movement failed to protect the Qing Dynasty from collapse. Since the economic reforms began, the CCP also has led China down a similar path. On the one hand, it has opened the door to foreign investment but, on the other hand, it has railed against "spiritual pollution." This time around, China's absorption of things foreign has certainly been much deeper than earlier attempts. But the pragmatic spirit that imbued the CCP during Deng's rule is now being drowned out by a more ideologically driven CCP. The CCP looks more and more out of tune with the needs of a modern economy.

Chinese business leaders plainly see how the autocracy stymies innovation. As a SOE board director put it to me:

> "Innovation is about challenging things, it is like rebelling. If you don't have democracy then you won't dare to rebel. If an official has a good idea, then his first consideration is will I get into trouble with the party's Disciplinary Commission, will I be put under house arrest. Therefore, people keep silent."[18]

A senior Chinese banker explained to me the need to complement economic progress with political reform:

> "I accept that the last 30 years' development has been made possible by dictatorship. But in the future the economy needs political reform—openness, accountability, an independent judiciary, open networks. Institutional reform is the key but it will bring many challenges."[19]

There is a deadening effect due to increasing government monitoring and restriction of the internet. The government has installed the so-called Great Fire Wall of China (GFWC), which filters and blocks internet traffic with the rest of the world. Websites are closed down almost as quickly as they are put up. Crude and arbitrary trawling of topics to be stopped catch general traffic and slows the internet. More and more Chinese are forced to use virtual private networks (VPNs) to circumvent the GFWC. In its cat and mouse game with internet users, the China government is threatening to disable VPNs. At certain times, the internet is simply taken down. This happened for six months in 2009 in Xinjiang against the background of attacks by Uighur separatists, forcing businessmen who relied on the web for their commerce to travel to neighboring Gansu province to conduct their transactions. In order to stifle any conceivable threat to its power, the CCP restricts intellectual discourse and basic telecommunications, even at the cost of hampering economic growth. If, as is likely, social tensions grow, the prospect is that the restrictions will be increased, further undermining China's participation in the world's knowledge economy.

We also see a radical tightening of controls on foreign technology. Responsibility for regulating government procurement is being moved from the government to entities under the CCP. Technology procurement has become an ideological issue, not just a commercial or scientific one. It is ideological in the sense it has to do with national cybersecurity. Foreign high-tech products are seen as a threat.

The CCP is perfectly happy to accept some medium-term negative impact on the economy as a cost of supporting the paramount goals of national security. Foreign firms find it hard to comply with the new rules on technology procurement, leaving Chinese banks scrambling to find local technology suppliers that can meet their mission-critical standards, even though purchasing from them may well increase their security vulnerability. Chinese banks also estimate that this may reduce their efficiency in handling bank transactions by 20% to 30%. Once again, political power takes priority over economics.

With the long-term campaign against corruption has come a wave of fear among SOE leaders and government officials that is debilitating for the economy, freezing decision-making and deterring risk-taking and innovation.

As the post-Mao reforms took shape, the CCP exhibited a deep pragmatism, dynamism, and willingness to learn, thus creating the conditions in which *the China paradox* could emerge and unleash China's economic growth. However, while showing extraordinary adaptability, the CCP also proved unwilling to entertain changes to its political role. Now that Chinese society (or at least a significant part of it) has achieved relative wealth and pushes for more transparency and accountability from government, the CCP looks increasingly out of step with a modern economy. The CCP's overconfidence, growing assertiveness, and deepening social repression puts the delicate balance between CCP power and the forces of economic and social change at serious risk.

The CCP will still have the flexibility, adaptability, and experience to sustain its present modus operandi in the medium term, over the next 10 to 15 years. But that is very different from saying the CCP will be able to lead China to the next level of development.

Despite its key role as architect of the reforms, the CCP may represent as much a liability as an asset for China in the longer term. The CCP's deft navigation of uncharted waters up to now should not blind us to the risks it faces. What makes it difficult for those running the CCP is that they are boxed in, since both paths—reforming the CCP role or maintaining the status quo—present serious dangers to its rule.

The collapse of the CCP, let alone the Chinese nation-state, does not seem on the horizon. But at the same time the direction that the CCP is taking makes it hard to share the optimism of a prominent Chinese professor who foresaw a China that, while still a one-party state, "will be more pluralistic and diversified politically, and will strengthen its legal system and find ways to protect human rights."[20]

It will take a yet-to-be-discovered extraordinary leader or group of leaders in the CCP to let their grip on power relax even slightly. As the CCP continues to ride the Chinese tiger, it surely feels there is no convenient or safe time to dismount from the beast.

In maintaining the status quo and continuing to tighten its grip, the CCP runs the risk of not only undermining its credibility and social relevance, but also of stifling China's creative side. The danger is that it may feel that the economic reforms have run their course, but have created what is imagined to be a sustainable model. Having saved itself from near-death after the failure of the Mao years, is the CCP somehow prematurely declaring victory?

As China seeks to move up the developmental ladder and join the global knowledge economy, success will necessarily require further opening up, both economically and politically, not less. The current trajectory of the CCP is neither bold, nor wise. Its recent hunkering down is dangerous and short-sighted. The political dimension in China is the most critical factor and the prognosis is gloomy.

The Rule of Law

The weakness of the rule of law in China is closely related to the CCP and China's flawed governance. China has a strong legal framework, but it falls down in its ability or willingness to enforce the law.

China uses the Chinese term yifa zhiguo, which translates best as the "rule by law," in contrast to true "rule of law." To quote the highly-respected lawyer Jerry Cohen, the CCP "totally dominates the legal system, including the education, training, and day-to-day operation of its personnel and institutions. 'Judicial independence'… is the enemy and forbidden by party rulers even to be discussed in law schools."[21] He also sees a further deterioration:

> "The law reform spirit of the earliest years of this century began to die in China during the Hu Jintao era…. It came to an end with the ascension of Xi Jinping, despite the greater professionalization of the judiciary…. Most new laws produced … are designed to expand the party's repressive policies."

Barring changes to the role of the CCP, true rule of law will be a pipe dream in China.

In China, the theft of intellectual property rights (IPR) is all-pervasive. Foreign firms operating in China complain bitterly. It constrains them from deploying their core technology in China. For example, because of the risk of IPR theft, GE refused to transfer to China the production of aircraft engine turbine blades at the front of the engine, which require special coating and hardening to withstand high-speed impacts.

Chinese courts threw out the suit brought by US semiconductor producer AMSC after Chinese turbine maker Sinovel was caught red-handed stealing source code.[22] GM filed an unfair competition lawsuit in Shanghai against Chery Auto, claiming that Chery's QQ "shared remarkably identical body structure, exterior design, interior design, and key components" with the Matiz produced by GM's Daewoo in South Korea. GM even had strong evidence that Chery brazenly used the original Daewoo model for crash testing to get its own model approved in China! But an out-of-court settlement was the best GM could get.

Other foreign auto makers have sued Chinese firms in Chinese courts: Toyota (against Geely), Honda (against Shuanghuan, claiming that its local S-RV looked exactly like Honda's CRV), and Nissan (against Great Wall Auto). All these lawsuits were either thrown out by the Chinese courts or settled out of court. These examples demonstrate why China's judiciary has been deemed to be unreliable and certainly not independent.

However, there are signs that China's enforcement of IPR is improving, largely reflecting national self-interest and the need to protect the IPR of emerging Chinese companies. As an economics professor at Peking University put it to me:

"China has abundant talent and capital. The bottleneck is IPR protection.... IPR protection is vital for start-ups, for trade secrets. This issue has a big impact on China's ability to innovate... [As a result] finance is not directed at innovation."[23]

While foreign firms make the most noise on IPR protection, arguably the bigger story is the harm that such wanton IPR theft has wrought on Chinese firms, serving as a serious disincentive to the pursuit of innovation. This affects large firms, such as technology giant Huawei, which seeks to defend its large portfolio of patents, or a small publisher of trade directories, whose chief editor shared with me his frustration at not being able to use IT to expand his sales because of the risk of IPR theft.

There are also signs that in response to rampant patent infringement, Chinese courts are becoming more receptive to suits, even those lodged by foreign firms. Foreign plaintiffs have been winning more than 80% of their patent-infringement suits against Chinese companies, though it should be added that they "only sue in China if they are confident they can win."[24]

The Chinese government does deserve some credit for its awareness of the need for a stronger legal underpinning of business transactions and a more even-handed application of laws relating to property and contracts.

But that treatment does not extend to society more broadly. Calls for the nation's constitution to be upheld are punished as an attack on CCP rule. Without radical changes to the way the CCP controls China's legal system, it is hard to see how the rule of law can be dramatically improved.

China's weak rule of law will continue to hamper innovation and to drive Chinese firms and individuals to hold assets and wealth offshore. Foreign firms will still invest in China due to the market opportunities, but will continue to hold back on deploying some of their most sensitive or valuable technology. This is all to the detriment of China's progress.

Culture, Education, and Civil Society

China today suffers from a poorly functioning civil society. One litmus test of this cultural dissonance is to consider how Chinese function when transplanted into other societies. Chinese educated and living in the US and Europe, for instance, display a greater propensity for creativity and innovation than their brethren who remained in China.

Chinese business leaders are acutely conscious of China's cultural problems, and prominent on their list of concerns is an aversion to risk-taking. As the head of a Chinese private equity firm put it to me:

"China's entire education system discourages peoples from taking risk. People are afraid to take risk. Innovation needs to be driven by entrepreneurs."[25]

As an explanation for the dearth of innovation, others point to China's fast-growing market, which has no shortage of business opportunities and where success has not depended on breakout thinking or risk-taking. "There is lots of easy money to be made without R&D. You can make money in other ways."[26]

A Cocktail of Confucianism and Leninism

China also carries a heavy load of cultural baggage. Contributing to the lack of bold long-term thinking are the two schools of statecraft that have intersected in modern China—the Confucian tradition and Leninism (or Stalinism).

Modern China has seen repeated efforts to replace traditional values. In the early 20th century, Chinese intellectuals began an assault on what they saw as the oppressive ethics of Confucian society in which the people were subservient to their ruler, the child to the father, and the wife to the husband. On taking power in 1949, the CCP took up that theme and the new Marriage Law of 1950 freed Chinese women from arranged marriages and concubinage. But the CCP also systematically destroyed the traditional Chinese extended family, including the ancestor worship that underpinned it and the ancestral halls where tablets recording family histories were held and offerings made. The ancestor-oriented Qingming Festival (involving grave sweeping) was banned.

The CCP demanded exclusive loyalty and would not accept the extended family as an alternative focus for the people. At times during the Mao years, the CCP went even further by undermining the nuclear family through, for instance, encouraging children to turn in their parents for activities deemed to be "counterrevolutionary."

In place of Confucian values, the CCP instilled loyalty to the party. Love of the party was deemed to be the only path to love of the nation. A regimen learned from Stalin's Russia was put in place under which nobody was trusted, where everybody was watched, and those who were not *active* supporters of the new order were hunted down and severely punished. The CCP pioneered new psychological techniques, "brainwashing," to force confessions and to drive people into a full mental embrace of the "New China."

Many older Chinese today will express nostalgia for that period since there was a high degree of predictability and it was in some ways less stressful than today. But it came at a high social and economic cost, and not just because wealth generation was weak. Throughout society, from factory directors to research institute heads and university lecturers, the instilled culture was dominated by the fear of failure. Conformity and caution were valued over new ideas or risk-taking. Everybody looked over his or her shoulder, paying attention to any shift in the political climate.

While the CCP did a thorough job of eradicating Confucian institutions, in other respects its actions had the effect of reinforcing old cultural norms, such as the concept of "obedience" (fuzong), but with the CCP as its new focus. The content of education changed, but the ethos and methods used in education owe much to the past. Many Chinese will tell you that the driving principle underlying social behavior is still the Confucian tenet called the Doctrine of the Mean (zhongyong zhi dao), which encourages conformity to a middle way and deters bold thinking.

With Mao's death, Marxism-Leninism retreated and was relegated to near irrelevance. Although the autocratic statecraft learned from Lenin and Stalin have remained firmly in place, the Chinese are free to participate in the economy and privately express their opinions within certain limits. The Chinese people breathed a sigh of relief and began to revert to building their lives with minimal interference from the CCP.

But the years of the socialist straitjacket, coupled with the legacy of traditional philosophy, have left their mark on Chinese businesses, especially in the SOE sector. The corollary of the aversion to risk-taking is a tendency to hide behind collective actions as a way to avoid personal responsibility for leadership decisions. A key factor holding China back is "a wish for consensus, not being willing to make a decision, thus slowing things down. They are not willing to make a mistake, while in the US you can make a mistake as long as you get things back on track."[27]

Anything Goes, as the Market Latches onto Newfound Freedoms

While large SOEs may stick to a deadening consensus approach that stifles decisive action, at the other end of the spectrum certain segments of society have embraced the newfound freedoms in ways that have been described variously such as laissez faire, frontier capitalism, hedonism, free-for-all, market "anarchy." All these fit to a certain extent. Now that the former externally imposed moral and ideological straitjacket has been removed, it is as if the Chinese people are now struggling to find their own internal moral compass.

Countless Chinese firms blazon the word trust (Chinese: <u>xin</u>), a key Confucian value, across their websites. Many Chinese CEOs display on the walls behind their desks the calligraphy for the Confucian word <u>ren</u>, which translates into something like "not bearing to see the suffering of others." These words are unfortunately simply aspirational. There is precious little "trust" or "ren" in China today.

While sound strategy and strong legal documentation are increasingly the norm, Chinese businesses still rely too heavily on traditional and often crooked "relationships" (<u>guanxi</u>), which often speed things up, but may become a shaky approach once the official who facilitated matters changes job or, worse, is arrested.

Fortunately, in between those two extremes of stifling consensus and unbridled "grab what you can" there is an impressive coterie of Chinese firms that are enthusiastic about modern management skills and keen to play according to acceptable standards.

Corruption, Moral Turpitude, and Social Alienation

Corruption, which tracks back to the privileges enjoyed by the educated official class in traditional society, has come back on a scale unseen in world history. Like many of the cultural aspects being discussed here, corruption saps the life out of business, rewarding those who are well-connected rather than those who innovate.

The Chinese press is full of examples of moral turpitude. We have seen examples of passers-by on the street walking past an injured or sick person for fear of the legal consequences, even though they had no part in that person's condition. Caught on a video surveillance tape, a driver accidently ran over a child and then reversed back over it to ensure the child was dead.

Chinese people are dismayed by these aspects of the new society but largely feel powerless to change it for the better, and they mouth the ubiquitous words "nothing can be done" (<u>meiyou banfa</u>). Despite all the liveliness, joy, and color that have flooded back into Chinese society, there remains a troubling alienation.

In 1922, the radical Chinese writer Lu Xun described Chinese society as "an iron house without windows, absolutely indestructible, with many people fast asleep inside who will soon die of suffocation." That nadir was followed by a new pit of despair during the first decades of the PRC under Mao. Although today the ideological baggage of the Mao era has been largely shed, the tools and levers of social control, propaganda, and coercion, the habits learned from Stalin's paranoia, all remain well-oiled and in daily use. Though Chinese citizens today get on with life, there is still a strong undercurrent of alienation and frustration.

Below is a work by contemporary Chinese painter Su Xinping.[28] The room has windows, certainly an improvement on Lu Xun's room. But the alienation and stifling atmosphere of China today shouts at us. There is a deep mood of yearning, yearning to be somewhere else.

The Chinese government is acutely mindful of this moral vacuum. It has shown some appetite for nurturing religion (while showing anxiety over the fast-growing Christian church). There is even (albeit limited) discussion about allowing religious believers into the CCP, much as capitalists were recently welcomed in. In an effort to strengthen the institution of the family, which it ironically spent decades undermining, the CCP has restored a series of public festivals that have roots in the old Confucian society.

We should also note that nationalism serves as a vital bonding agent in China today. Nationalism has been an integral element of Chinese communism, just as it was with communism in Russia, Vietnam, and Cuba. Now that China has abandoned social revolution and economic collectivism, we are left with nationalism and the goal of China's revival (zhenhua) as a key cultural element that serves as the glue holding the Chinese people together. Nationalism and patriotism energize and define Chinese society. The Chinese feel a "national mission and passion."[29] The CCP is perfectly happy to cynically utilize international tensions to rally public support. With that often comes ugly anti-foreign feelings that lie not far below the surface in China.

Education Falls Short

There is also a strong perception among Chinese that education is failing to deliver the needed results. Starting from the 7th century during the Tang Dynasty, the Chinese used a complex imperial examination (keju) system to select government officials. While this was not the meritocracy some paint it as (only a tiny proportion of Chinese were able to write characters and thus compete in the exams), it was nonetheless highly efficient and stood the test of time, eventually being abolished in 1905.

But the efficiency of the examination system came at social cost. As one Chinese scholar has observed, it "diverted scholars, geniuses and thinkers away from the study or exploration of modern science" and was:

> "designed to reward obedience, conformity, compliance, respect for order, and homogeneous thinking.... It was an efficient means of authoritarian social control.... Success on the keju enforced orthodoxy, not innovation or dissent."[30]

While China's educational system owes much to the borrowed Soviet model, it remains influenced by the old imperial system and emphasizes rote learning and orthodoxy. At its heart today is the gaokao, the countrywide examination used to select students for the universities.

Having been suspended during the Cultural Revolution, the gaokao was reinstated in 1977. In 2015, nearly 9.5 million students took the test, competing for some 7 million places. Wide swaths of the Chinese population motivate their children to study for long hours late into the evening. They struggle to accumulate wealth to pay for their children's tutorials.

But although Chinese schools outperform the world in scores, "where they fall short is creativity, originality, divergence from authority."[31] The tests are "a well-designed and continuously perfected machine that effectively and efficiently transmits a narrow content and cultivates prescribed skills."[32]

One Chinese university student wrote with courage and earthy eloquence:

> "In elementary school, they rob us of our independent values; in middle school, they take away our capacity for independent thought; and in university they take away our dreams and idealism. Thus, our brains become as empty as the underpants of a eunuch."[33]

Chinese universities still face the lingering post-1949 Soviet-style emphasis on engineering, manufacturing skills, and hardware, at the expense of management, design, and marketing—that is, software (in the broadest sense), which lubricates industry and commerce.

Foreigners, perhaps having come to China with low expectations and having been surprised by the quality of the Chinese they recruit or deal with, tend to single out the education system as a key factor for China's continued economic success.[34] Meanwhile, Chinese business people still feel the burden of the past and fault China's education for not inculcating entrepreneurial attitudes.[35]

China's emerging middle class is increasingly looking overseas for their children's education. Applications for Chinese universities actually peaked at 10.5 million in 2008 and since then have been declining. According to the Ministry of Education, about 1 million upper-middle school students opted not to take the gaokao, mainly because they intended to study overseas. The number of students going overseas is increasing 20% annually. Since China's economic reforms began in 1978, about 2.6 million Chinese have gone abroad to study, and the annual rate today is around 400,000.[36] The majority go on to find jobs overseas, marry, and put down roots; so far, only 1.1 million out of 2.6 million have returned to China.[37] That said, those that do return play a vital, transformative role.

Business Education Flourishes

A total of 184 universities provide courses for a Master of Business Administration (MBA), with annual enrollment of 30,000 MBAs and 7,000 Executive MBAs (EMBA).[38] The EMBA approach has been an invaluable tool for sharpening the knowledge and skills of business managers who had missed out on education often due to the Cultural Revolution. Many Chinese, typically already having strong business experience, are enrolling at top business schools around the world, from Wharton (the US) to INSEAD (France) and the London Business School.

As we evaluate the impact of this current flourishing of business education, it is not just a question of numbers (by that measure China leads the world), but also about quality.

A decade ago China's press was full of complaints about the poor quality of the country's business education. However, since then enormous progress has been made. The clear leader has been the China Europe International Business School (CEIBS), established by the European Union and the Shanghai government. It has a staff of 400 in Shanghai, Beijing, and Shenzhen, as well as a new campus in Ghana. CEIBS' alumni now total 11,000. It is ranked as having the 15th best MBA program in the world, ahead of Tuck (Dartmouth), Judge (Cambridge, UK), Stern (NYU), and Said (Oxford). Three business schools based in Hong Kong also make the list of top 100 MBAs.[39] Chinese business schools are also making it into the 100 top Master of Science in Management programs (a notch below MBAs).[40]

Even with the expanding volume and quality of home-grown graduates, plus the returnees, there will to be a continued, perennial shortage of business talent. This in turn puts great pressure on Chinese and foreign firms to develop sophisticated programs to attract, train, and retain the staff needed to fuel future growth and innovation.

Economic and Financial Stability

For several decades, it seemed that China's reformed economy would continue to exceed all expectations. Each year, China shot the lights out. That heady period has now passed.

China's economy is going through a painful but necessary adjustment, striving to switch from smoke-stack industry to the knowledge economy. China does not want to remain the "factory of the world." It also seeks to move from a government investment-led model to one that relies on consumer demand. All of this implies structural change.

While the slowdown of China's growth reflects this period of healthy "rebalancing," it also has set off alarm bells across the world. Is the global reaction to the cooling of the Chinese economy justified or an overreaction? Most of China's economic metrics or vital signs remain healthy by global standards.

GDP growth is declining but, at 6.9%, remains one of the highest in the world. The latest government Five Year Plan (2016–20) has set an annual GDP growth target of 6.5% to 7.0%, still a significance pace. Even though this is way below former double-digit growth rates, the actual growth is still massive since the denominator of the ratio is so much greater. Moreover, if the government can manage economic growth to a more sustainable level while maintaining social stability, that would be a massive achievement in its own right. So why is there so much angst about the Chinese economy?

The scene on the ground in China seems to belie the dark predictions that China's economic and financial system is a tower of playing cards and close to collapse. While much of the global concern arises from an unreasonable expectation that China could sustain super high growth, it also justifiably arises from a troubling deterioration of those hitherto healthy metrics.

Although China's foreign exchange reserves (excluding gold) were over US$ 3 trillion at the end of 2015, compared with only US$ 2.3 billion in 1977 and US$ 1 trillion in 2006, making them by far the largest in world, in 2015 they had declined by US$ 500 BN. Though China has a growing trade surplus, this is driven not only by increasing exports but also by declining imports, as the domestic economy cools. China's planned budget deficit is around 3%, not an issue given China's borrowing capacity, but still more in line with US levels than the healthier 1% deficit only two years ago. Fiscal revenues continue to grow, but they are outstripped by fiscal expenditures to stimulate the economy.

The main concern is China's debt burden (public and commercial), described in the foreign press as a "ticking time bomb." The concern is focused not just on the amount of debt, but also its rapid growth.

Public debt has been fueled by a lending binge designed to sustain GDP growth during the last global downturn. In 2008, China launched a stimulus program of around US$ 600 BN, which led to a ballooning of local government debt. An estimated 10,000 local government financing vehicles (LGFVs) were permitted to raise funds through bonds and loans. My experience with LGFVs is that their opaque corporate governance and ill-defined and overlapping roles make them fertile ground for corruption and a recipe for financial disaster. The government is moving urgently to rein them in. Meanwhile, one LGFV has already defaulted on seven bonds with a value of RMB 3.1 BN.[41]

The problem with China's public debt is that it is not clear to anyone, including the government itself, just how large it is. Current estimates of China's ratio of public debt to GDP range from less than 50% (IMF estimate) to 80%. China's National Audit Office revealed the disturbing trend that local government debt was US$ 3.23 trillion in 2013, way up from the US$ 1.75 trillion, or 25% of GDP, in 2010. The concern is how to manage the breakneck growth of China's pubic debt down to a reasonable level.

Officially recorded commercial debt is also a serious headache, said to be about US$ 11 trillion, or 125% of GDP. On top of that we need to include the unofficial so-called "shadow banking," estimates of which range from US$ 2 trillion to US$ 6 trillion (or 70% of GDP). Shadow banking covers a range of financial services: "wealth management products" (investment packages offered by banks, off-balance sheet), pawn shops, and "popular loans" (informal, high interest loans between individuals or companies).

There are factors that can mitigate the risks of the Chinese financial system buckling under the debt load and which are grounds for modest optimism.

Ongoing urbanization will sustain wealth generation at the local level. As urbanization rises from the current level of 51% to the target of 70%, there will be new waves of development and wealth creation moving into the Western interior. This will likely create land price appreciation and the ability to service and repay debt used to finance the infrastructure development.

Residential real estate does not resemble the US bubble. Much of the 2008–09 stimulus financing went through infrastructure projects into real estate. In some places, the construction got ahead of demand, creating empty, so-called "ghost cities." But the financial stress it created relates mainly to the indebtedness of the LGFVs, not to that of the consumer. As one Chinese investment fund head put it to me:

> "In real estate, the problem is not on the market [demand] side. Real estate is red hot. But China's financial fundamentals are good. With home mortgages, buyers

have to put down 30% on their first home and 60% down on their second home. The leverage is low."[42]

That said, the falling value of residential property is undermining the wealth of not just the new rich, but also of many ordinary citizens who plowed their capital into property. Were property prices to go into a deep decline, then China's financial risk, and with it political risk, would be greatly magnified.

China has little or no overseas debt. This means that it can resolve issues of excessive indebtedness or nonperforming loans within its own system and at its own pace, if necessary through the recapitalization of the state banks as has happened in the past.

Much of China's shadow banking plays a useful role. About 20% of shadow banking is highly risky off-balance sheet "wealth management products." The government has described these as Ponzi schemes and one, involving US$ 7.6 BN of online investment products, affecting 900,000 investors, has already been closed down. It is easy to see that if these financial products were to continue to unravel on a larger scale, the resulting public outcry could undermine political stability. But importantly, "80% of [shadow banking] is simply filling the gap that the official system does not want to fill."[43]

The key will be to bring shadow banking out of the shadows, so that the true risks can be understood and addressed. Interest rate reform (ending the floor on lending rates and the cap on deposit rates) is undermining the rationale for shadow banking and reducing its growth. As one foreign investment banker put it:

> "Chinese banks are finally addressing the financing needs of SMEs [small- and medium-sized enterprises]. There is greater flexibility in interest rates that can be charged. If SMEs were paying 18% interest to shadow banking, they surely will be willing to pay 10% interest to official banks. The official banks are now able to eat the rice bucket of shadow banking. Now with flexibility on interest rates, official banks can lend at interest rates that reflect the true risk."[44]

In addition to the risk-mitigating factors outlined above, we can also layer in our knowledge of how China has over the last four decades successfully handled complex economic and financial risks. But while there was until recently a widespread confidence that the CCP had mastered the levers of running a modern economy, we are finding that it is looking more like a novice and, at times, out of its depth when it comes to market-driven economics. Its fumbling during a stock market meltdown drove home just how skin-deep many of the newfound skills are.

Confronting the Environmental Crisis

China's breakneck growth has been accompanied by catastrophic environmental destruction.

Twenty years ago, the key catchphrase from Deng Xiaoping was that "development is a rigid principle." The drive for "development" to pull China out of poverty and stagnation left little room for debate about what kind of development to adopt. China embraced an automobile-centric approach that relied on the broad impact of the auto production value chain in pulling up the rest of the economy. Back then, when I asked a Chinese official about the environmental impact of mass car ownership, he shrugged off the issue, pointing out that the pollution sent the positive message that China was achieving economic takeoff. The government bristled at concern over China's greenhouse gas emissions, seeing it as an attempt to stop China from achieving its legitimate national goals of wealth and strength.

China's environmental crisis has come to a head: air pollution, unsafe drinking water, water shortages, poisoning from metals, contaminated baby formula, poisoned former industrial sites, and more. Plus, of course, there is China's impact on global climate change.

This is an area where public opinion has flexed its muscle. The government has belatedly but vigorously taken up the issue of environmental protection. In 2006, it published a report showing that environmental degradation and pollution represented an annual cost to the nation of more than US$ 80 BN, or 3% of GDP, a sum that should be subtracted from reported GDP to arrive at a true "green GDP." These figures have continued to be monitored and the cost was said to be US$ 248 BN, or 2.5% of GDP, in 2010.

Although adding green GDP targets to local government performance objectives were abandoned due to resistance from officials and disagreement over methodology, nonetheless the central government remains committed to drawing a line under the "development at any cost" model and is rebalancing priorities.

Car ownership is being restricted. Capital and government subsidies are being plowed into developing electric vehicles (EVs) and batteries for them. Polluting industries—aluminum smelting, for instance—are being relocated to the less populated interior and with cleaner, more efficient technology. Fines imposed on polluting companies have been increased to a level that hurts. China is also tackling the critical issue of how it generates its power—its energy mix. Although coal is used to produce 60% of China's electricity (and 80% of all energy needs, if we include direct use for industry such as cement or steel), hydro and wind already account for 20% and 5% of electricity generation capacity, respectively.[45]

While by 2030 the total power generation capacity is projected to more than double, coal-fired generation will fall to around 44% of the much larger total, while solar and wind power will account for 13% and 14%, respectively. These new sources of energy, plus biomass and geothermal, will together contribute to a lowering of China's CO_2 emissions. Nuclear power will account for around 6% of electricity production by 2030.[46] Though nuclear waste disposal issues remain unresolved, concerns over safety are in part addressed through China's mastery of Generation III technology, which permits passive safety, thus reducing the risk of meltdown.

The priority given by the government to renewable energy sources has also propelled China into a strong global position in the manufacturing that supplies this industry. Chinese wind turbines and solar power equipment account for about 20% and 26% of the global market, respectively. In solar, China is present throughout the value chain, from producing its own polysilicon to photovoltaic (PV) cells and modules.

China will likely not only be the largest producer and user of electric vehicles (EVs), but is also set to become the world's fastest adopter of new urban mobility solutions using internet social media platforms to provide consumers with access to fleets of EVs as an alternative to private car ownership.[47]

While *the China paradox* opened up the path to development, the powerful combination of unleashed commercial forces and a CCP exercising a light, noninterventionist hand had the unintended, but perfectly predictable, disastrous impact on the environment. Now, as the central government struggles to reverse this trend, it meets heavy resistance from vested interests at the local level. In a striking admission of this issue, the Ministry of Environmental Protection, in an attempt to control its local agencies, has set up regional bureaus with staff from the central ministry.

The Mega Domestic Market

For China, its domestic market is a strategic advantage that distinguishes it from other Asian economies, such as South Korea, Taiwan, and Thailand. The market is not only already very large, but will continue to grow. In the wake of the economic takeoff of the coastal cities, the central and Western regions present wave-upon-wave of development potential. As urbanization moves from around half the population to the target of 70%, there is the prospect of further decades of wealth creation.

The scale of the domestic market accords China a series of major key competitive advantages.

China is not heavily export-oriented. Its ratio of exports to GDP is about 30%, compared to 74% and 57% in Taiwan and South Korea, respectively. Moreover, if you compare China's exports with GDP on a value-added basis, the ratio falls to around 10%. That's because the proportion of product imported for assembly and re-export has been growing as Chinese exports become increasingly high tech. As China becomes even less reliant on exports, it is creating built-in resilience against the impact of global downturns.

The large domestic market gives China *the ability to attract foreign investment and technology*. Though it is tough to do business in China and may put one's technology at risk, the scale of the Chinese "opportunity," however illusory, has proven to be a powerful magnet for attracting foreign investment.

Chinese firms use the domestic market to launch, test, and improve their products; to develop management skills and organization; to achieve economies of scale; and to accumulate capital to support growth. It provides a low-risk test ground prior to taking on tougher global markets.

Gleaming New Ground Transportation Infrastructure

China's new ground transportation infrastructure—its expressways, ports, bridges, tunnels, high-speed rail, subways, and its future EV fleets—will be of critical importance to China's future growth, not only linking China to the world, but also helping crucially to integrate the highly regional and fragmented domestic economy.

This excellent infrastructure marks China off from India, which is held back by its poor ground transportation. President Obama expressed admiration for China's transportation infrastructure, saying it is "embarrassing" when he compares it with that of US. Though, as part of the hangover from the developmental spurt, China's cities are snarled with traffic jams, overall its transportation is a strong foundation for future growth.[48]

China has built the largest expressway system in the world, totaling 105,000 km, compared to the 77,000 km in the US. Its high-speed rail system (defined as speeds of greater than 200 kmh) is 16,000 km long, the largest in world. China accounts for seven of the world's top container ports.

The expansion of Shanghai port, now the largest in the world with an annual throughput of 33MM containers (twenty-foot equivalent unit, or TEUs), was achieved through constructing the new Yangshan deep-water port, which is linked to the mainland by a 33 km sea bridge, the longest in the world. Shanghai's old city (Puxi), on the west bank of the Huangpu River, has been connected to the Pudong New Development Area on the other side by 7 bridges and 12 tunnels.

Most major Chinese cities now have a subway system. Shanghai has 14 lines and is the longest system in the world. Beijing, with 17 lines, is the world's second in length and the world's busiest in terms of ridership, handling 3 *billion* journeys per year and holding the world record for one day— 11 million! Guangzhou already has 8 lines and plans a total of 21. China is also making great strides in other modes, for instance bus rapid transit (whereby buses run along routes segregated from the other traffic), which is operating in 20 Chinese cities and is planned for 9 more. New urban mobility solutions using EVs will begin to reduce pressure for private car ownership.

The CCP has shown pragmatism in inviting foreign companies to operate its public transport, such as in subways and buses, as a way to introduce new capital, management skills, and to raise efficiency (and in turn to reduce government subsidies). Should the service underperform, the foreign operator is held responsible, deflecting criticism away from the government.

Government-Sponsored Research and Development

China's expenditure on research and development (R&D), excluding that for the military, has seen double-digit growth over recent years, reaching

US$ 193 BN, or just over 2% of GDP. In value terms, this is larger than that of Japan and Europe. It is currently around 60% of the US expenditure and projected to match that of the US by 2022.[49]

Only about 22% of China's R&D is directly government-funded, surprisingly low compared to about 30% in the US. But to capture the full impact of the Chinese government's role in orchestrating China's R&D we need to also consider the multiple ways in which it supports R&D, in addition to just funding.

Under the Soviet-style central planning system, R&D had been concentrated in research institutes divorced from the factories, defined by bureaucrats rather than by consumer or market needs. Upstream, pure research was neglected in favor of practical application-focused R&D, thus starving the nation of the life blood of fundamental innovation.

Since the reforms, the government has dealt effectively with that dysfunctional legacy. In 1985, the CCP admitted the old system hampered "the full use of the intelligence and creativity of scientists and engineers." Deng called for "an atmosphere in which top-notch persons can show their true potential."

The bloated scientific bureaucracy was scaled back and research pushed down to enterprises. The Chinese Academy of Sciences (CAS) was reformed, with cuts to its 60,000 employees and a consolidation of its 120 overlapping institutes.[50] There has been a migration of scientists and engineers into the business sector, which now dominates China's R&D.

Chinese planners today call for the nation to:

"Promote industrial upgrading by scientific innovation. Guide the investment, talents and technology flow to enterprises, promote the strategic union of production and R&D, and increase the industrial core competitiveness."[51]

The "union of production and R&D" addresses the issue of R&D being over-concentrated in research institutes, completely divorced from the companies that would ultimately produce the goods. In recent decades, government R&D investment has been channeled to enterprises, either through direct grants or loans from state-owned banks. Many government research institutes have grasped the opportunity and become commercial entities. Notable among these is the world-leading computer maker, China's Lenovo, which started life as an institute under CAS.

This shift of R&D from research institutes to companies may have gone too far since it has reduced basic research while encouraging commercial applications, thus ironically stifling the innovation that can spawn new generations of products.

The Chinese government's role in spurring R&D and innovation has borne a strong resemblance to the earlier efforts of other Asian economies, such as Japan, South Korea, and Taiwan, to move up the technology ladder.

Japan's Ministry of International Trade and Industry (MITI) funded research and investment that contributed to Japan's postwar economic "miracle."[52] In the 1970s, MITI actively intervened in Japan's machine tool industry, leading to Japanese global dominance of a new breed of numerically controlled machine tools and machining centers.[53] Korea's Economic Planning Board in the 1970s provided low-interest loans and tax holidays, which were instrumental in creating the shipbuilding industry dominated by the likes of Hyundai and Daewoo. In 1973, the Taiwan government established the Industrial Technology Research Institute (ITRI),[54] which was instrumental in creating Taiwan's dominance in semiconductors and PC computers, especially laptops.

The Chinese government's science and technology program for 2006 to 2020 took as its slogan "indigenous innovation, leapfrogging in priority fields, enabling development, and leading the future."[55] It defined "indigenous innovation" as including not only "original innovation" (a very high target), but also the revealingly termed "re-innovation based on the assimilation and absorption of imported technology" (a much more achievable target). "Re-innovation" (from learning, improving, and licensing all the way through to outright IPR theft) is a key aspect of China's economic catch-up strategy.

Government support for R&D comes in many forms. First there is policy setting and economic planning, handled by the NDRC, the Ministry of Science and Technology (MOST), plus the MIIT. Once the specific plans are approved from the Ministry of Finance, funds are directed to projects at the institute or at the enterprise level through some 70 government agencies, the largest of which are MOST, CAS, and the National Natural Science Foundation of China; and also through loans from state-owned banks.

The 863 State High-Tech Research and Development Plan launched in 1986 by MOST covered biotech, space, IT, automation, and energy. Over 16 years, RMB 11 BN of funds was disbursed to 5,200 R&D programs employing 40,000 researchers in 200 institutes, 100 universities, and 100 enterprises. Results from the plan included supercomputers and the Shenzhou spacecraft.[56] In 1997, the 973 Program, China's National Basic Research Program, focusing on energy (including nuclear), natural resources, and environmental protection, was launched, and in the period to 2008 it invested RMB 8.2 BN into 382 projects. In 2013, MOST provided RMB 22 BN of R&D funding through the main 863 and 973 programs.[57]

New efforts with a focus on the underlying technology, rather than mainly on manufacturing, require a much more costly approach. In 1995, the government launched Project 909 to reduce China's dependence on semiconductor imports, but with only mixed results. The government more recently pledged RMB 1 trillion to basic chip design in an effort to become less reliant on foreign firms. The NDRC has made available US$ 20 BN to Chinese firms acquiring foreign semiconductor companies. In 2012, the government announced investment of US$ 1.5 trillion to support a program to address strategic emerging industries, which as of 2017 included 11 areas including next generation IT, biotechnology, and new energy vehicles. [58]

How then does government support for companies mesh with the market economy? In the ICT sector, the two market leaders are Huawei and ZTE, producers of telecom infrastructure equipment, one a private firm and the other state-owned, both based in Shenzhen. They have a very strong rivalry, and each has its own R&D, unique products, and branding; and they compete for customers and for talented engineers and salespeople.

But that should not lead us to miss the reality that, in such a strategic sector as ICT, ultimately the interests of the nation transcend the competition between companies and converge behind the scenes into a centralized and single-minded approach, driven by the CCP. The competition that does exist pushes each company to improve, innovate, and excel, but at the end of the day it is as if they are just different runners on the national athletics team.[59]

Where do things converge behind the scenes into what we can call China, Inc.? Given the rivalries between government ministries, this convergence and the setting of broad goals occur principally at a higher level, through the State Council's Leading Groups, led by the premier or vice premiers, or increasingly within the CCP top echelons. Foreign ICT companies face not only well-run Chinese firms, but a behind-the-scenes approach coordinated by the Chinese government that can call the shots when needed.

The Mobile Handset Example

China's mobile handset sector is an example of how the government has actively nurtured "national champions." In 1991, it launched a plan to create locally made and Chinese-branded mobile handsets, providing RMB 1.4 BN in state grants over five years to SOE players such as Xiahua, Kejian, Soutec, and EastCom. It took some time to show results. But in 1998, CCP head Jiang Zemin triumphantly made a call from a GSM handset made by the Chinese firm Xiahua. Foreign competitors took a while to wake up to the challenge.

In 1999, when the Chinese share of the China handset market was only 5%, the government set market share targets of 10% for 2001 and 21% for 2003. As it turned out, Chinese players in fact achieved a market share of 21% in 2001 and a stunning 56% in 2003, before falling back to 48%, as the Koreans gained traction and incumbent players such as Motorola found ways to deliver a lower-priced product in the Chinese mass market.

The government carefully limited the issuance of manufacturing licenses to nine Chinese firms out of 30 that had applied, with the goal of achieving some "managed competition" while allowing room for these nine firms to grow. It set company-specific quotas limiting the import of mobile phone kits for assembly in China with the goal of spurring local production.

Moreover, by 2000, access to mobile handset technology had greatly improved, dramatically favoring new entrants. Foreign suppliers of integrated circuit "chipsets," (which are the guts of a handset), such as Lucent, Motorola, Philips, and Siemens had strong relationships with Chinese firms. Motorola provided chipsets to EastCom not just for its production of Motorola-branded product but also for EastCom's own new handset. Foreign suppliers, impatient at the slow progress being made with CDMA and 3G infrastructure in China, were willing to sustain their chip sales through selling into the Chinese low-end market, even though they were unwittingly building competitors who would quickly ascend the quality ladder and take them on.

Other components, such as ear pieces, antennae, and casings, were all readily available. Since handset production on a subcontracted basis was migrating to China, there was no shortage of firms that could supply Chinese former subcontractors, now turned competitors.

Chinese handset makers came from varied backgrounds and sought to take advantage of their domestic sales channels. Telecom switchgear manufacturers, such as EastCom, ZTE, Bird, and Huawei, sought to utilize their close links with the telephone companies. Others, such as Konka, Xiahua, Kejian, and Haier, had a consumer goods background and could make effective use of their efficient distribution channels to sell the handsets.

At the heart of the problem for the foreign handset brands was a rapidly changing market structure. There was explosive 95% annual growth in mobile phone subscribers (they went from 10 million in 1997 to 100 million in 2001). In the same period, China's mobile phone penetration rate rose from less than 1% to 6%. Indicative of the growth potential in China, this compared to South Korea's penetration rate, which in 2001 stood at 56% and that of North America and Europe at around 100%. As mobile phone ownership shifted from business managers to workers, small traders, and students, an enormous mass market was being created.

The Chinese handset producers were successful in addressing this mass market, selling attractive looking handsets at a price far lower than the foreign brands, but still with comparable functionality. Quality issues, such as notoriously poor ear pieces, were successfully dealt with.

Market incumbents in China, such as Nokia and Motorola, responded aggressively to the body blows rained down on them from Chinese entrants and adopted new strategies to address the emerging mass market in China. They achieved a lower price point through the redesign of their phones, outsourcing more of the production and simplifying their overly complex distribution chain. The foreign players made a successful comeback. While the rich profit margins became a thing of the past, on the plus-side the market was by then so much larger.

Today the situation in China with smartphones shares some similarities with what we saw developing in the year 2000 with the earlier generation of mobile handsets. However, the government role is *not* a defining factor in this.

There is now a plethora of Chinese smartphones on the market, based on the Android operating system (OS), competing against the likes of Apple and Samsung. But compared to 15 years ago, market success is defined not just by manufacturing skills, but also by the ability to create designs and apps that satisfy the consumer. This skill set is something still being developed by Chinese firms and does not lend itself to the old style of government support and funding.

Nonetheless, this has not stopped the Chinese government from interfering and complaining that that 97.7% of China's 300 smartphone producers are Android-based. "Even though the Android system is open source, the core technology and technology roadmap is strictly controlled by Google," with the result that Chinese firms "constantly face Google's commercial discrimination, including the delay of timing on code sharing due to agreement restrictions."

The government's interest in creating China's own smartphone OS, coupled with efforts to restrict the Android system, lies in a desire to gain access to mobile phones for security reasons and has little to do with commercial factors. This move has met with skepticism from Chinese smartphone manufacturers, which are perfectly happy with the Android OS and are beginning to make their mark overseas. Few believe a new China-developed OS is needed or desirable.[60] In this instance, government involvement in R&D would hold Chinese business back. Fortunately, this irrational effort looks unlikely to bear fruit.

Furthermore, while the earlier reverse engineering of the old GSM mobile handsets demonstrated the decisive power of the government to incubate new production that could compete with global incumbents, it still did not stack up as an innovation breakthrough. In light of the history of meager returns from massive government investment in technology and the serious issues of governance and corruption, there is good reason to be skeptical about China's R&D potential.

China's R&D Results Are Patchy

China has achieved a great deal in its space program. It grew out of China's nuclear weapons program, which achieved its first atomic bomb explosion in 1964, followed by a nuclear bomb test in 1967, plus ballistic missiles to deliver them. On the civilian side, China has put its first man into orbit, and plans a manned space station by 2020 and exploration of the Moon and Mars. Other examples of strong R&D results include China's leading the world in large-scale gene sequencing.

Moreover, by some standards, China's R&D performance appears impressive, be it patents filed, academic articles published, or the volume of funds directed into R&D. But such statistics can mask underlying structural issues.

Despite the rapid growth in overall R&D expenditure in China, there has been decline in scientific research in favor of product development with identifiable commercial outcomes. Between 1995 and 2011, expenditure in China on basic research fell from 5.2% to 4.7% of all R&D funding, while for applied research there was a precipitous fall from 26% to 12% of the total during the same period. A Chinese academic has written:

> "The low share of scientific research expenditure has negatively affected China's innovation capability and may jeopardize China's ambition to become an innovation-oriented nation. The shrinking of applied research is a serious problem, because applied research links basic and development research."[61]

Great weight has been put on creating manufacturing capability, while the push upstream into the science, design, and software that make the manufacturing possible has been neglected. The government is mindful of this issue, as can be seen from its evolving approach to the semiconductor industry.

In 1995, Project 909 was launched to reduce dependence on semiconductor imports and it achieved major success in attracting investment into China by semiconductor producers such as Japan's NEC and firms from Taiwan and the US. But with the exception of some low-end "commodity chips" used for certain consumer products, this knowledge transfer excluded access to strategic skills in *chip design*, which remained largely offshore and in the hands of the foreign firms such as Intel, Samsung, and Qualcomm. In addition to paying royalties for chip designs, China today spends heavily on semiconductor imports. China also is active in global markets seeking to acquire firms with that expertise.

Some aspects of the governance of China's R&D, notably the role of the CCP, are unlikely to change:

> "The restrictions that hinder innovation ... permeate deeply into the Chinese economy. They are ties that bind. They create a constrained environment for Chinese engineers, an environment that would be unacceptable to their peers in other industrialized countries. They limit innovation by favoring ideas that emphasize stability rather than transformation. You find this atmosphere in universities, of course, but it is also prevalent in laboratories, offices, and engineering professional societies."[62]

Recently, light has been shone on how endemic corruption has inevitably reached into China's state-funded R&D. The anti-corruption campaign has netted more than 50 scientists and two senior CCP officials in Guangdong, who were accused of siphoning off government R&D funds. In another case, leading scientists (including one academician) were accused of diverting funds from projects and two were sentenced to ten years in prison.[63] Only 40% of China's total government R&D budget actually gets to the research it was allocated to, while the rest is accounted for by business expenses. To quote a Chinese academic: "If China spends so much money, why haven't we achieved more significant accomplishments? Part of the reason may be that much of the money is stolen."[64]

In 2014, the Chinese government announced that "government will no longer directly manage technology projects"[65] and that MOST would lose its current role in this. This bombshell was aimed at addressing the problem that competitively bid projects—that is, the largest ones—are awarded "on the basis of personal connections, not scientific validity."[66]

It is easy to see how MOST was forced to announce its withdrawal from active management of R&D funding. MOST is generally recognized as having underperformed over the years. It worked closely with the Ministry of Railways on high-speed rail. Although China's high-speed rail is functioning well after a disastrous accident involving poor oversight over a research institute responsible for signaling, this was at the cost of massive corruption that left the railways under a massive pile of debt. The former Minister of Railways is serving a life sentence for corruption.

Still there is the prospect that, although enterprises will continue to be the biggest spenders on R&D, principally on product-related development, the government will remain the key force driving the broader hunt for "indigenous innovation" and technology leap-frogging that has so far largely eluded the nation.

Connecting with the Consumer

Whether it involves cars or mobile phones, Chinese firms now have easy access to the technology and components needed to produce consumer products, especially since many of the foreign component suppliers have migrated to China. What has proved more challenging for China has been mastering the design skills needed to create attractive products that resonate with the consumer. But if we look at smartphones, there are encouraging signs that Chinese players will finally be able to break out of the trap of low-quality, low price, and poor design (feel and look) that have bedeviled them to date.

The China smartphone market is the largest in the world but is very crowded. Chinese brands such as Huawei and Xiaomi (sales of 108MM and

70MM handsets in 2015, respectively) jostle for market leadership with foreign players such as Apple and Samsung. Other Chinese firms, such as Coolpad and Lenovo, are also competing strongly.

Given the China smartphone market's competitive intensity, profitability is becoming an issue. Yulong, the manufacturer of Coolpad, despite its market strength in the high end, saw its net profit margin decline to 2.3%. Xiaomi also has razor thin margins. Predictably, Chinese smartphone producers are increasingly looking to overseas markets to sustain their growth. This move is a vital test of whether Chinese consumer design can take on the world.

Huawei is selling its new Ascend P6 in 100 countries, including across Europe. It has many of the features of the latest iPhones and Samsung phones, but is a good deal cheaper.[67]

Chinese smartphones use the Linux-based Android operating platform, to which they have free and open access despite Android being owned by Google. Globally 64% of smartphones and tablets now run on the Android platform, which is customizable by manufacturers. A wide array of application software written specifically for the platform is available.

Low-end smartphones sold by Huawei, ZTE, Yulong, and other Chinese firms have come under heavy criticism from American consumers. While Yulong sells a full range of models in China, including a high-end one with a titanium case, in the US it has focused on "budget shoppers," with a price of US$ 99 for a noncontract phone with prepaid service. In online reviews of this phone, most opinions were at the lowest level (one star) with comments such as, "This phone is horrible," "stay away from this turkey," "please beware," "sucks."[68]

With smartphones, the design aspect is critical: the thickness, size of the screen, shape, color, all combine with the functionality and software of the phone to produce a consumer experience, a feel and touch that appeals.

Huawei has sought to innovate in design and functionality, building the world's thinnest smartphone, for instance, a water-resistant model, and one with the largest display—6 inches. Having plugged away patiently,[69] Huawei shows clear signs that it may be turning the corner in the US, where its high-end phone has received positive reviews:

> "Apart from being the slimmest smartphone yet at 6.2 millimeters thick, many will find the Ascend P6 to be the most beautifully designed Android OS mobile device as well. This is quite surprising for a manufacturer that generally has not cared one bit about the design of its phones in the past. This is why Huawei has managed to get the interest of possible purchasers with this truly beautiful product."[70]

Consumer feedback must be music to the ears of Huawei executives:

> "The P6 shows that Huawei can build high-quality phones. What goes inside those phones can easily be improved, but making something that feels and looks good is a harder skill to nail. Huawei appears to have made good ground here.... The takeaway message here is that Huawei means business."

Chinese smartphones are achieving the hitherto missing design quality, permitting them to compete against the iPhone, which, although assembled in China, is advertised as "designed by Apple in California."

Prospects of Deepening Economic Reform?

Once Hu Jintao's leadership ended, the era of massive infrastructure investment was widely and openly criticized as being fundamentally unsustainable, a wasteful, inefficient, environmentally polluting, and often corrupt way of supporting economic growth. The Xi Jinping regime that followed was left with the task of "cleaning up the mess" (as one Chinese observer put it to me) from the earlier stimulus program. A rebalancing of the economy was begun.

There began a consolidation of industry where massive overcapacity had reduced or eliminated profitability. The government has instructed companies in 19 sectors, including coal mining, steel, aluminum, and shipbuilding to cut capacity and reduce production.

The current regime shows some determination to force things to happen. "Zombie enterprises" are being merged, reorganized, having their debt restructured, or even bankrupted and liquidated. Although this process is expected to entail several million redundancies, the hope is that the unemployment will be sucked up by the services sector, which is growing faster than the rest of the economy and now exceeds 50% of GDP.

Massive mergers have already taken place, including that of Cosco Shipping and China Shipping, the nation's two largest shipping firms, which created a firm with combined assets (ships, wharfs, shipbuilding, etc.) of RMB 600 BN. Baosteel is merging with Wuhan Iron and Steel to create combined steel capacity of 60 MM tons. The same process is under way in the cement industry. But it remains to be seen just how effective these mergers will be in forcing consolidation. The danger is that rather than reducing capacity, this is simply creating even larger bad companies that will not be allowed to fail.

Chinese citizens still save about half of their income to cover health, education, and retirement. Though the weak social safety net is being improved, in the short term it is unrealistic to expect a huge uptick in consumer spending. So, inevitably, propping up economic growth through infrastructure investment will continue. But those funds may be allocated more smartly and efficiently with an emphasis on smaller cities and townships, rather than creating unlivable megacities.

Steps are being taken to reform the "residency permit" (hukou) system, which has been in place since 1958 and restricts the ability of rural citizens to gain residency in cities, seriously hampering rational flows of labor and talent. Without a hukou, there is no access to city health benefits or children's education, creating an underclass of illegal urban migrants.

Although hukou reform is challenging since it places a heavy burden on public finances needed to cover the new residents and meets with resistance from existing urban residents, pilot programs are already under way. It is estimated that if 160 million migrants could obtain city hukou, then the nation's consumption would increase by 11.8%.[71] The expectation is that even if China's GDP growth were to slow to as low as 3% to 4%, the more consumption-led economy would provide the needed additional wealth creation.

If the CCP can wean China off the previous hyper-growth while maintaining wealth creation and avoiding civil disorder through a smooth rebalancing of the economy, then it would be a massive contribution to the reform process and a remarkable achievement.

The CCP also continues "structural reforms," including the reduction of the bureaucratic burden on businesses. It calls for further diversification of SOE ownership through inviting investment from private firms. It pledges a more rational and fair allocation of bank financing to POEs on conditions similar to those enjoyed by SOEs.

These are useful changes but amount to tinkering around the edges rather than taking on the bigger, overarching issue of the CCP's role in the economy. This is not a new topic. In 1980, Deng argued that the CCP should reflect on whether the role it plays in a given enterprise is constructive or useful. If not, then the CCP should pull back and avoid "having a finger in each pie," and thus "the party's prestige will grow."[72] In 1987, CCP head Zhao Ziyang stressed that CCP power should be separated out of factories and universities.[73]

At the height of the reforms (under Premier Zhu Rongji), the CCP maintained its presence in SOEs but used a light hand, minimizing its interference in business matters. But during the "lost ten years" of the Hu Jintao regime, the CCP beefed up its hold on enterprises. Although policy statements under the current Xi administration call for further SOE reform, actions speak louder than words. SOE leaders feel strongly that, in fact, the CCP is drastically tightening its grip on their firms, further "going backward" and reverting to a pre-reform model. They will tell you in private that the "separation of party and enterprise" (<u>dangqi fenkai)</u> is a crucial unfinished piece of the reforms. They express frustration at the way that even the stock market-listed part of their SOE is subject to interference by the CCP, in the setting of salaries and bonuses, for instance.

Some liberal, highly market-oriented Chinese economists openly urge the government to pursue further reforms that will stop the interference of the CCP in business governance. They vigorously oppose China's new version of socialism, which is seen as an unholy alliance between the SOEs, the state banks, local government, and the CCP.

One such liberal who is a former SOE chairman and still, remarkably, a member of the CCP recently stated:

> "China's current problem is that the government-dominated economic structure has led to the collusion of public power and capital, and hence special interest groups have been formed.... The key to achieving this goal is to change the functions of the government, which means the government's role must transform from dominating the economy to a role to provide public goods and services."[74]

He went on to say:

> "China's market-oriented reform still has a long way to go. The promotion of the rule of law, and a new round of comprehensive reform in the political system and in social governance is inevitable."[75]

He is correct when he says that a true market economy is a long way off, but he is surely over-optimistic with regard to the inevitability of political and social reform. Assuming that the CCP is still in power, there is little prospect of the end game being anything remotely like liberal capitalism. One senior Chinese business leader during a one-to-one meeting with me characterized the system as state capitalism (a commonly held view) and then smiled and added candidly that "some even talk about it being like prewar [World War II] Germany."

Another SOE manager put it to me: "SOEs are driven by political interests. If there is no political reason they will not act on anything. One party [the Communist Party] monopolizes resources."[76]

The views by that liberal Chinese economist quoted above are remote from those of China's current leadership. When economic reform entails, as he puts it, "comprehensive" reform of the political order, then it will meet a brick wall since it goes to the heart of the CCP's monopoly of power. One may speculate that his view was either naïve or perhaps, more plausibly, a careful part of the Chinese government's deceptive soft power messaging to the West.

The current rebalancing of the economy is a reshaping of reforms in a more sustainable direction, a significant retuning or refining of the economic model underlying *the China paradox*. But the optimism over a true deepening of the reforms that accompanied Xi's appointment has been replaced by a gloomy opinion that the CCP has little intention of pursuing that route. The CCP remains focused on its own survival and views any dismantling of its role in the economy as a slippery slope to irrelevance and a fate similar to that of the Soviet Union under Gorbachev.

We should not imagine for one minute that the CCP is looking to either create a true Western-style market economy or for that matter would agree to take a back seat. Even more concerning, it today seems bent on reasserting itself in SOEs and, in so doing, undermining the past achievements of the reforms.

It is of course possible that Xi is first regaining full control of the nation to ensure there is sustainable short-term progress, with the sincere intention of later reinvigorating and deepening the reform process. But the evidence does not point in that direction. In contrast to what we saw at the peak of the reforms when the CCP exhibited a willingness to experiment and learn, its leaders today show an overconfidence, rigidity, and autocratic spirit that does not bode well for the sustainability of *the China paradox*.

It is as if the CCP—having dismantled central planning, put the state sector back on its feet, and created a hybrid economy with some room for the private sector—is declaring the victory with a new viable version of one-party autocratic socialism. Unfortunately, this posture flies in the face of China's urgent desire to move up the economic ladder toward an innovative knowledge economy. The CCP's "locking down of the information environment" in response to the "digital subversion of the PRC" is the kind of action that will prevent China from achieving its true economic potential.[77]

Chapter 10
Conclusion

China's history is littered with examples of failed attempts to create true change. Typically, the forces of conservatism massively outweighed the impulses for economic modernization. In 1949 China passed up a half-chance to put itself on the path to prosperity. Instead, under Mao, it imported the dysfunctional Soviet system lock, stock, and barrel, and on top of that fostered brutal internal conflict. That lethal cocktail set China back decades.

Since Mao's demise, China has given birth to *the China paradox*, which has proved so far to be a winning formula. China's hybrid developmental model has worked well since the forces of change, of entrepreneurialism, of innovation have enjoyed a productive equilibrium with the ruling CCP, which, while not abandoning its autocratic instincts, has displayed remarkable pragmatism in leading the economic reforms. Incompatible forces unexpectedly became mutually supportive and aligned. Hence, *the China paradox*.

In launching the economic reforms, Deng Xiaoping was sailing into uncharted waters. It was about learning through doing, an ad hoc experimentation and a search for what might work. It was a seat-of-the-pants exercise that ultimately delivered beyond all expectations. The reforms unleashed creativity and energy throughout Chinese society. The pent-up energy of the Chinese people could find expression after being kept for so long under lock and key.

Deng's bold pragmatism was critical in drawing a line under the Mao era and sending the signal to society that there were very few limits on what could be considered. But that should not lead us to conclude that Deng did not have a vision. Through the twists and turns, he never deviated from his core vision of a prosperous China that continued to be ruled autocratically by the CCP. What he did not have was a clear path to that goal.

The fundamental goal of the CCP is to stay in power. When we acknowledge that simple but core fact, then China is less puzzling. Things fall into place. People ask why a ruling autocratic communist party would provide the business class room to grow. The answer is that wealth creation underpins the longevity of CCP rule. What seems a paradox is perfectly logical.

DOI 10.1515/9781501507212-010

The reforms were chaotic, with a stop-and-go pattern of rapid progress followed by clampdowns or readjustments to reign in what was seen as "market anarchy" and also to put a lid the rising democratic expectations of civil society. As the old straitjacket of central planning was dismantled, power was devolved to the local level, where, despite China's unitary legal system, almost federal style variations were permitted. As the government fretted over how to resolve the problem of the SOEs, the private sector of industry emerged and proved vital in creating wealth and jobs. This bought time for the government to sort out the heavy legacy of the Mao years. Civil society started to stir, spurred on by the internet and social media. Environmentalists prodded the government, which belatedly began to admit the air pollution crisis. Religion flourished, filling the gap left by the retreat of Marxism. Private commerce returned and the street cries of small traders again rang out in the alleys of Beijing.

The positive balance of forces within *the China paradox* was at times disrupted. In 1989, in response to a perceived challenge to its rule, the CCP has no compunction about turning its guns on its citizens. Officials who abhorred the free-wheeling new order quickly sought to roll back the reforms. But the cat was out of the bag. The Chinese had grasped their new-found economic freedom. Deng, doggedly sticking to his thesis that growing prosperity was the key to the CCP's survival, fought back to restore momentum to the reform process.

Many younger Chinese are today not aware of the vibrancy, fresh air, and relative openness of the first decades of the reforms. It was a heady time of experimentation and breakthroughs. I worked with reformist officials who pushed through new regulations permitting foreigners to own their whole investment and not have to form a JV. Firms that had been forced to hide under the smokescreen of being a TVE had their private status recognized under law. The CCP began to welcome private businessmen into their ranks. Senior CCP leaders abandoned some of the opacity that surrounded one-party rule. Zhao Ziyang (CCP head, 1987–89) held press conferences in which he talked without notes for two hours. Zhu Rongji (premier, 1998–2003) boldly forced SOEs to modernize and risked his political life by pushing for accession to the WTO. The government played a vital role in China's emerging business models, which we have documented.

The China paradox emerged as a hybrid model with a mixture of spontaneous economic activity and bureaucratic guidance. The model was humming with positive energy while underpinned by the government as the backstop to prevent any meltdown.

Until a few years ago, China's rise seemed all but inevitable. The CCP faced challenges but always seemed to muddle through and come out as an unlikely hero. It had managed the mixed-economy effectively, achieved smooth political succession and allowed civil society some space to grow. Today, the verdict has swung from adulation to serious concerns.

While *the China paradox* proved successful in kick-starting the economy, there has been a heavy cost to this model, resulting in China actually turning out to be an underperformer. Unbridled development has left China with a serious hangover. Unprecedented wealth creation is a mixed blessing since it opened the door to corruption on a grand scale that amounts to nationwide kleptocracy. While hundreds of millions of Chinese have indeed been pulled out of (or have pulled themselves out of) poverty, much of the wealth has gone missing, siphoned off into the families of top leaders, salted away in real estate in London or New York.

The problems stem from Deng's laissez-faire tactics encapsulated in his slogan "development is a firm principle," allowing things to rip, so that change could take hold. The CCP looks less and less like the architect of a new order that can stand the test of time. It missed the opportunity to learn from other societies' experience while reveling in the economic takeoff. Growing air pollution back then was seen as a badge of honor, a sign that China had somehow mastered the principles of "development." Things having been permitted to rip, it has proven hard to rein them in. Regulations on environmental protection, industrial consolidation, illegal local taxes, and a host of other aspects are systematically obstructed by local interests. The CCP, which had seemed to have learned the ropes of importing foreign concepts such as the stock market, has more recently looked incompetent and out of its depth, shaking our faith in its economic governance.

If China's recent track record looks rather tattered around the edges, the future is even more challenging.

We have looked at key factors that could continue to drive China forward and others that might derail that progress. China's excellent newly built transportation infrastructure sets it apart from nations such as India. China's educational system still suffers from the Confucian and communist legacies but functions well nonetheless. Coupled with the impact of students returning from overseas, China is able to make good use of its nation's brain power. Scientific research and industrial R&D benefit from government support.

China is busy addressing its environmental crisis, seeking to "turn a bad thing into a good thing" by not only leading the world in adopting renewable energy sources, but also becoming a leading supplier of the wind turbines and solar panels needed for this. China will likely become a leading producer and user of electric vehicles.

China's financial condition is a bone of contention and remains murky and hard to fathom. Although its financial risk is manageable as it stands, the deeper concern is the deterioration of the vital economic signs. But in China the buck ultimately stops with the government. While the government still has the financial resources to navigate these risks, collapse does not look to be in the cards.

Based on the above factors, one might imagine that China's success story will progress unimpeded. Not at the crazy pace of past decades while China caught up, but still growing steadily and in ways that are more sustainable.

But the risks all track back to the CCP, which in theory holds all the levers that might avert economic disaster. So the critical uncertainty in China is the nation's governance—that is, the ruling CCP. Our once-cautious confidence in the CCP as an institution we hoped had adapted and morphed from Stalinist cadres into technocratic custodians of *the China paradox*, has been seriously dented by economic fumbling and bungling, by the factional infighting in the CCP, and by a clampdown on dissent stronger and more systematic than we have seen in decades. We have been forced to rethink China's prospects.

Having reaped the benefits of the reforms, the CCP is revealing its longer-term vision on how it plans to rule. Its goal is to restore more of its central authority and play a stronger coordinating role in the economy. This does not mean a revival of the discredited central planning, but it implies a move from an improvised system, like jazz, in recent decades, to one more like classical music, with a conductor, in the future. Of course, the CCP is the sole conductor.

Early hopes that Xi Jinping would usher in a period of revived reform have been dashed. A cold wind blows through civil society. Not a return to Mao's "red terror," but certainly many steps backward. Civil rights lawyers are imprisoned. Those who call for true respect for the state constitution are treated as enemies. China is rapidly balkanizing its internet, blocking certain services, and in so doing isolating its scientists and academics from international discourse.

On the economic front, things too are bleak. Xi has concentrated power in his hands and in so doing sidelined his premier, who by tradition should be in charge of the economy. Authority has been transferred from government institutions to organs of the CCP. The CCP is ramping up its interference in the management of old-style SOEs. The CCP vision is for the SOE sector to absolutely dominate the economy under the close control of the CCP. This is essential to the CCPs raison d'etre since it can claim it presides over a new, more successful iteration of "socialism," and not a version of capitalism.

We are at a watershed in China's development. Having stumbled so badly during the Mao period, Deng and his successor reformers appeared to have learned many lessons and exhibited less hubris and more practical common sense than the CCP had in the past. Whether it was in insisting on a truly collective CCP leadership, in tolerating a burgeoning private economy, or in permitting the entry of global firms that could easily outshine local SOEs, the reformers showed wisdom and pragmatism. It did the trick and *the China paradox* created the illusion that China had somehow broken the code for making "socialism" work, where Lenin, Stalin, and Mao had failed. It seemed that China had created what has been described as the "perfect dictatorship."[1] That success may be more short-lived than anticipated.

As the CCP experimented with this hybrid system, it was prepared to try many formulas, to explore ways to further liberate the productive forces and drive technological and business innovation. It showed a true inquisitiveness about how things work in other societies. It exercised restraint in how it handled political control, with, of course, certain egregious exceptions, such as the crushing of the democracy movement in 1979 or the Tiananmen Square Massacre in 1989. In the early phases of the reforms, its leaders were in the main tentative, cautious, and mindful of not disrupting the economic forces they had liberated.

Unfortunately, the now super-confident and bullying CCP threatens the continuing functioning of *the China paradox*, undermining the balance between economic liberalization and political autocracy, which relies on the CCP wielding a light hand.

Unfortunately, the CCP is less adaptable or evolved than we had imagined. Few doubted its resolve to maintain its tight grip on China. But what we witnessed is a progress from the early chaotic and exploratory period of post-Mao China toward a truer expression of the innate violent and bullying instincts of the CCP. Since the last decade and in particular since Xi took over, it is as if the CCP feels massively confident and less constrained. Xi is not only consolidating his own personal power, but also ensuring that the CCP is preeminent across society, including in the SOEs. He turns the screws on civil society and on a country that has slowly been finding its voice.

On the international front, China struts around threatening its neighbors and stealthily building its military might, ranging from aircraft carriers to future hypersonic missiles launched from outer space. A virulent strain of Chinese nationalism courses through the veins of ordinary Chinese.

On an individual basis, many CCP members, be they at a leadership level or just ordinary citizens, display admirable decency in their views. The issue is that once gathered together, the CCP is collectively bound by its traditional brutal ethos. Just swapping a Mao suit for a Western one made of Italian cloth does not change the core values.

Though the model underlying *the China paradox* during the past four decades did have its weaknesses, it fit China's political legacy and permitted an orderly and gradual dismantling of the old economic model. The CCP welcomed foreign technology and business ideas while holding the lid on the Chinese pressure cooker of a society. Beyond that there was always a ray of hope that China would also evolve politically, that somehow there would be a gradual convergence between universal human values and the Chinese model. The contrary seems to be happening. China has played a strong game of poker, leaving the world guessing as to where it was going. Now the highly confident CCP flexes its muscles.

The balancing act that has served China so well is looking fragile. Social fissures continue to open up, such as tensions with Muslim Uighurs and the Tibetans, a civil society that has found its voice despite internet controls, factionalism in the CCP, burgeoning religion, not to mention the widening gap between rich and poor. What if, for instance, there was an outbreak of rebellion that was exploited by a charismatic, messianic figure. In fact, the well-oiled Chinese security apparatus should be able to handle most eventualities. But the required clampdown would undermine economic progress.

Events outside the China mainland could also trigger such a clampdown. It could be heightened dissent in Hong Kong or a push toward fuller independence in Taiwan. It could be a standoff in the South China Sea. The CCP will not stand by and permit what it deems to be attacks on China's sovereignty. Military action, or just the threat of it, would disrupt trade and air and sea transportation, sending tremors through the Chinese economy. Just as with the domestic economy, the CCP's survival trumps the economy and could throw China into a tailspin.

Growing CCP interference in the economy and the focus on creating "national champions" and barriers for foreign firms do not bode well for the future. Given the pace of change, one can never declare victory in the acquisition or development of technology. Today, you may achieve self-sufficiency, but tomorrow you may find yourself left behind. Integration into the global economy is the best way forward. The Great Fire Wall of China erected by the CCP to block ideas deemed to be poisonous hampers intellectual exchange, including in science and technology. Again, the CCP's political survival trumps economic development and gnaws away at the equilibrium with *the China paradox*.

How should we rate the chances that the CCP could manage to transform itself? Today, it is a secretive, opaque institution that outranks the government and the national constitution. Organizationally, it adheres to Leninist principles while its behavior on the ground often resembles that of the Mafia. Designed for an insurrectionary program that won power nearly 70 years ago, the CCP seems an anomaly in a modern industrialized society. In view of the historical lessons etched in its psyche from the collapse of the Soviet Union, the CCP refuses to take even a baby step towards its own reform.

Barring an unlikely change of heart by the CCP, we should expect to see increasing friction between China's flawed governance and the needs of the modern economy, with the result that China will continue to underperform and be held back from its true potential. The notion that China will, in the near future, become the next superpower is wide of the mark.[2] History also tells us to expect unanticipated events that could derail the Chinese economy and might even force the current CCP leaders to move aside.

So, the CCP is at, or close to, a crossroads. A figure or group of people within the CCP may summon the courage and foresight to gradually and carefully shape a new political order that will not become a roadblock to future economic progress and give China the ability to extricate itself from the current trajectory. The CCP might even change its name to reflect the new economic reality. However, the CCP is more likely to try to sustain the status quo. Indeed, a new set of leaders might well choose to further roll back the reforms.

If the trends we have identified in China's governance continue without political reform, we can still have moderate confidence that China will muddle through for another 10 to 15 years. That confidence is derived from China's entrepreneurial energy, which can be sustained despite the CCP.

Looking out beyond that 10-to-15-year time frame, the risks become greatly magnified. The CCP is already hunkering down rather than stepping out boldly. The CCP that functioned effectively during the peak of the reforms would become the fundamental obstacle to China's development and come under severe pressure. As it stands, it seems that the CCP would rather double-down and live with that risk than take preemptive action.

So how will the issues with China's governance play out in the business world at a more microlevel? On the positive side, the Chinese government will continue to play its valuable role as sponsor of "national champions" in key sectors. It will continue to force the pace of technological "catch up" and to foster innovation, providing deep pockets for long-term investment.

But on the negative side, the CCP, in response to decades of centrifugal, decentralizing forces during the reforms, is seeking to claw back its all-encompassing authority. For large old-style SOEs, this will mean that their already weak corporate governance will increasingly be held hostage by the plans of bureaucrats. Some government measures may be rational and needed, but others exhibit the lingering legacy of the planned economy, creating an atmosphere that hampers legitimate risk-taking.

When it comes to new-style SOEs such as Lenovo and Haier the story is refreshingly different. Strong CEOs, who had built their firms from humble beginnings or rescued them from oblivion, have achieved a high degree of autonomy, which should be unassailable. They have a good chance of keeping the predatory CCP in the background. With their blend of personal and government ownership, they look and act more like private firms. Given their management skills, which compare favorably with those of their global peers, they will continue to compete strongly on the world stage.

Chinese POEs came out of the shadows and helped prop up the economy while the government worked out what to do with the SOEs. Although some with a strategic role, such as in high-tech, will find themselves increasingly a *de facto* part of China, Inc., there is a raft of others that have established a strong culture of independence. They will of course look over their shoulders, watchful of CCP intentions and playing a visible game of token participation in the political process. But they can stand on their own feet. State banks are now willing to finance them. They show the ability to integrate and turn around foreign firms they have acquired. All this bodes well for the future.

As we look at what China will become, we should be cautious not to overestimate the ability of the CCP and the vestiges of the old order to strangle or debilitate the free-market element of the Chinese economy. The CCP's effort to strengthen its hold is precisely because it senses its waning relevance. The CCP is bluffing when it says that without it China has no future. We should have confidence that the new economy has taken root and is underpinned by the new middle class and the buying power of the consumer.

The strong performance and sustainability of the private sector, as well as of the new-style SOEs, will counterbalance the ponderous and wealth-draining state sector. Longer term, we shall likely see the new economy grow at the expense of the old one.

Though the old economy has been reshaped and given a corporate veneer, it remains a series of fiefdoms of the CCP, often functioning in cozy duopolies and loaded up with debt that the government will never let them default on. As it becomes clearer that the issues of the old economy were not fully dealt with during the reforms, the CCP may have to consider according the new economy a more central role.

The first time around, in the earlier reforms, the CCP grudgingly allowed the new economy to carry the load. This time around, a positive scenario would be that it has to accept a rebalancing of the equilibrium whereby it takes more of a back seat. This would imply that the CCP is willing to reform itself, signaling that China is finding a way to peacefully evolve. It would represent an enlightened re-igniting of the reform process whereby the hybrid model is fine-tuned and overhauled to fit new conditions. Unfortunately, such positive change looks remote.

If the economy were to deteriorate dramatically, the CCP might be forced rethink its current iteration of the developmental model or face pressure to hand off to a new set of leaders or, worse, a meltdown toward a failed state. Unfortunately, the odds are that the CCP would default to an even harder line, putting at risk the fruits of the reforms and leading to a downward spiral of the economy.

We should hope, of course, that the trends prove us wrong and that *the China paradox* has longevity and is not unravelling. But the evidence points in the other direction. There is still time for these trends to be reversed. China is not on the brink of collapse but is certainly in a more precarious condition than could have been imagined only a few years ago. Fortunately, the trends are perfectly visible to the Chinese themselves, with whom we share a deep commitment to avoiding China's failure, an event that would be catastrophic for both China and the world.

Endnotes

Chapter 1

1 How reformist Chinese economist Xue Muqiao characterized the first decades of the PRC. See Xue Muqiao, *China's Socialist Economy*, Beijing, 1981, p.236.

Chapter 2

1 G.E Morrison, *An Australian in China*, London, 1902, p.4.
2 E.A. Kracke, Jr., Sung Society—Change within Tradition, In *The Far Eastern Quarterly* (August 1955).
3 Max Weber, *Religion of China: Confucianism and Taoism*, Macmillan, 1951.
4 Etienne Balazs, *Chinese Civilization and Bureaucracy: Variations on a Theme*, Yale, 1967.
5 Ho Ping-ti, The Salt Merchants of Yang-Chou: A Study of Commercial Capitalism in Eighteenth-Century China, In *Harvard Journal of Asiatic Studies*, Vol. 17, Nos. 1–2 (1954).
6 Albert Feuerwerker, China's Early Industrialism: From Feudalism to Capitalism, In *Journal of Asian Studies*, Vol. 18 (1959).
7 Henry McAleavy, *The Modern History of China*, Weidenfeld and Nicolson (1967), pp. 127–8.
8 Albert Feuerwerker, *China's Early Industrialization, Sheng Xuan-huai (1844–1916) and Mandarin Enterprise*, Harvard, 1958, pp. 1–29.
9 For further discussion of Wu Zhihui and these issues refer to Paul Gilmore Clifford, *The Intellectual Development of Wu Zhihui: A Reflection of Society and Politics in Late Qing and Republican China*, Unpublished Ph.D. Thesis, University of London, 1978.
10 Wu Zhihui, Wuzhengfu zhuyi zhi xiantian, In *Xinshiji* magazine, No.49, Paris, 1908. Facsimile reprint, Daian, Tokyo, 1966.
11 Wu Zhihui, Qingnian yu gongju, In *Xinqingnian* magazine (October 1, 1916), Wu Zhihui xiansheng quanji, Vol. 4, pp. 404- 409 Taibei, 1969.
12 Wu Zhihui, Xin xinyang, *Ibid*, Volume 1, p. 70.
13 *Nanjing linshi zhengfu gongbao*, No. 8, Feb. 5, 1912, quoted in Yu Heping, *zouxiang xiandai de licheng* (jingjijuan, 1900–1949), p. 615.
14 *Hunan: Shiye Zazhi*, No.9. Quoted in Yu Heping, *zouxiang xiandai de licheng* (jingjijuan, 1900–1949), p. 616.
15 Yu Heping, *zouxiang xiandai de licheng* (jingjijuan, 1900–1949), p. 616.
16 John King Fairbank, Edwin Oldfather Reischauer, Albert M. Craig, *East Asia: The Modern Transformation*, Houghton Mifflin (1965), pp. 691–692.
17 Albert Feuerwerker, *The Chinese Economy 1912–1949*, University of Michigan (1968), p. 120.
18 McAleavy, *Ibid.*, p. 128.
19 Yu Heping, *Ibid.* (jingjijuan, 1900–1949), p. 620.

DOI 10.1515/9781501507212-010

20 Albert Feuerwerker, *The Chinese Economy 1912–1949*, University of Michigan (1968), pp. 81–120.
21 *Ibid.*, p. 120.
22 *Ibid.*, p. 125. Quoted in "Growth and Changing Structures of China's Twentieth Century Economy," in Dwight H. Perkins, ed., *China's Modern Economy in Historical Perspective*, Stanford, 1975.
23 Yu Heping, *Ibid.*, (jingjijuan, 1900–1949), p. 622.

Chapter 3

1 Mao Zedong, On New Democracy, In *Selected works of Mao Tse-Tung*, Vol. 2, p. 358.
2 *Ibid.*, p. 353.
3 Gunther Stein, *The Challenge of Red China*, Pilot Press (1945), p. 88.
4 Frank Dikötter, *The Tragedy of Liberation: A History of the Chinese Revolution 1945–1957,* Bloomsbury Press (2013), p. 227.
5 Liu Shaoqi, *zai Tianjinshi gongshangjie zuotanhui shang de jianghua*, in Liu Shaoqi, *Lun xinzhongguo jingji jianshe*, pp. 96–109.
6 Kenneth Lieberthal, *Revolution and Tradition in Tientsin, 1949–52*, Stanford (1980), p. 164.
7 Liu Shaoqi, *Ibid.*, p. 97.
8 Lieberthal, *Ibid.*, p. 168.
9 Jurgen Domes, *The Internal Politics of China 1949–1972*, C. Hurst & Company (1973), p. 43.
10 Justin Yifu Lin, Fang Cai, Zhou Li, *The China Miracle: Development Strategy and Economic Reform*, The China University Press (2003), pp.34–35.
11 Lin et al., *Ibid.*, pp. 38–40.
12 Lin et al., *Ibid.*, p. 40.
13 Wu Jinglian, *Dangdai zhongguo jingji gaige jiaocheng*, Nanjing (2010), p.33.
14 Liu Guoguang and Wang Ruisun, Restructuring of the Economy, in Yu Guangyuan (ed.) *China's Socialist Modernization*, Foreign Languages Press (1984), p. 91.
15 *Ibid.*, pp. 86–7.
16 Wu Jinglian and Mao Guochuan, *Zhongguo jingji gaige – ershjiang*, Beijing (2012), p. 25.
17 Wu Jinglian, *Ibid.*, p. 45.
18 Xue Muqiao, *China's Socialist Economy*, Foreign Languages Press (1981), p. 205.
19 Joseph C.H. Chai, *China: Transition to a Market Economy*, Oxford University Press (1998), p. 35.
20 See Yang Jisheng, *Tombstone: The Great Chinese Famine, 1958–1962*, Farrar, Straus and Giroux (2008.
21 Ezra F. Vogel, *Deng Xiaoping and the Transformation of China*, Belknap Press (2011), pp. 78–79.
22 In 1969, Lin Biao had been appointed Vice Chairman and Mao's chosen successor, but died in 1971 in an air crash while fleeing from China, after an alleged coup attempt. In 1973, a campaign called the Criticize Lin Rectification was launched. Early in 1974, that campaign morphed into the "Criticism of Lin Biao and Confucius," with Confucius serving as a proxy for attacking the Left's arch enemy Premier Zhou Enlai.
23 Paul Clifford Photo Collection.

24 *Ibid.*

25 Chinese statistician Li Chengrui's analysis in 1983, cited in Zhang Zhuoyuan and others, *Xinzhongguo jingjishigang (1949–2011)* (2012) p. 102; and Chinese Academy of Social Sciences, Research Institute of the Central Committee of the CCP, *zhongguo gongchandang lishi*, Vol. 2 (1949–1978) (2012), pp. 906–907.

26 Downfall of a Newborn Counter Revolutionary, *Peking Review*, Vol. 28, No. 40, September 30, 1977, pp. 24–27.

27 Chinese Academy of Social Sciences, Research Institute of the Central Committee of the CCP, *zhongguo gongchandang lishi*, Vol. 2 (1949–1978) (2012), p. 907.

28 Paul Clifford Photo Collection.

29 Kai-Yu Hsu *ed.*, *Twentieth Century Chinese Poetry, An Anthology*, Doubleday (1963), p. 379.

30 Raymond Zhou and Huang Yiming, A Harvest of Security for Those Who Returned, *China Daily*, March 16, 2012.

31 Michael R. Godley, The Sojourners: Returned Overseas Chinese in the People's Republic of China, In *Pacific Affairs*, Vol. 62, No. 3 (Autumn 1989), p. 330.

32 *Wuming huaqiao nongchang "630" shijiande zhenxiang*, in blog *Guxi rensheng*, April 16, 2014.

33 Dai Shiqiang, *huainian Qian Weichang*, on *Lixue tudi* website, July 31, 2010.

34 Zou Chenglu, *Chemical Synthesis of Crystalline Bovine Insulin: A Reminiscence*, The Ho Leung Ho Lee Foundation, November 18, 2004.

35 *Technology Transfer to China*, US Congress, Office of Technology Assessment, 1987.

36 Yang Jisheng, *Ibid., p.* 344.

37 Mikhail A. Klochko, *Soviet Scientist in Red China*, F.A. Praeger (1964), pp. 177–178.

38 *Ibid.*, p. 184.

39 Edward Crankshaw, *The New Cold War. Moscow v. Pekin*, Harmondsworth (1965), p. 188.

40 Paul Clifford, *Los Fertilizantes Quimicos En China, Nexo Vital Entre los Hidrocarburos y la Agricultura*, In *Estudios de Asia y Africa*, El Colegio de Mexico (1979), pp. 146.

41 *Ibid.*, pp. 142–143.

42 *Ibid.*, p. 143.

43 *Ibid.*, p. 146 and p. 156.

44 *Farm Mechanization Targets for 1980*, *Peking Review*, No. 8, February 24, 1978, p. 12, cited in Paul Clifford, Los Fertilizantes Quimicos En China, Nexo Vital Entre los Hidrocarburos y la Agricultura, *Estudios de Asia y Africa*, El Colegio de Mexico (1979), p. 149.

45 *Peking Review*, Vol. 20, No.10, March 1977.

46 Research Institute of the Central Committee of the CCP, *zhongguo gongchandang lishi*, Vol. 2 (1949–1978), pp. 825–826.

47 Justin Lin et al., *The China Miracle*, Ibid., p. 71.

48 *Ibid.*, p. 74 and p. 82.

49 Author's interview with John Gittings, journalist and writer on China, July 10, 2014.

50 E.L. Wheelwright, Bruce McFarlane, *Chinese Road to Socialism: Economics of the Cultural Revolution*, Monthly Review Press (1971).

51 Peng Kuang-hsi, *Why China Has No Inflation*, Foreign Languages Press (1976).

52 Mao (who had recently died) was not included in the Gang. While he was to be roundly criticized for "serious mistakes" (not crimes) committed in his later years, the CCP left his overall reputation largely intact, since they needed and still need his mantel for legitimacy. Although there is an undercurrent of opinion in China which calls it the "Gang of Five," to include Mao Zedong, that is not part of CCP orthodoxy.

Chapter 4

1 Xue Muqiao, *Ibid.*, p. 236.

2 Although this term is closely associated with Deng, it is thought to have first been coined by Deng's reformist colleague Chen Yun at a CCP work conference in December 1980.

3 Born in Sichuan in 1904, in 1919 Deng had travelled as a 16-year-old to France where, under the auspices of the Work-Study Movement started by Chinese anarchists, he worked in factories including Renault. He joined the CCP and, after studying in Moscow, he returned to China where he devoted himself to the revolution, joining the CCP's Long March and ultimately taking up senior positions in the Party after the PRC was established. During the Cultural Revolution his strong relationship with Mao permitted him to avoid death in prison but did not prevent him from twice being removed from power.

4 Deng Xiaoping, The "Two Whatevers" Do not Accord with Marxism, From *Selected Works of Deng Xiaoping* (1995), Vol. 2, pp. 51–52.

5 Deng Xiaoping, Speech at the All-Party Conference on Political Work, in *Selected Works of Deng Xiaoping* (1995), Vol. 2, pp. 124–136; Hold High the Banner of Mao Zedong Thought and Adhere to the Principle of Seeking Truth from Facts, *Ibid.*, pp. 137-139, Emancipate the Mind, Seek Truth from Facts and Unite as One in Looking to the Future, *Ibid.*, pp. 150–163.

6 Li Zhisui, *The Private Life of Chairman Mao*, Random House (1994), p. 376.

7 Deng Xiaoping, We Can Develop the Market Economy Under Socialism, in *Selected Works of Deng Xiaoping* (1995), Vol. 2, p. 238.

8 Deng Xiaoping, *zai quanguo kexuedahui kaimushishang de jianghua*, in *Deng Xiaoping xuanji*, Vol. 2, pp. 85–110.

9 Deng Xiaoping, We Should Use Foreign Funds and Let Former Capitalist Industrialists and Businessmen Play Their Role in Developing the Economy, in *Selected Works of Deng Xiaoping* (1995), Vol. 2, p. 166.

10 *Ibid.* pp. 85–110.

11 Deng Xiaoping, Adhere to the Principle of "To Each According to his Work. In *Selected Works of Deng Xiaoping* (1995), Vol. 2, pp. 112–113.

12 Deng Xiaoping, *yong xianjinjishu he guanli gaizaoqiye*, in *Deng Xiaoping xuanji*, Vol. 2, pp. 129–131.

13 Deng Xiaoping, *shixin kafang zhengce, xuexi shijie xianjin kexuejishu*, in *Deng Xiaoping xuanji*, Vol. 2, pp. 132–133.

14 Paul G. Clifford, *China en 1979*, *Estudios de Asia y Africa*, Vol. XV, No. 3, El Colegio de Mexico (1980), pp. 649–650.

15 Victor Nee and Sonja Opper, *Capitalism from Below: Markets and Institutional Change in China*, Harvard University Press (2012), p. 38.

16 Xue Muqiao, *Ibid.*, p. 54.

17 *The Sixth Five-Year Plan of the PRC for Economic and Social Development (1981–1985)*, Foreign Languages Press (1984), p. 115.

18 Deng Xiaoping, *yong xianjinjishu he guanli gaizaoqiye,* in *Deng Xiaoping xuanji*, Vol. 2, pp. 129–131.

19 Deng Xiaoping, *Selected Works of Deng Xiaoping,* Vol. 3, pp. 360 and 362

20 Deng Xiaoping, *Selected Works of Deng Xiaoping*, Vol. 3, p. 361.

21 Jiang Zemin, *Sangedaibiao shi women dang de lidang zhi ben, zhizheng zhi ji, liliang zhi yuan,* in *Lun "sangedaibiao"* (2001), pp. 13–14.

22 Xi Jinping, Push Ahead with Reform Despite More Difficulties, February 7, 2014, in *Xi Jinping, The Governance of China*, Foreign Languages Press (2014), p. 113.

23 *China's Twelfth Five Year Plan (2011–2015),* translated by the Delegation of the European Union in China, May 2011.

Chapter 5

1 Xue Muqiao, *Ibid.*, pp. 211–218.

2 In common with other writers and to avoid confusion over a relatively small semantic point, I stick to State-owned Enterprises (SOEs) throughout the book, even in the earlier chapters.

3 Paul G. Clifford, *Project notes*, 1993.

4 For an excellent account of this endemic issue in China, see Jeremy R. Haft, *Unmade in China. The Hidden Truth About China's Economic Miracle*, Polity Press (2015).

5 OECD, *State Owned Enterprises in China: Review of the Evidence,* p. 3.

6 Paul G. Clifford, *Project notes*, 2001.

7 *Ibid.*

8 *Ibid.*

9 Gabriel Wildau, China Kicks Off Second Round of Privatisation Reform, In *the Financial Times*, August 10, 2014.

10 Unirule, quoted by on *Caixin.com*, March 3, 2011.

11 Gavekal Dragonomics, quoted in China Kicks Off Second Round of Privatisation Reform, In *the Financial Times*, August 10, 2014.

12 Gordon G. Chang, *The Coming Collapse of China,* Random House (2001), p. 45.

13 Interview with Professor Feng Lu, Peking University, May 2013.

14 Terril Yue Jones, Q&A: Chinese Computer Giant Showcases Capitalist Credentials, In *Los Angeles Times*, May 4, 2006.

15 *Ibid.*

Chapter 6

1 Yingyi Qian and Jinglian Wu, *China's Transition to a Market Economy: How Far Across the River?,* Stanford University (2000), p. 4.

2 "Collective" means owned jointly by the local farmers or local government. Considered part of the "socialist" economy, but not part of the State sector.

3 Jon Sigurdson, Rural Industry and the Internal Transfer of Technology, in S.R. Schram (ed.) *Authority Participation and Cultural Change in China*, Cambridge University Press (1973), p. 216.

4 *Ibid.*, pp. 217–218.

5 *Ibid.*, p. 218.

6 Qian and Wu, *Ibid.*, p. 9.

7 Paul G. Clifford, *Project Notes*, May and June 1995.

8 Victor Nee and Sonja Opper, *Ibid.*, p. 49.

9 Nee and Opper, *Ibid*, p. 41.

10 Wanxiang America Corporation is the lead investor in Geneva Glen Capital.

11 Jean Lee and Hong Li, *Wealth Doesn't Last 3 Generations: How Family Businesses Can Maintain Prosperity*, World Scientific Publishing (2008), p. 282.

12 Andy Rothman, China's Corporate Landscape, *Matthews Asia*, October 1, 2014.

13 *Ibid.*

14 *Ibid.*

15 Paul G. Clifford. Confidential interview with the China representative of a US investment bank, 2013.

16 Paul G. Clifford, Confidential interview with a Chinese private equity fund head, 2015.

17 *Haobudongyao jianchi woguo jiben jingjizhidu, tuidong gezhong suoyouzhijingji jiankangfazhan*, in *Beijing Ribao*, March 5, 2016.

Chapter 7

1 Deng Xiaoping, *Jiaqiang sixiang jiben yuanze jiaoyu, jianchi gaigekaifang zhengce*, February 1987, In *Deng Xiaoping Wenxuan*, Beijing (1993), Vol. 3, p. 200.

2 AmCham China, *White Paper 2005*, p. 22.

3 AmCham China, *2010 White Paper*. p. 22.

4 US-China Business Council, *2014 China Business Environment Survey*, Washington (2014).

5 For example, this is the view expressed boldly by Ma Xiuhong, former Deputy Ministry of Commerce, whom I knew in the 1980s when she was in charge of that ministry's department responsible for foreign investment approvals.

6 Paul G. Clifford, *Project Notes*, 1988.

7 Keith Bradsher, Ford's Signal to the Auto World: Here Comes China, *The New York Times*, June 21, 2017.

8 Ding Junfa, *Zhongguo wuliu*, China Logistics Publishing House (2002), pp. 2–3.

9 Paul G. Clifford, *Project Notes*, October 1993.

10 *Logistics in China: An All-Inclusive Market?*, PricewaterhouseCoopers (2012), p. 9.

Chapter 8

1 Liang Xionghui, COO, Lifan Group, quoted in Tian Ying, *China's Plans for Its Own Car Brands Stall*, In *Businessweek*, August 30, 2012.

2 Mathew Strabone, *Nuclear Options: What Explains U.S.-China Cooperation on Thorium? Georgetown Public Policy Review*, November 6, 2014.
gppreview.com/2014/11/06/nuclear-options-explains-u-s-china-cooperation-thorium

3 Sandra Ferguson, Open Letter to PM Tilman Thomas, March 6, 2010.

4 Confidential interview with US government economist specializing in the Chinese economy, September 2013.

5 Dan Breznitz and Michael Murphree, *Run of the Red Queen: Government, Innovation, Globalization, and Economic Growth in China*. Yale, 2011, p.3.

6 *Ibid.*, p.4.

7 Liang Xionghui, *Ibid.*

8 Paul Clifford, August Joas, Frank Leung, A New Vroom for China's Auto Market. In Mercer *Management Journal*, Number 19, 2004.

9 Keith Bradsher, China Hints at Effort to Export Cars to West, In *The New York Times*, October 18, 2013.

10 Paul Mozur, Using Cash and Pressure, China Builds Its Chip Industry, In *The New York Times*, October 26, 2014.

11 Stacy Higginbotham, Qualcomm Forms Joint Venture in China to Take on Intel, *Fortune.com*, January 17, 2016.

12 TrendForce Reports XMC to Be China's Memory Base as It Gathers Technologies and Coordinates Nation's DRAM Industry Development, In *Trendforce.com*, June 29, 2015. press.trendforce.com/press/20150629-1969.html#CUQKfjxv8zLzpgQe.99

13 China Set to Challenge Global Chipmakers with Huge State-Led Project, In *Asia.nikkei.com,* November 4, 2015.

14 Paul G. Clifford, Confidential interview with senior leader of a major global PE firm, October 23, 2014.

15 Prof. Li Hongchang, quoted in Lan Xinzhen, Train Exports on Track, In *Beijing Review,* November 21, 2013 (updated September 2, 2015).

16 William Poirier, Westinghouse VP for Nuclear Plants, China, quoted in Nuclear Power in China, How the Red Dragon Will Lead the World, In *Power Engineering International*, October 1, 2010.

17 Alex Morales, Jessica Shankleman, and Rachel Morison, Is China's Role in Hinkley Point Really a Security Threat? In *www.bloomberg.com*, August 5, 2016.

18 Peter Nolan, *Is China Buying the World*?, Cambridge, 2012.

19 Zhang Xiaoji, ed., *Qianyan wenti*, Beijing, 2003, pp.87–90.

20 Gina Qiao and Yolanda Conyers, *The Lenovo Way,* McGraw-Hill, 2014, p. 43.

21 *Ibid.*, p.75.

22 Lenovo Group Ltd, Annual Reports, cited David Shambaugh, *China Goes Global,* Oxford, 2013, pp. 198–199.

23 *Ibid.*, p. 136.

24 Paul G. Clifford, Interviews with BestBuy sales staff, New Jersey, December 2014.

25 Lenovo has a fiscal year ending March 31st. The year referred to is the year in which the year-end falls. Hence FY 2006 is the same as FY 2005/2006.

26 Lenovo Group Ltd, Annual Reports.

27 Roger Kay, How Lenovo Can Turn Liabilities into Assets, In *Forbes*, May 12, 2014.

28 Lenovo Says 'Hypergrowth' in China Smartphones Ending, In *Bloomberg News,* November 6, 2014.

29 Lieke Wang, A Case Study of the Acquisition of Swedish Volvo by Chinese Geely, Master's Thesis, 2011, p. 28.

30 Niklas Pollard, Volvo Cars Says Begins XC60 Production in China, In *Reuters*, November 9, 2014.

31 Michael Bathon, Wanxiang Wins US Approval to Buy Battery Makers A123, In *Bloomberg*, January 29, 2013.

32 US Congress, *China's Foreign Aid Activities in Africa, Latin America and Southeast Asia*, 2009.

33 Teresa Hayter, *Aid as Imperialism,* Penguin, London, 1971.

34 Much to China's chagrin, at the national stadium's opening ceremony, the local band played the Taiwan anthem, not that of the PRC.

35 For an excellent profile of CDB see Henry Sanderson and Michael Forsythe. *China's Superbank*, Wiley, 2003.

36 Erin Conway-Smith, Chinese Autos Suffer the 'Fong Kong' Curse in Africa, In *Global Post*, May 18, 2012.

37 Wang Chao, Liu Lu, Textile Industry at the Crossroads of Change, In *China Daily*, December 15, 2014.

38 China Lianhe Rating Company, *xinyong dengji baogao* (on AFECC medium term notes), 2013, p. 25.

39 *Ibid.,* pp. 2–3.

40 Sandra Ferguson, Open Letter to PM Tilman Thomas, March 6, 2010.

41 Peter Hess, *In Mozambique, China Is Encroaching*, UT Texas, blog, September 1, 2013.

42 *Ibid.*

43 Caiphas Chimhete, Villagers Sue Diamond Firms for Pollution, In *The Standard* [Zimbabwe], September 9, 2012.

44 China Lianhe Rating Company, *xinyong dengji baogao* (on AFECC's medium term notes), 2013, p. 18.

45 Alastair Fraser, *Boom and Bust in Zambian Copper Mining: Donors, Multinationals, China and the Populist Response*, University of Oxford, 2006.

46 Michael Sata was President of Zambia from 2011 until his death in 2014.

47 Dan Breznitz and Michael Murphree, *Run of the Red Queen: Government, Innovation, Globalization, and Economic Growth in China.* Yale, 2011, p. 42.

48 Professor Robert Cywinksi from Huddersfield University, quoted in *Ibid.*

49 Paul G. Clifford, Interview with Prof. Stephen Thomas, Professor of Energy Policy, Public Services International Research Unit (PSIRU), University of Greenwich, London, February 22, 2015.

50 Paul G. Clifford, Interview with David Martin, Chief Executive of the Alvin Weinberg Foundation, London, February 25, 2015.

51 *Ibid.*

52 Mathew Strabone, *Nuclear Options: What Explains U.S.-China Cooperation on Thorium? Georgetown Public Policy Review*, November 6, 2014.
gppreview.com/2014/11/06/nuclear-options-explains-u-s-china-cooperation-thorium

53 Stephen Chen, Chinese Scientists Urged to Develop New Thorium Nuclear Reactors by 2024, In *South China Morning Post*, March 18, 2014.
http://www.scmp.com/news/china/article/1452011/chinese-scientists-urged-develop-new-thorium-nuclear-reactors-2024

Chapter 9

1 A word of clarification on the term "stability." Here it is used in the broadly accepted way and we distance ourselves from how the Chinese government and CCP uses the maintenance of the "social stability" (shehui wending) as an excuse to suppress legitimate dissent.

2 John Wilson Lewis (ed.), *Party Leadership and Revolutionary Power in China*, Cambridge University Press (1970), p. 1.

3 Richard McGregor, *The Party: The Secret World of China's Communist Rulers*, Penguin Books (2010), p. 31.

4 For pessimist views on the short-term future of the CCP, see Gordon G. Chang, *The Coming Collapse of China*, Random House (2001), p. 3.

5 McGregor, *Ibid.*, p 31.

6 McGregor, *Ibid.*, p. 265.

7 *China Private Equity 2014*, p. 23, published by China First Capital.

8 David Shambaugh, *China's Communist Party: Atrophy and Adaptation*, University of California Press (2008), pp. 3–5.

9 McGregor, *Ibid.*, p. 216.

10 Gabriel Wildau, China Anti-Corruption Sleuth Brags of Conquests in Leaked Speech, *The Financial Times*, October 27, 2015. The reference was to Ma Zehua, CEO of China Ocean Shipping (Cosco).

11 Xiao Gongqing, quoted in Suisheng Zhao, *Xi Jinping's Maoist Revival*, in *Journal of Democracy*, July 2016, p. 11.

12 Such as Hu Shuli (veteran editor and publisher, she has opposed the assault on the already limited media freedom) and Ren Zhiqiang (real estate developer and CCP member who rejects the drive for blind obedience to the CCP).

13 Chen Yi, *dujia chuanwen kanfa zhonggong 9 hao wenjian*, In *Mingjingbao*, 20 August 2013.

14 The other six topics rejected were "universal values," "civil society," "neo-liberalism" (meaning "total privatization and complete market economy"), the "Western view of the press," "historical nihilism" ("that seeks to negate the history of the CCP and of the New China"), and finally "calling into question the Reforms and Opening Up and the socialist nature of Socialism with Chinese characteristics."

15 Christopher K. Johnson, President Xi's Assault on China's Security Services: Grasping Tightly the Key Levers of Power, in *MERICS Papers on China No.1.*, posted on *Sinocism.com*, July 21, 2016.

16 *Ibid.*

17 Didi Kirsten Tatlow, In Book, Xi Jinping Taints Ousted Rivals with Talk of Plot, In *The New York Times*, January 27, 2016. The book referred to is *Edited Excerpts of Discussions by Xi Jinping on Tightening Party Discipline and Rules.*

18 Paul G. Clifford, Confidential interview with Board Member of the listed part of a large Chinese SOE.

19 Confidential interview by Paul G. Clifford with senior executive of a Chinese bank, Beijing, September 2013.

20 *Interview with Wang Jisi by Yoichi Funabashi, Editor-in-Chief, Asahi Shimbun, The Listener*, June 12, 2010, also quoted in Martin Jacques, *When China Rules the World*, Penguin Books (2012), p. 286.

21 Jerome Cohen, *Interview: Jerome Cohen, The Diplomat*, September 1, 2016.

22 Jianxiang Wang, Sinovel Claims Court Win over AMSC, *Wind Power Monthly*, June 9, 2015.

23 Professor Yao Yang, Dean, National School of Development, Peking University, Director, China Center for Economic Research, Interviewed by Paul G. Clifford on March 28, 2013.

24 Jack Nicas and Josh Chin, Stronger Chinese Patent Laws Also Help U.S. Companies, *The Wall Street Journal*, July 20, 2016.

25 Paul G. Clifford, Confidential interview with managing director of a Chinese private equity fund, March 25, 2013.

26 Paul G. Clifford, Confidential interviews with managing director of a Chinese private equity firm, March 25, 2013.

27 Confidential interview with senior executive of nuclear power engineering firm, July 19, 2013.

28 Su Xinping, *Vacation No.7*, painted in 2000. From the Clifford Collection.

29 Interview with David Sovie, Partner, Accenture, July 19, 2013.

30 Yong Zhao, *Who's Afraid of the Big Bad Dragon? Why China Has the Best (and Worst) Education System in the World*, quoted in Diane Ravitch, The Myth of China's Super Schools, *The New York Review of Books*, November 20, 2014.

31 Ravitch, *Ibid.*, p. 26.

32 Yong Zhao, quoted in Ravitch, *Ibid.*, p. 27.

33 Zhong Daoran, from *I do not forgive: China's education after a 90-criticism and reflection*, quoted in Ian Johnson, Class Consciousness, *The New Yorker*, February 3, 2014.

34 Paul G. Clifford, Confidential interviews conducted with senior executives in energy and consulting sectors, July 2013.

35 Paul G. Clifford, Confidential interviews in China, March 2013.

36 Plight of the Sea Turtles, in *The Economist*, July 6, 2013, p. 41.

37 *Ibid.*

38 Haiyong Ma, Research on the Existing Problem of China's MBA Education and the Countermeasures, in *Journal of Management and Strategy*, Vol. 1, No. 1, December 2010, p. 1.

39 http://rankings.ft.com/businessschoolrankings/global-mba-ranking-2013.

40 http://rankings.ft.com/businessschoolrankings/masters-in-management-2012.

41 Zhang Yuzhe, Investors Seek Liaoning Debt Boycott as Bond Default Battle Heats Up, English Caixin, July 19, 2016.

42 Paul G. Clifford, Confidential Interview with head of a Chinese private equity fund, March 27, 2013.

43 *Ibid.*

44 Paul G. Clifford, Confidential interview with Chief Representative of a US investment bank in China, March 22, 2013.

45 Simon Gos, Power Statistics China 2016: Huge Growth of Renewables Amidst Thermal-Based Generation, in *Chinese European Energy News*, February 9, 2017.

46 Sophie Vorrath, Graph of the Day: China's Future Generation Mix, in *Reneweconomy.com*, August 28, 2013.

47 As an indication of this future wave, see the firm Future Mobility Corp., established in 2016 by Tencent and Foxconn.

48 Barack Obama, remarks to Business Round Table, Washington, December 3, 2014.

49 Batelle/R&D survey, in *R&D Magazine*, December 2013.

50 OECD, *Review of Innovation Policy, China*, 2007, p. 35.

51 Delegation of the European Union in China, *Translation of China Five Year Plan (2001–2015)*.

52 Chalmers A. Johnson, *MITI and the Japanese Miracle: The Growth of Industrial Policy, 1925–1975*, Stanford University Press (1982).

53 In the 1970s, I was involved in research commissioned by the UK government into why the UK's machine tool industry had all but been wiped out by Japanese competition. The answer lay partly in the UK machine tool producers' low investment in R&D. But MITI's guidance of and support for Japanese firms was the decisive factor.

54 http://www.itri.org.tw/eng/

55 PRC State Council, *The National Medium and Long Term Program for Science and Technology (2006–2020)*.

56 http://www.most.gov.cn/eng/newsletters/2004/200411/t20041130_17780.htm

57 Cao Cong and Yu Taosun, quoted in Christine Larson, Overhaul of Chinese Science Spending Looms, in *Science*, http://news.sciencemag.org/asiapacific, October 23, 2014.

58 http://www.reuters.com/article/2012/07/23/; http://www.chinadaily.com.cn/china/2012-07/24; National Development and Reform Commission, *zhanluexing xinxing chanye zhongdian chanpin he fuwu zhidao mulu*, February, 2017.

59 The foreign competitors in ICT are allowed to participate in the race since they force change on the Chinese firms and provide the opportunity for Chinese firms to learn to learn from, imitate, and copy them. Somewhere, out of sight, things converge at a point where government has its say, for instance through limiting the foreign firm's market share by rationing government procurement contracts

60 *Jingji guancha wang*, May 20, 2012.

61 Cao Cong, quoted in China's Reform of R&D Budget Management Doesn't Go Far Enough, in *Science*, http://science.sciencemag.org/content/sci/suppl/2014/08/27/345.6200.1006.DC1/1253479.Sun.SM.pdf, August 29, 2014.

62 David Alan Grier, *The Ties That Bind: The Chinese Misunderstanding of Innovation*, Brookings Institution, September 17, 2014.

63 Jan Qiu, Scientists Caught in China Anti-Corruption Sweep, in *Nature*, http://www.nature.com/news/scientists-caught-in-chinese-anti-corruption-sweep-1.16152, October 16, 2014.

64 Cao Cong, quoted in Gwynn Guilford, *China Is Spending a Fortune on Science—and Is Getting Robbed Blind by Corrupt Scientists*, QZ.com, February 21, 2014.

65 *Xin de zhongyang caizheng keji jihua ganglifangan jiangchutai, zhengfu buzai zhijie guanli keji xiangmu*, In *Renmin ribao*, October 21, 2014.

66 *Pillars of Reform*, editorial in *Nature*, October 29, 2014, www.nature.com.

67 Eric Pfanner, China Taps a Growing Phone Market, In *The New York Times*, July 6, 2013, pp. BI, B6.

68 Amazon.com, July 12, 2013.

69 http://money.cnn.com, May 3, 2013.

70 http://www.brighthand.com, July 12, 2013.

71 Prof. Yao Yang, address to conference on China economy, NYSE, January 7, 2013.

72 Deng Xiaoping, *Selected Works of Deng Xiaoping* (1995), Vol. 2, p. 270.

73 Zhao Ziyang, *Guanyu_dangzheng fenkai*, October 14, 1987, xinhuawang.

74 Dr. Qin Xiao, address to conference on China economy, NYSE, January 7, 2013.

75 *Ibid.*

76 Paul G. Clifford, confidential interview with Board Member of a large Chinese SOE, Beijing, April 2014.

77 Suisheng Zhao, *Xi Jinping's Maoist Revival*, in *Journal of Democracy*, July 2016, p. 7.

Chapter 10

1 Stein Ringen, *The Perfect Dictatorship: China in the 21st Century,* Hong Kong University Press (2016).

2 For extensive discussion of China's underperformance as a global power, see David Shambaugh, *China Goes Global: The Partial Power,* Oxford University Press (2013).

Index

A

Absorption 5, 6, 35, 184
Academician 33, 190
Accession 99, 160, 198
Accountability 51, 72, 164, 165
Accounts 59, 60, 67, 74, 97, 98, 180
Accusations 136, 141
Acquisition 129, 131, 132, 133, 134,
    135, 203
– foreign 122, 130
Activist 158, 159
Actors 149
Adaptability 57, 157, 162, 166
Addressing Ownership and Govern-
    ance 62, 63, 65, 67, 69, 71, 73
Aeronautics Industry 61
AFECC 142, 143, 144, 145, 146
AFECC Organization Chart 143
AFECC to court for polluting 145
AFECC workers 142
AFECC's activities 143
AFECC's chairman 142
AFECC's headquarters building dates
    142
AFECC's overseas construction pro-
    jects 142
AFECC's role 145
Afoul 32, 45
Africa 12, 80, 93, 136, 137, 140, 141,
    142
Age 12, 45, 85, 136, 157
Agenda 41, 53, 80, 153, 155
Agility 82, 135
Agreements 49, 113, 144
– government-to-government 136
Agriculture 13, 20, 21, 36, 149
Agro-industrial conglomerate 77
Aid 22, 136, 138
– promised 119, 144
Air 85, 86, 203
Airports 3, 140, 143, 144
Alienation 171, 172
Allay 19, 45, 129
Alleys 114, 198

Ally 18, 19
American Chamber 95
American Motors 100, 102
Anarchy 61, 171
Ancient Chinese philosophy 163
Android 187, 188, 191
Android system 188
Anhui 142
Anjin 146
Annual rates 35, 96, 174
Anshan 16, 43
Anticorruption 53, 77
Anxiety 3, 19, 45, 156, 159, 163, 172
AP 127, 128
Apple 187, 191
Applications 10, 174, 184
Approval, official 49, 114
Aquifer 119, 144
Architect 14, 27, 39, 52, 166, 199
Areva 127, 128, 129
Army 43, 46, 91, 163
– modern 11, 12
Arrest 45
– house 114, 164
Arrival 10, 20, 27, 76, 140
Arsenals 11
Ascend P6, 191
Asia 6, 53, 122, 142, 152
Asian economies 181, 184
Aspirational 53, 171
Aspiring Chinese professionals 114
Assault 19, 169
Assembler 89, 135
Assemblies 89, 90, 100, 102, 106,
    181, 186
Assets 50, 67, 69, 166, 168
Atmosphere 58, 183, 189, 204
– stifling 4, 172
Autarky 25
Authority 45, 46, 48, 74, 81, 154, 156,
    158
– local 67, 158
Auto 99, 100, 121, 123, 125, 127
Auto components 89, 106, 135

Auto industry 100, 107, 109, 111, 115, 121, 134, 135
- fast-developing Chinese 89
- indigenous Chinese 119
Auto JVs 100
Auto makers
- dispersed Chinese 90
- emerging Chinese 122
Auto sector 100, 101
Autocracy 40, 82, 154
Autocratic China 90
Automobiles 59, 100
Autonomy 50, 78, 79, 94, 154, 204
Aversion 66, 168, 170
Avert 152, 200

B
Backseat 77, 79
Backsliding 27, 82, 154
Backward 21, 49, 61, 85
Backwardness 39, 108
Balance 1, 4, 74, 201
Balance sheet 60, 70, 93
Banks 69, 86, 93, 144, 177
- commercial 138
- foreign 75, 76, 139
- official 178
- state-owned 89, 183, 184
- west 87, 182
Barriers 6, 7, 23, 95, 106, 203
Barring 105, 167, 203
Batteries 89, 135, 150, 179
Battle 26, 48
Bearings 12, 89, 104
Beer 60, 63
Behavior 6, 149, 203
Beijing 27, 28, 29, 30, 31, 32, 49, 131
Beijing Jeep Factory 28, 29
Beijing Jianzhong Machinery Company 58
Berths 147
Biannual 24, 89
Biochemistry 32
Biotechnology 54, 185
Bleakness 37
Bloated workforces 99, 115
Block 62, 67, 115, 149

Blowing 37, 114, 162
Boards 160
Bode 77, 162, 195, 203, 205
Boldness 4, 5
Bonding agents 104, 173
Bonds 133, 176, 177
Booming Chinese 62
Bottlenecks 63, 102, 107, 109, 168
Boundaries 44, 46, 47, 49, 114, 116, 150
Branding 106, 185
Brands 80, 90, 122, 124, 129
- foreign 124, 187
Brazil 103, 126
Brewery 59, 60, 62, 63
Bribery 9, 19, 125
Bribes 109, 144
Bridges 65, 133, 140, 144, 181, 182
Britain 32, 92
Building materials 143, 144
Bureaucracy 44, 71, 150
Bureaucrats 26, 33, 60, 94, 183, 204
- local Chinese 146
Bureaus, local government tax 60
Buses 182
Business activities 70, 144, 160
Business focus, clear 64, 68
Business innovation 95, 201
Business lines 64, 68, 70
Business managers 175, 187
Business Model in Emerging Markets 148
Business Models 119, 120, 122, 136, 137, 138, 140, 148
Business philosophy 80, 89
Business processes 4, 80, 115
Business strategy 64, 65
Businesses 11, 14, 15, 67, 134, 153, 154, 159
- international 94, 126
- restructured 61, 69
Businessmen 22, 43, 52, 87, 165
- private 19, 198
Bustling 20, 98
Buyers 60, 97, 177

C

CADFund (China-Africa Development Fund), 138
Cake 99, 101, 103, 105, 107, 109, 111, 113
Cambridge 32, 175
Campaign 26, 27, 28, 29, 30, 46, 66, 163
- anticorruption 77, 154, 163
- political 24, 28, 29, 31, 39
Capacity 16, 59, 63, 77, 102, 123, 174, 176
Capital 10, 11, 63, 86, 87, 88, 89, 91
- initial 78, 138
Capital flight 94, 154
Capitalism 40, 42, 47, 51, 52, 61, 81, 201
Capitalists 19, 45, 173
- emerging Chinese 15
Carats 146
Cars 13, 100, 105, 122, 129, 141, 190
Cat 42, 48, 99, 164, 198
- out of the bag 48, 99, 198
Caveats 42, 136
CCP 1, 154, 156, 158, 159, 165, 166, 203
- ruling 81, 197, 200
CCP Committee 72, 160
- firm's 160
CCP Head 41, 52, 198
CCP leaders, current 53, 203
CCP leadership 18, 26, 51, 162
CCP meetings 76, 160
CCP power 42, 83, 165, 193
CCP rule 43, 153, 168, 197
CCP secretary 66, 86, 160
CCP sets 41, 53
CCP's ability 158
CCP's Politburo 112, 113
CCP's role 155, 193
CDB 138, 140, 143, 145
CEIBS (China Europe International Business School), 175
Cement 22, 49, 180
Cement industries 77, 192
Cement plants 140, 141

Central planning 23, 25, 47, 48, 60, 61, 62, 100
Centrally Planned Economy 23, 40, 52
Century 3, 5, 9, 10, 12, 164, 167, 169
CEO 66, 71, 72, 160
CFIUS (Committee on Foreign Investment in the US), 130, 133
CFLP (China Federation of Logistics and Purchasing), 108
Chambishi copper 146, 147
Changchun 62, 63, 90, 101, 103, 151
Chaos 3, 17, 25, 26, 28
Chemicals 19, 145
- toxic 86, 97
Chengdu 31, 59, 63
Chery 105, 141, 142, 167
Child 43, 54, 169, 171
China 2, 34, 99, 121, 123, 126, 127, 176
- animated 153
- celebrate 4
- center of excellence in 111
- confronted 13
- creating 188
- customers penetrate 110
- domestic market accords 181
- economic order 17
- fit 202
- forced 10
- free 39
- hand 116
- housed 33
- imperial history 9
- launched 39
- left 32, 44, 114, 199
- lethal cocktail set 197
- liberated 16
- liberating 40
- linking 181
- made in 123
- manufacturing-heavy 140
- measure 175
- moved 40
- northeast 49
- peaceful 156
- permitted 1, 3

– plague 21
– post-Mao 202
– postwar 18
– propelled 180
– propelling 121
– prosperous 197
– pull 179
– rebuilt 17
– served 155, 202
– shoehorn 129
China Academy of Sciences 33
China accounts 182
China afloat 83
China autos 141
China coast 11
China complain 167
China deal 127
China debt 148
China Development Bank 89, 93
China Development Bank Corporation
    138
China entry 102
China Europe International Business
    School (CEIBS), 175
China Exim Bank 137, 143, 144, 147,
    148
China Export & Credit Insurance Cor-
    poration 140
China Federation of Logistics 108
China Federation of Logistics and Pur-
    chasing (CFLP), 108
China for foreign electronics manufac-
    turers 130
China government 165
China handset industry 134
China handset market 186
China handsets 134
China International Contractors Asso-
    ciation (CHINCA), 140
China logistics market 110
China logistics players 110
China mainland 202
China market 102, 104, 105, 125, 131,
    132, 134, 135
– domestic 97, 138
China Merchants Steam Navigation
    Company 10

China Merchants/Sinotrans and Cosco
    Logistics 110
China Mobile 81
China Neglect Logistics and Resist
    107
China Nonferrous Metal Mining Corpo-
    ration 146
China ODI 130
China ODI set 130
China operations 116
China Paradox 1, 2, 4, 39, 153, 154,
    155, 195
China profits 114
China projects 128
China sail 37
China shines 120
China Shipping 192
China shot 175
China smartphone market 190, 191
– tough 133
China struts 202
China Telecom 81
China to Africa and Southeast Asia
    141
China Unicom 81
China Welcome FDI 96, 97
China winning 126
China-Africa Development Fund (CAD-
    Fund), 138
China-developed HSR 126
China-foreign link-up in nuclear power
    129
China/Japan 34
China's accession 52, 62, 74
China's activities 147
China's activity in emerging markets
    141
China's adoption 5, 6
China's aid 136, 138
China's anti-monopoly law for rigging
    prices 116
China's auto industry 101, 102, 106
China's Auto Industry Growth 107
China's banks 77
China's banks sign loan agreements
    137
China's bearings industry 84

China's breakneck growth 179
China's burst of activity in ODI 129
China's capital 21
China's Capitalists 18, 19
China's computer market by reducing import tariffs 131
China's dependence 150, 185
China's development 37, 201, 204
China's developmental model 4
China's Economic Planning 53, 55
China's economy 15, 36, 37, 115, 175
– left 17
China's economy and society 1
China's Emergence 119, 120, 122, 124, 126, 128, 129, 130
China's exercise of soft power 144
China's expenditure on research and development 182
China's exports 97, 181
China's Fault Lines and Tensions 161
China's FAW 141
China's First Five Year Plan 22
China's GDP 35, 40, 52, 83, 97, 98
China's GDP growth 52, 193
China's governance 155, 204
China's growth 116, 176
China's history 3, 6, 42, 197
China's imperial system 10
China's indigenous auto industry 122
China's innovation capability 120, 189
China's interest rate regime 93
China's isolation 95
China's judiciary 167
China's leaders 107, 109, 110, 161
China's leaders for increased enterprise autonomy 50
China's Left 34
China's Lenovo 183
China's Logistics 108
China's logistics capability 108
China's market 72
China's mastery of Generation III technology 180
China's mobile handset sector 186
China's mobile phone penetration rate 187

China's MSR program 151, 152
China's National Audit Office 177
China's National Basic Research Program 184
China's northeast 63, 69
China's officials and economists embracing 107
China's Post-Mao Economic Reforms 41
China's progress 6, 32, 162, 168
China's pulsating economy 13
China's rail freight system 109
China's ratio 177
China's R&D 183, 188, 189
China's R&D performance 188
China's R&D Results 188
China's reformers 5
China's Reforms 41, 53
China's research and development 149
China's revival 173
China's rulers 40
China's ruling CCP 74
China's Self-Strengthening Movement 10
China's semiconductor industry 34, 123
China's SOE sector 71, 75
China's SOE-dominated economy 55
China's SOEs 23, 57, 81, 122
China's stage of development 34
China's State Pharmaceutical Administration 61
China's strident nationalism and growing military assertiveness 6
China's top leaders 49, 113, 142
China's transportation infrastructure 182
China's zeal for acquiring foreign technology 120
China/Zimbabwe chrome for telecom equipment deal 139
CHINCA (China International Contractors Association), 140
Chinese 3, 13, 26, 31, 121, 125, 170, 173
– private 94, 138

– traditional 89, 169
Chinese Academy of Sciences 32, 78, 183
– Government-owned Chinese Academy 130, 132
Chinese anti-Qing revolutionaries 12
Chinese authoritarian legacies 5
Chinese auto brands 106, 122
Chinese auto industry 122
Chinese auto makers 122, 123
Chinese banks 75, 137, 165, 178
Chinese brands 106, 190
Chinese business and political leaders 65
Chinese business leaders 164, 168
Chinese business people 174
Chinese business schools 175
Chinese business visitors 120
Chinese businesses 99, 146, 153, 170, 171, 188
Chinese businessmen 11, 18, 19
Chinese cities 182
Chinese citizens 98, 172, 193
Chinese companies 130, 153, 168
Chinese courts 167, 168
Chinese developmental model of recent decades 2
Chinese dynasties, established 18
Chinese economist 23, 36, 155
– leading 57
– liberal 195
Chinese economist Xue Muqiao 25, 47
Chinese economy 24, 104, 176, 189, 203, 205
Chinese enterprises 17, 36, 80, 86
Chinese equipment suppliers 127
Chinese factories 14, 17, 44, 141
Chinese firms 96, 130, 138, 140, 141, 153, 154, 185
Chinese government 61, 62, 64, 75, 76, 111, 112, 116
Chinese government and CCP 136
Chinese government and SOEs 82
Chinese government concessional loans 143
Chinese government data 93

Chinese government funding 140
Chinese government level 125
Chinese government policy 146
Chinese government procurement 133
Chinese government's role in orchestrating China's R&D 183
Chinese government's role in spurring R&D and innovation 184
Chinese government's science and technology program 184
Chinese institutions 28
Chinese intellectuals 12, 14, 169
Chinese IPR enforcement 95
Chinese leaders 10, 33, 45, 101, 137, 148
Chinese logistics firms focus 110
Chinese low-end market 186
Chinese manufacturers 102, 109, 110, 141
Chinese market 122, 132
– large 132, 134
Chinese model 40, 155, 202
Chinese money 139, 148
Chinese ODI 129, 130
Chinese partners 99, 111, 121
Chinese people 1, 3, 6, 39, 42, 170, 171, 173
Chinese players 106, 122, 186, 190
Chinese POEs 94, 204
– large 93, 160
Chinese press 131, 171
Chinese pressure cooker 156, 202
Chinese ratings agency 142
Chinese reactors 127
Chinese reform 149
Chinese revolutionaries 12
Chinese scholar 173
Chinese schools outperform 174
Chinese semiconductor industry 111
Chinese side's hunger and enthusiasm 115
Chinese smartphone manufacturers 188
Chinese smartphone producers 191
Chinese smartphones 187, 191, 192

Chinese society 4, 5, 159, 165, 171, 172, 173, 197
Chinese SOE governance 70
Chinese SOEs 66, 68, 72, 74
Chinese students 14
Chinese suppliers and customers 59
Chinese turbine maker Sinovel 167
Chinese universities 5, 43, 174
Chinese workers 140, 141
Chinese-branded mobile handsets 186
Chinese-branded vehicles 106
Chongqing government 104
Cisco 91, 92
Cities 14, 86, 88, 90, 104, 112, 113, 193
– coastal 98, 181
Citizens 4, 17, 29, 37, 46, 61, 159, 162
Civil society 168, 169, 171, 173, 198, 199, 200, 202
Cladding 48, 49
Classes, capitalist 43, 44, 52
Clean break 16, 17
CNMC 146, 147
CNR 124, 125, 126
Coal 16, 29, 147, 151, 180
Code 29, 156, 188, 201
Commerce 4, 5, 13, 14, 19, 20, 21, 23
Commercialize 78, 150
Commitment 13, 57, 128, 205
– long-term 119, 152
Committee on Foreign Investment in the US (CFIUS), 130, 133
Companies 67, 68, 69, 70, 77, 78, 125, 144
– bad 69, 77, 192
– private 83, 89, 91, 132
Compensation 59, 124
Competition 26, 43, 62, 74, 99, 154, 185
– foreign 99, 110, 131, 160
Competitive Chinese automakers 106
Competitiveness 50, 57, 65, 67, 135
Competitors 67, 82, 105, 121, 132, 186
– foreign 131, 186
Complaining 13, 188

Complexity 2, 57, 68, 105
Components 102, 106, 126, 127, 128, 131, 186, 190
Concept 34, 42, 81, 150, 170
Confident 2, 72, 83, 85, 95, 103, 168, 202
Conflict 48, 49, 164
Conformity 170, 173
Confucian society 12, 169
Confucianism 163, 169
Confucius 12, 27, 28, 30
Congo 143, 145
Consensus 65, 66, 170
Consolidation 16, 54, 67, 77, 134, 183, 192
Construction 21, 34, 49, 126, 127, 135, 142, 177
Consultants 32, 65, 66
Consumer 21, 24, 26, 105, 106, 177, 190, 191
Consumer products 15, 20, 36, 59, 84, 124, 189, 190
Contact, direct 23, 24
Contracts 108, 127, 140, 168
Contribution 42, 83
Control 3, 4, 23, 25, 26, 27, 48, 116
– central 14, 49
– operating 96, 112, 113
– political 73, 201
– social 4, 16, 172, 173
Controversy 92, 144
Copper 129, 143, 146, 147
Corruption 51, 53, 73, 75, 76, 77, 163, 171
Cost 70, 124, 127, 128, 133, 146, 147, 165
– high 63, 119
Cotton 9, 29, 85, 136
Countries 91, 125, 126, 130, 136, 141, 142, 147
– emerging 6, 136, 142, 148
– industrialized 119, 189
– recipient 136, 145, 147, 148, 149
Coup 26, 28
Crimes 42, 45, 156
Crisis 35, 158, 159
– environmental 179, 200

Criticize Lin Biao and Confucius 27,
28, 30
Cronyism 41, 75, 76, 156
CSR 124, 125
Cultural Revolution 26, 31, 32, 36, 37,
43, 45, 46
Culture 4, 25, 42, 74, 168, 169, 171,
173
– corporate 73, 78, 160

D
Dalian 49, 62, 88, 113, 123
Dalian factory 49, 50
Danger 51, 166, 192
Death 45, 46, 114
Debt 60, 76, 125, 131, 144, 146, 190,
192
Deepening Economic Reform 192,
193, 195
Degree 58, 64, 71, 74, 78, 80, 81, 91
Democratic Republic 143, 145
Deng 27, 41, 42, 43, 44, 45, 51, 52
Deng Xiaoping 1, 2, 27, 35, 37, 39, 95,
96
Denunciation 19, 27, 28, 46
Design 105, 106, 107, 122, 123, 189,
190, 191
– product 122, 124
Desktops 132, 133
Development 18, 120, 149, 150, 179,
180, 181, 182
– industrial 11, 15, 87
Development zone 97, 147
Developmental ladder 157, 166
Developmental model, hybrid 1, 197
Diamonds 139, 143, 145
Direct investment, foreign 6, 44, 83,
95, 98, 121
Director 32, 63, 64, 112
Disappointment 37, 121, 123, 125,
127, 128
Disappointment in Auto and Semicon-
ductor 121, 123, 125, 127
Disrupt 155, 156, 158, 160, 162, 164,
166, 168
Disruption 1, 29, 30, 50, 148
Dissent 45, 46, 107, 154, 173, 200

Dogs 62, 63, 64
DOI 1, 9, 17, 38, 39, 57, 83, 95
Domestic market 49, 89, 115, 181
– large 121, 126, 181
Domestic trade 108, 109
Dues 102, 103
Dynasty 12, 44, 156, 163
– late-Qing 11, 12
Dysfunctional Soviet Model 20, 21,
23, 25

E
EastCom 186, 187
Economic development 2, 36, 46,
137, 203
Economic forces 39, 201
Economic front 162, 201
Economic growth 21, 37, 47, 156, 161,
165, 192, 193
Economic ladder 53, 195
Economic model 17, 20, 26, 36, 37,
40, 195
Economic order 58, 83
Economic policies 27, 39
Economic progress 44, 157, 164, 202,
203
Economic reforms 35, 39, 40, 41, 50,
51, 52, 197
Economic success 4, 174
Economic system 5, 42
Economics 151, 165, 179
Economies of scale 60, 102, 131, 132,
181
Economy 51, 53, 93, 154, 165, 192,
193, 205
– global 6, 203
– mixed 19, 42, 47, 62
– modern 14, 23, 26, 39, 107, 164,
165, 178
– old 205
– private 83, 88, 201
Education 43, 167, 168, 169, 170, 171,
173, 174
– children's 174, 193
Education system 169, 174
Educational system 173, 199
Electric vehicles. *See* EVs

Electronics Industry 111, 112, 140
EMBA (Executive MBAs), 175
Emergence 3, 17, 39, 49, 86, 93, 96, 106
Emergence of Chinese Firms 153
Emerging Chinese companies 167
Emerging markets 134, 135, 137, 138, 139, 140, 141, 148
Empire 9, 10, 11, 12, 13, 14, 15, 16
Employees 58, 59, 70, 74, 77, 79, 88, 91
Encirclement 19, 20
Enemy 4, 18, 19, 46, 167, 200
Energy 3, 4, 85, 86, 151, 153, 180, 184
Engine 84, 85, 103, 167
Engineers 78, 115, 183
Enterprise level 50, 184
Enterprises 48, 58, 74, 84, 183, 184, 193, 194
– collective 79, 88
– foreign-owned 111, 160
– medium-sized 93, 178
– modern 11, 79
Entities 61, 66, 67, 69, 103, 124, 125, 142
– commercial 124, 183
– listed 70, 72
Entrants, foreign 14, 62, 111, 112, 122
Entry 99, 100, 105, 106, 201
Environmental protection 179, 180, 185, 199
Equity 96, 100, 122, 123, 128, 133, 142, 146
Especially 87, 89, 91, 96
Establishment 10, 13, 16, 19, 61, 98, 122, 123
EV fleets 180, 181
EVs (electric vehicles), 89, 90, 107, 123, 150, 179, 180, 182
Exactions, official 10, 11
Excess 59, 70
Experts 13, 34, 152
Export 103, 125, 127, 137, 138, 141, 147, 181

F
Factories 23, 24, 50, 59, 61, 90, 124, 125
Failures 3, 5, 23, 39, 122, 166, 170
Farmers 21, 26, 32, 43, 88
– local 46, 85
Fate 18, 19, 64, 156, 162, 195
FAW (First Auto Works), 101, 103
FDI (foreign direct investment), 44, 95, 96, 97, 98, 100, 115, 116
Fees 107, 109
Fertilizers 15, 34
FIEs (foreign-invested enterprises), 160, 161
Financial risks 178, 200
Firms 81, 92, 93, 94, 99, 154, 186, 189
– large 80, 160, 168
– local 96, 115, 126
– multinational 97
First Auto Works (FAW), 101, 103
First Decades 17, 18, 20, 22, 24, 26, 28, 30
Five Year Plan 24, 48, 54
Fixed assets 57, 60, 101
Flourish 5, 9, 42, 54, 78, 79, 82, 83
Flourishing 154, 156
Foreign auto firms 100, 101, 122
Foreign companies 63, 86, 115, 121, 126, 182
Foreign direct investment. *See* FDI
Foreign exchange 21, 48, 50, 102, 103
– shortage of 102, 103
Foreign firms 96, 99, 100, 110, 115, 116, 125, 168
Foreign investment 95, 96, 108, 109, 110, 112, 113, 181
Foreign investors 96, 97, 102, 113, 114, 115, 116, 121
Foreign technology 4, 6, 15, 44, 115, 121, 125, 126
Foreigners 10, 15, 18, 31, 44, 99, 100, 121
Foreign-invested enterprises (FIEs), 160, 161
Fuel 21, 89, 91, 150, 175
Functionality 122, 187, 191
Funding 68, 76, 94, 138, 183, 187

G

Gang of Four 35, 37, 42, 44, 45
Gaokao 43, 173, 174
GDP 144, 146, 148, 177, 179, 181, 183, 192
GDP growth 36, 53, 176
Geely 134, 135, 141, 167
Generation III 82, 126, 127
Generation III technology 127, 180
Generations 18, 33, 119, 184, 185, 187
GFWC (Great Fire Wall of China), 164, 203
Ghana 141, 143, 175
Glass exports 49, 50
Gleaming New Ground Transportation Infrastructure 181
GM 100, 102, 103, 104, 105, 106, 167
Goods 29, 50, 120, 136, 147, 183
– white 79, 81
Google 133, 134, 188, 191
Governance 62, 63, 65, 71, 72, 73, 188, 189
Government 47, 53, 71, 77, 81, 144, 185, 198
– central 48, 49, 50, 54, 63, 79, 81, 84
– city 29, 63
– nationalist 18, 156
– previous 76, 145
Government agencies 99, 184
Government approvals 57, 130
Government buildings 143, 144
Government ministries 81, 185
Government officials 12, 144, 165, 173
Government ownership 20, 204
Government patronage 6, 81, 154
Government research institutes 150, 183
Government schools 88
Government subsidies 11, 106, 179, 182
Government support 106, 129, 134, 185, 187, 200
– central 112, 142
Government/CCP 64, 75, 81, 135, 136
Government-dominated economic structure 155, 194
Government-Sponsored Research 182, 183, 185, 187, 189
Great Fire Wall of China (GFWC), 164, 203
Grenada 119, 137, 143, 144
Grip 4, 39, 41, 50, 166, 194, 201
Growth 36, 83, 84, 85, 105, 133, 175, 176
– fast 114, 133
– profitable 103, 130
– rapid 80, 89, 176, 189
– slowing 77, 140
Guangzhou 45, 89, 100, 182
Guidance 13, 54, 160

H

Haier 79, 80, 94, 187, 204
Handsets 80, 111, 186, 187, 191
Hangzhou 29, 35, 87
Heart 1, 2, 3, 4, 5, 6, 7, 136
Heart of China's Emergence 119, 120, 122, 124, 126, 128, 130, 132
Hefei 90, 142
High-speed rail. *See* HSR
Hiring 92, 162
Historical legacies 1, 4
History 6, 18, 39, 136, 139, 149, 156, 159
– modern Chinese 27, 157
Home 13, 85, 87, 98, 154, 178, 179
Hong Kong 31, 52, 69, 70, 98, 124, 161, 175
Honor 107, 108, 199
Hotel 129, 144
HSR (high-speed rail), 3, 54, 82, 124, 125, 181, 190
Huawei 91, 92, 93, 94, 185, 190, 191, 192
Hybrid economy 153, 195
Hybrid Model 1, 2, 3, 4, 5, 6, 7, 198

I

IBM 116, 130, 131, 132, 133, 134
IBM executives 131, 132
IBM's PC division 131, 132
Illegal tolls 109, 110
Implications 4, 153, 160, 162

Imports 5, 21, 32, 34, 35, 44, 103, 105
Inc 91, 93, 135, 137, 141, 147, 148, 153
Independence 9, 83, 202, 204
Industrial base 15, 34
Industrial production 15, 29, 120
Industrial Technology Research Institute (ITRI), 184
Industrialization 9, 10, 11, 12, 13, 14, 15, 16
Industry 13, 14, 15, 20, 21, 43, 101, 180
– heavy 20, 21, 22, 36
– light 20, 24, 36
– private 16, 19
Inflation 37, 58, 59
Infrastructure 11, 23, 54, 97, 105, 111, 147, 186
Infrastructure investment 53, 193
Infrastructure projects 76, 177
Innovation 4, 6, 120, 164, 165, 168, 169, 184
– indigenous 99, 184, 190
Institutes 32, 151, 183, 184
Institutions 4, 5, 55, 156, 159, 167, 173, 200
– financial 135, 137
Instrumental 14, 184
Intel 123, 132, 189
Intellectual property rights (IPR), 128, 167
Intellectuals 17, 30, 42, 43
Interest rates 54, 93, 137, 178
Interference 50, 71, 77, 80, 135, 154, 194, 201
Internet 145, 149, 158, 164, 165, 180, 198, 200
Investment 36, 96, 146, 147, 148, 183, 184, 185
– government R&D 183
– government-sponsored 136
– massive government 188
– primary China 111
Investment capital 115, 129
Investment funds 96, 102
Investors 57, 69, 70, 72, 95, 97, 104, 113
IPhones 191, 192

IPO 64, 65, 69, 70, 72, 77
IPR (intellectual property rights), 128, 167
IPR protection 168
IPR theft 167, 168, 184
Iron ore 11, 12, 129
ITRI (Industrial Technology Research Institute), 184

J
Japan 11, 13, 14, 16, 34, 123, 183, 184
Joint ventures. *See* JV
Joy 30, 171
JV (joint ventures), 49, 99, 103, 105, 121, 123, 124, 125

K
Kawasaki 125, 126
Kejian 186, 187
Key sectors 75, 129, 163, 204
Kits 102, 103
Km 45, 62, 85, 104, 109, 125, 182
Knowledge 5, 13, 32, 42, 65, 175, 178
Knowledge economy 157, 164, 175
– global 116, 166
Korean War 19, 20, 156

L
Laptops 132, 133, 184
Large SOEs 57, 64, 65, 74, 76, 77, 82, 160
Law 87, 112, 166, 167, 168, 198
– rule of 6, 166, 167, 168, 194
Layers 3, 4, 16, 24, 178
Leaders 12, 13, 14, 137, 160, 162, 163, 201
Leadership 27, 51, 52, 76, 150, 162
– current 4, 195
Learn and catch-up model 119, 122
Legacy 23, 25, 57, 76, 78, 101, 110, 115
Legal system 166, 167, 168, 198
Lending 69, 93
Lenovo 78, 79, 130, 131, 132, 133, 134, 135
– permitted 132
Lenovo CEO 78, 132

LGFVs (local government financing ve-
hicles), 176, 177
Li Tieying 111, 113
Lid 3, 156, 198, 202
Life 20, 25, 39, 45, 46, 51, 171, 172
Light water reactors. *See* LWRs
Lin Biao 27, 28
Lin Biao and Confucius 28, 30
Lines 12, 67, 182
Loans 58, 60, 136, 137, 138, 140, 183,
184
– low-interest 21, 184
– nonperforming 69, 178
Local government 85, 86, 90, 93,
136, 138, 158, 159
Local government debt 176, 177
Local government financing vehicles
(LGFVs), 176, 177
Local level 25, 48, 50, 71, 158, 159,
177, 180
Localism 103, 104
Location 43, 87, 97, 104, 113, 150
Logistics 50, 80, 99, 100, 107, 108,
109, 110
– modern 107, 108
Low-end 133, 189
Lu 88, 89, 90, 91
Lu Guanqiu 88, 90
LWRs (light water reactors), 150, 151

M
Machine tools 12, 22, 84
Machinery 15, 20
Machines 12, 13
– washing 48, 59, 79
Magnet for Foreign Investment 95,
96, 98, 100, 102, 104, 106, 108
Malawi 143, 145
Management 11, 14, 15, 63, 70, 71,
72, 78
– merchant 10, 85
– senior 14, 66
Management consultants 73, 131
Management skills 96, 99, 115, 153,
181, 182, 204
Management team 72, 78
Managers 14, 28, 43, 79, 86, 115

Manufacturers 104, 108, 111, 115, 121,
191
Manufacturing 90, 91, 99, 100, 110,
114, 185, 189
Manufacturing skills 174, 187
Mao 18, 19, 22, 26, 27, 37, 42, 197
Mao Zedong 1, 2, 4, 18, 19, 37
Maputo 143, 144
Market 60, 61, 105, 106, 109, 110,
116, 187
– export 86, 89
– free 50, 87
– global 80, 82, 123, 128, 132, 180,
181, 189
– international 92, 128, 131
– largest 105, 127
– mature 132, 133
– stock 69, 93, 96, 115, 160, 199
Market demand 55, 80, 96, 102, 106
Market economy 52, 185
– socialist 47, 52, 61
– true 55, 194
Market entry 97, 104
Market forces 50, 52, 53
Market mechanisms 20, 21
Market reputation 65, 79
Market segments 106, 110
Market transitions 130, 133, 135
Market-oriented economies 40, 75,
108
Master of Business Administration
(MBAs), 175
Materials 23, 24, 25, 50, 61, 84, 104,
108
Materials science 33, 152
MBAs (Master of Business Administra-
tion), 175
MEI (Ministry of Electronics Industry),
58, 111, 113
Melt 81, 82
Members 27, 92, 95, 112, 113, 140,
158, 194
Merchants 9, 10
Mergers 154, 162, 192
Middle class 107, 161, 205
MIIT (Ministry of Industry and Infor-
mation Technology), 54, 184

Milestone 41, 61, 87, 113
Mining 140, 142, 147
Minister 13, 112, 113, 158
Ministry 24, 48, 49, 50, 60, 71, 116
– central 23, 49, 71, 180
Ministry of Aeronautics Industry 61
Ministry of Education 61, 174
Ministry of Electronics Industry (MEI),
    58, 111, 113
Ministry of Foreign Economic Rela-
    tions and Trade (MOFERT), 112,
    113
Ministry of Industry and Information
    Technology (MIIT), 54, 184
Ministry of International Trade and In-
    dustry (MITI), 184
Ministry of Railways. See MOR
MIS (management information system),
    67
Mistakes 3, 42, 44, 66, 116, 170
MITI (Ministry of International Trade
    and Industry), 184
MNCs (multi-national corporations),
    110, 129
Mobility solutions, urban 180, 182
Model 2, 120, 121, 135, 136, 141, 148,
    149
Model works 124, 135
Modern China 5, 169
Modernization, economic 10, 36, 197
MOFERT (Ministry of Foreign Economic
    Relations and Trade), 112, 113
Molten salt reactors. See MSRs
Money 37, 57, 93, 102, 122, 133, 169,
    190
MOR (Ministry of Railways), 124, 125, 190
Motorola 111, 112, 113, 114, 186, 187
Motorola Mobility deal 133, 134
Motorola project 112, 113, 114
Motorola's choice 112, 113
Mozambique 143, 144, 145
MSRs (molten salt reactors), 119, 150,
    151, 152
Multiclass alliance 18, 19
Multi-national corporations (MNCs),
    110, 129
MW 151

N
Nation 14, 16, 42, 148, 149, 156, 157,
    183
– recipient 136, 149
National champions 6, 54, 91, 115,
    116, 129, 203, 204
National Development and Reform
    Commission. See NDRC
National economy 84, 107, 144
National unity 45, 156
Nationalism 12, 173
Nationalization 19, 20
Natural resources 16, 129, 137, 140,
    184
NDRC (National Development and Re-
    form Commission), 54, 71, 184,
    185
Network 3, 64, 109
New China 18, 32, 169
New Democracy 18, 19
Newfound freedoms 68, 170
Nigeria 126, 141
Ningbo 87, 88
North China 19, 30, 85, 113, 124
Nuclear power 6, 54, 124, 126, 127,
    128, 129, 151
Nuclear proliferation 150, 151

O
ODA (overseas development assis-
    tance), 136
ODI (outbound direct investment), 129
Off-balance sheet 177, 178
Officials 9, 10, 14, 17, 27, 28, 107, 108
– local 63, 86, 87, 97
Old-style SOEs 74, 78, 79, 154, 201
– large 73, 75, 204
Onward 20, 52, 74, 75, 77, 104
Open door 95, 115, 116
Opportunity 181, 183, 199
Opposition 27, 51, 66, 74, 94, 152,
    163
Optimism 3, 5, 152, 166, 177, 195
Options 59, 68, 83, 152
Outbound direct investment (ODI), 129
Output 15, 21, 35, 49, 50, 103

Overseas 5, 14, 129, 140, 154, 174, 200

Overseas development assistance (ODA), 136

Overseas factories 80, 88

Overseas markets 129, 191

Overseas-Chinese State Farms 31

Ownership 61, 62, 64, 71, 142, 179, 180, 182

P

Pace 3, 6, 18, 40, 176, 178, 203, 204

Parent, unlisted 70, 72

Parent companies 64, 70, 134

Paris 12, 14

Participation, undermining China's 165

Partners 96, 100, 104, 122, 123, 126, 154

– foreign 95, 115, 124, 128, 129

Party 52, 58, 71, 162, 167, 169, 194, 195

Path 10, 66, 68, 152, 153, 163, 164, 166

PC business 131, 134

PCs 131, 132

Peace 37, 155, 157, 159, 161, 163, 165

People's Republic 17, 18, 20, 22, 24, 26, 28, 30

People's Republic of China. *See* PRC

Peugeot 100, 102, 122

Phase 40, 41, 52, 62, 139, 141

Phones 50, 54, 187, 191, 192

Picking 129, 131, 133

Picture 50, 93, 144, 153

– true 66, 67, 75

Planned economy 24, 44, 45, 46, 47, 51, 52, 57

Planning 25, 52, 90, 94

Plants 15, 16, 25, 43, 84, 85, 120, 123

– small 34

Players 135, 136

– foreign 96, 121, 126, 187, 191

PMI (post-merger integration), 131, 132

POEs (privately owned enterprises), 84, 85, 87, 88, 90, 91, 93, 94

POEs Flourish 87, 89, 91

Political order 10, 45, 46, 155, 195, 203

Pollution 107, 127, 179

Ponderous 24, 25, 79, 82, 99, 205

Population 3, 21, 35, 63, 87, 156, 157, 158

Port 19, 87, 108, 136, 137, 147, 181

Post-Mao 1, 35, 37

Post-merger integration. *See* PMI

Post-reforms 109, 159

Poverty 3, 21, 37, 39, 47, 179, 199

Power 2, 16, 17, 30, 31, 40, 153, 158

– concentrated 26, 53, 201

– political 40, 42, 46, 77, 162, 165

– public 155, 194

– technological 151

Power generation 75, 152

Power stations 138, 140

Power technology, nuclear 126, 127

Pragmatism 1, 3, 42, 83, 144, 165, 197, 201

PRC (People's Republic of China), 5, 15, 16, 19, 37, 144, 156, 158

Premier 41, 74, 76, 185, 198, 201

Preservation 42, 43

Pressure 47, 54, 60, 63, 104, 105, 204, 205

Prices 21, 50, 54, 63, 65, 89, 187, 191

Private capital 18, 76

Private Economy Emerges Unannounced 83, 84, 86, 88, 90, 92, 94

Private enterprises 47, 52, 54, 83, 86, 87, 88, 91

Private firms 75, 76, 78, 86, 87, 91, 93, 94

Private sector 45, 47, 74, 75, 81, 83, 84, 94

Privately owned enterprises. *See* POEs

Privatization 62, 63, 64

Producers 24, 49, 111, 124, 135, 185

Production 36, 58, 59, 84, 85, 86, 101, 102

Productive forces 44, 201

Productivity 5, 50, 57, 103

Profitability 10, 60, 68, 84, 100, 114, 116, 135
Profits 67, 68, 85, 87, 93, 94, 131, 132
Program 18, 19, 29, 31, 125, 175, 184, 185
– economic reform 45
Projects 65, 66, 67, 128, 137, 138, 142, 150
Promises 16, 18
Proposal 111, 112
Prospect 67, 69, 107, 165, 181, 190, 194
Province 13, 30, 33, 62, 69
Public debt 176, 177

Q
Qingdao government 79, 80, 81
Qualcomm 123, 189

R
Railways 6, 9, 126, 136, 137, 140, 147, 190
Ratio 34, 76, 176, 181
R&D 90, 91, 149, 150, 182, 183, 184, 188
R&D funding 185, 189, 190
Reactors 127, 128, 150, 151
– nuclear 126, 127
Real estate 94, 177, 199
Recession 132, 133
Red Guards 26, 27, 29
Reform process 50, 51, 96, 153, 156, 193, 195, 198
Reformers 61, 201
Reforms 40, 41, 47, 51, 53, 58, 195, 205
– comprehensive 194, 195
– enterprise 73
– gradual 50, 74
– political 44, 46, 164, 204
– post-Mao 14, 165
Reforms Take Shape 39, 40, 41, 42, 43, 44, 45, 46
Regime 14, 18, 156
Regulations 6, 11, 58, 87, 110, 124, 198, 199
Re-innovation 120, 121, 126, 184

Ren 91, 92, 171
Republic 9, 10, 11, 12, 13, 14, 15, 16
Republic of China 12, 14
Republican period 14, 15, 31, 58
Research 32, 33, 34, 150, 151, 182, 183, 190
Research institutes 33, 34, 104, 130, 183, 190
Resolution 69, 70
Resources 88, 119, 136, 152
Responsibility 54, 58, 72, 145
Restaurants 20, 144
Restrictions 90, 95, 99, 105, 125, 164, 165, 189
Returnees 31, 32, 150, 175
Revenues 57, 59, 60, 88, 90, 138, 142, 146
Revive China 19, 31, 47
Righted 39, 40, 41, 42, 43, 44, 45, 46
Risk 72, 114, 115, 161, 166, 169, 200, 204
– high 149
RMB 21, 52, 63, 70, 87, 88, 94, 184
Roads 98, 102, 109, 127, 137, 140, 147, 150
Roots 37, 77, 173, 174, 205
Rule 39, 53, 94, 153, 165, 166, 198, 200
Rulers 3, 4, 5, 82, 169

S
Safety 24, 106, 110, 127, 128, 152, 180
Sales 78, 87, 88, 89, 130, 131, 134, 135
– global 79, 91, 135
Samsung 114, 120, 187, 189, 191
SASAC (State-owned Assets Supervision and Administration Commission), 54, 71
Scenes 79, 114, 125, 146, 153, 176, 185
Schools 46, 88, 158, 159, 163, 169
Science 12, 13, 32, 33, 78, 150, 183, 184
Scientists 13, 17, 33, 42, 45, 150, 183, 189

– leading 32, 190
– trained 32, 33
Sea 35, 37, 86, 98
Sectors 81, 82, 93, 94, 99, 111, 115,
  129
– rail 124, 126
– strategic 125, 185
Security 53, 92, 93, 100
Self-Strengthening Movement 11, 12
Semiconductor imports 123, 185, 189
Semiconductor industry 59, 123, 189
Semiconductors 54, 111, 114, 121,
  123, 125, 127, 129
Senior Chinese government 17
Separation 58, 71, 81
Separation of party and enterprise
  58, 194
Service industries 110, 120
Service levels 67, 109
Services 66, 68, 92, 95, 109, 110,
  120, 122
SETC (State Economic and Trade Com-
  mission), 71
SEZs (Special Economic Zones), 97, 98
Shadow banking 93, 94, 177, 178
Shadows 94, 153, 178, 204
Shanghai 14, 15, 19, 103, 104, 105,
  124, 182
Shanghai Auto 101, 122
Shanghai government 103, 104, 124,
  175
Shanghai Institute of Applied Physics
  (SINAP), 150, 151
Shanghai VW (SVW), 103
Shenzhen 91, 97, 98, 158, 175, 185
Shipbuilding 13, 82, 192
Shortage 29, 71, 85, 86, 102, 103,
  169, 186
Silos 23, 24
SINAP (Shanghai Institute of Applied
  Physics), 150, 151
Skills 5, 67, 68, 95, 96, 97, 115, 116
Slogan 17, 18, 28, 42, 62, 75, 80, 184
Smartphones 134, 188, 190, 191
Social order 45, 155, 156
Socialism 18, 19, 26, 36, 42, 44, 47,
  52

Socialist system 44, 47
Society 1, 2, 3, 4, 168, 170, 171, 202
SOE governance 71, 76, 77
SOE leaders 64, 68, 77, 165, 194
SOE reform 41, 61, 62, 74, 75, 82,
  163, 194
SOE Reform Falters 74, 75, 77
SOE sector 62, 170, 201
SOEs (state-owned enterprises), 57,
  58, 65, 67, 69, 71, 72, 75
SOEs, new-style 81, 82, 94, 204, 205
SOEs control 57, 61
South Africa 103, 138, 141
South China 31, 45, 51, 97, 98, 112,
  124
South Korea 3, 120, 121, 167, 181, 184
Soviet advisors 15, 31, 32
Soviet Model 25, 26, 27, 29, 31, 33,
  35, 37
Soviet Union 16, 20, 32, 33, 34, 36,
  40, 157
Soviets 16, 17, 20, 22, 36, 37, 101,
  102
Spa 61, 66
Special Economic Zones (SEZs), 97, 98
Speeds 125, 126, 182
Stability 155, 157, 159, 161, 163, 165,
  189
– financial 133, 175, 177
Stadium, national 119, 137, 144
Staff 33, 34, 48, 69, 70, 71, 142, 175
Standards, living 36, 44
Stark contrast 5, 23, 105
Stars 1, 39, 50, 138, 191
State 50, 57, 58, 59, 64, 70, 71, 78
State banks 76, 89, 91, 93, 96, 178,
  194, 205
State Council's Leading Groups 112,
  116, 185
State Economic and Trade Commis-
  sion (SETC), 71
State enterprises 40, 42
State firms 58, 63
State ownership 47, 160
State Planning Commission 24, 48
State sector 45, 49, 52, 84, 85, 94,
  95, 97

– dominant 42, 83
State-owned Assets Supervision 54, 71
State-owned enterprises. *See* SOEs
State-Owned Enterprises 57, 58, 60, 62, 74, 75, 76, 78
Statistics 24, 26, 136, 188
Status quo 5, 9, 151, 166, 203
Steel 22, 23, 24, 25, 26, 29, 102, 192
Steel plant 11, 16, 142
Steel works 12, 29, 32
Stick 115, 116, 170
Stock 20, 52, 81, 91, 134, 194, 197
Stock market listings 57, 62, 64, 68, 86
Strategy 57, 65, 74, 76, 78, 114, 184, 187
– economic 20, 22
Strengthen 51, 52, 157, 162, 166, 173, 205
Strings 136, 138
Students 5, 43, 51, 173, 174, 187, 199
Subscale 25, 62, 63
Subsidiaries 59, 64, 66, 67, 135, 142
Subways 181, 182
Supermarkets 142, 143
Supervision, official 10, 85
Suppliers 23, 25, 34, 79, 89, 100, 135
– foreign 99, 104, 126, 128, 186
Supply 16, 23, 25, 85, 104, 123, 141, 180
– local 100, 102, 104
Supply chain 127, 128, 133
Support 50, 52, 54, 92, 93, 94, 158, 159
– financial 22, 88, 92
Surge 96, 97
Surplus, economic 21
Survivability 57, 157, 159
Survival 2, 13, 57, 58, 77, 157, 195
SVW (Shanghai VW), 103

T
Taiwan 31, 135, 137, 144, 147, 181, 184, 189
Takeoff, economic 1, 179, 181, 199
Teachers 27, 45, 46, 88

Team 32, 66, 150, 152
Technological Development Area. *See* TEDA
Technology 6, 120, 121, 125, 126, 129, 150, 151
– core 167, 188
– proprietary 120, 135
Technology Breakthrough 149, 151
Technology ladder 121, 184
Technology procurement 165
TEDA (Tianjin Economic Technological Development Area), 113, 114
Telecoms 74, 75, 82
Temperatures, high 150, 151
Terms 14, 15, 17, 18, 68, 93, 148, 164
– medium 149, 166
Theft 19, 92, 120, 122, 167
Thorium 150, 152
Thorium molten salt reactor (TMSR), 150, 151
Tiananmen Square Massacre 43, 114, 157, 201
Tianjin 15, 19, 31, 61, 85, 112, 113, 114
Tier 89, 90
TMSR (thorium molten salt reactor), 150, 151
Top management 66, 72, 125
Topics 163, 164, 193
Toyotas 100, 167
Tpy 16, 59, 63
Track 65, 100, 111, 132, 170, 171, 200
Traditions 4, 5, 87, 201
Transfer 21, 65, 99, 125, 167
Transformation, economic 4
Transparency 51, 57, 71, 72, 110, 165
Transportation 14, 21, 54, 75, 82, 108, 146, 182
Trial 37, 40
Trillion 40, 52, 76, 138, 176, 177, 185
Trucks 22, 59, 98, 101, 102, 109
– heavy 101, 102
Tunnels 181, 182
TVEs 83, 84, 85, 86, 87, 88, 89, 198

U
Underperforming Overseas Assets 129, 131, 133

Union, trade 112, 160
Universities 31, 32, 33, 173, 174, 175,
    189, 193
Upgrading, industrial 96, 183
Uranium 150, 152
Urbanization 177, 181
US 15, 106, 123, 132, 135, 151, 182,
    183
US government 100, 133
US market 79, 135

V
Value 5, 37, 43, 72, 97, 104, 177, 178
Vehicles 100, 101, 102, 103, 105, 106,
    109, 122
– local government financing 176
Ventures 98, 111, 112, 120, 161
Vibrant New China 1, 2, 3, 4, 5, 6, 7
Victims 12, 31, 45, 46
Violence 27, 31, 46, 74, 162
Virtual private networks (VPNs), 164
Vision 37, 64, 76, 111, 151, 197
Voice 2, 12, 72, 202
Volatility 3, 133
Volkswagen 100, 102
Volvo 106, 122, 134, 135
VW 100, 102, 103, 104, 105

W
Walls 17, 28, 131, 171
Wang 32, 157
Wanxiang 83, 88, 89, 90, 91, 94, 135
War, civil 29, 156, 157
Waste 80, 150, 151
Water 73, 145, 151
Waves 17, 26, 112, 128, 165, 177
Way Forward 78, 79, 81
Wealth 5, 10, 83, 87, 139, 174, 178,
    179
Wealth creation 36, 37, 39, 40, 177,
    181, 193, 197
Wealth management products 177,
    178
Weaning 57, 59, 61

Wenzhou model 87
Western powers 19, 20
Western society 12, 164
Western technology 12, 153
Westinghouse 127, 128, 129
WFOEs 111, 112, 113
Wife 35, 45, 46, 162, 169
Windows 48, 59, 95, 172
Winning 16, 112, 113, 135, 160, 168
Workers 13, 19, 28, 52, 60, 85, 146,
    147
Workforce 5, 59, 68, 70, 113, 160
World power 119, 152
Writers 30, 157
Wrongs 39, 40, 41, 42, 43, 44, 45, 46
WTO (World Trade Organization), 41,
    52, 62, 74, 99, 160, 198
Wu Zhihui 13, 24
Wuhan 9, 11, 15, 90

X
Xi Jinping 41, 53, 76, 154, 162, 167,
    200
Xiahua 186, 187
Xiamen 88, 98, 112
Xiaomi 190, 191
Xindu Brewery 59, 60
Xu 45, 46

Y, Z
Zambia 141, 143, 145, 146
Zhang Wei 113, 114
Zhang Zhidong 9, 11
Zhao Ziyang 41, 114, 198
Zhejiang 54, 85, 87, 88, 90, 135, 141,
    142
Zhu Rongji 41, 52, 74, 75, 76, 160,
    198
Zimbabwe 136, 138, 139, 141, 145,
    146
Zimbabwe-China political/economic
    139
Zones 98, 113
ZTE 98, 185, 187, 191